Charles Pritcha

SEPTEMBER 2000

W9-CRH-423

Leveraging the New Infrastructure

Leveraging the NEW Infrastructure

How Market Leaders Capitalize on Information Technology

Peter Weill and
Marianne Broadbent

HARVARD BUSINESS SCHOOL PRESS
Boston, Massachusetts

Copyright © 1998 by the President and Fellows of Harvard College

All rights reserved
Printed in the United States of America
02 01 00 99   5 4

Library of Congress Cataloging-in-Publication Data
Weill, Peter.
    Leveraging the new infrastructure : how market leaders capitalize
on information technology / Peter Weill and Marianne Broadbent.
        p.   cm.
    Includes index.
    ISBN 0-87584-830-3 (alk. paper)
    1. Information technology—Management.   I. Broadbent, Marianne.
II. Title
HD30.2.W45   1998
658'.05—dc21   98-11335
                                                                    CIP

The paper used in this publication meets the requirements of the American National Standard for Permanence of Paper for Printed Library
Materials Z39.94-1984.

CONTENTS

Part 3 | Managing and Maximizing Value

PREFACE

We have embarked on a new era of competition, one that is faster paced, more global, and increasingly volatile, simultaneously requiring that firms find new ways to differentiate and to create value while relentlessly reducing costs. Some of the most important investment decisions senior management can make to meet this challenge are in information technology. Such investment will be as critical for creating long-term shareholder value as were earlier waves of decisions affecting the physical infrastructure: locations, buildings, and plant.

This book grew out of our fascination with how some firms make wise information technology investment decisions and how they reap the benefits of those decisions. Very little is known about why some firms are far more successful at generating business value from their information technology investments than others, or about which investment strategies actually pay off. During our work with hundreds of executives and managers, many told us how unprepared they were for the large and important information technology investment decisions that have shaped their firm's competitive capability. They realized the significance of these investments but struggled with the choices and their business implications.

Information technology is the single largest capital expense in many firms today and integral to achieving business goals. In the service industries, information technology often accounts for more than half the capital investment. It is the new infrastructure for organizations that enables new products and services, new organizational forms, access to new markets, and innovative ways to deliver services faster. Managers must now have new skills to make business choices involving key competitive, financial, organizational, and technical capabilities. Decisions about technical capability in particular must be made with confidence and competence.

But many managers are ill prepared to make the important information technology investment decisions that will shape their firm's competitive capability. As a result, these key decisions are often relegated to technical staff or, worse, to vendors, whose understanding of the firm's specific strategic directions is less than complete.

To meet managers' need to rethink how to make decisions about the new infrastructure, we suggest conceiving of the firm's information technology as an investment portfolio. The information technology portfolio contains investments with different management objectives. Like any portfolio, it must be managed to achieve the firm's goals, while balancing risk versus return.

Leveraging the New Infrastructure explains how firms can develop and manage their information technology investment portfolio to create business value. The book is based on eight years of research on the role and value of different types of information technology investments, in more than 100 businesses within 75 firms in locations around the world—Australia, Canada, Hong Kong, Japan, Malaysia, Singapore, Switzerland, the United Kingdom, and the United States. The studies provide hard evidence about why some firms get more value from their investments. Our observations and interactions enabled us to identify how managers can make appropriate investment decisions suited to their firm's unique strategic context.

Who Should Read
Leveraging the New Infrastructure?

This book is for all senior business managers and all financial, marketing, and information technology executives who are involved in decision making about strategy, competitiveness, and the use of information technology. Our aim is to provide a vehicle for serious dialogue between business and information technology managers about long-term technology investments. We cannot stress enough the significance of *senior* management involvement. Senior management must determine the capabilities of the new infrastructure and set in place structures to govern and manage it.

This book's links between strategic objectives, their information technology implications, and approaches to justification and governance are of particular interest to managers who

- Are responsible for meeting the firm's longer-term strategic needs.

- Work for firms undergoing major change.

- Are involved in meeting the needs of multiple businesses or functional groups, or in creating synergies across these groups.

- Are reviewing their current infrastructure investments and rethinking their technology justification arguments.

- Are considering the strategic potential of electronic commerce and need to understand technology infrastructure's implications.

- Must demonstrate the value of their information technology investments to senior management.

Leveraging the New Infrastructure presents a common business language about information technology and business value that is meaningful and accessible to all managers. The book explains, from a general management perspective, how firms can generate business value by making sound information technology investment decisions, focusing on the most difficult decisions involving infrastructure investments. These often involve large amounts of scarce capital and underpin long-term business competitiveness.

Some Assumptions

Throughout this book we refer to the dollars applied to information technology in a firm as investments, not expenditures. We chose our words deliberately, to focus attention on information technology as an asset. Most managers are aware of their annual information technology budget, but many are less aware of the large amount of capital dedicated to information technology. Peter Keen suggests the useful exercise of creating an information technology balance sheet as a management report. The identification of all the money tied up in information technology resources can make for considerable work, but the result is often startling. Firms often expense software, and real liabilities, such as future operations and maintenance costs, are regularly not captured. For example, Keen argues that every dollar of investment in software incurs an annual liability of 20 cents in operations and 40 cents in maintenance costs (see note 13 in chapter 2). In addition, most firms' accounting systems are not helpful in valuing a database or critical software developed in house.

Many information technology assets have long lives. Firms are still operating transaction processing systems built 15 years ago and modified over the years with hundreds of programming hours. Databases holding details on the relationship between the firm and its customers are relevant for the lifetime of the customer. Each year the average bank invests around 15 percent of expenses in information technology and adds to its asset base. In many firms, the information technology asset is undermanaged given its size. If the investment decisions are poor, the investment can become a liability rather than an asset. But whether asset or liability, the investment is cumulative and must be managed judiciously.

The use of the term *information technology investment* rather than *information technology expenditure* is designed to emphasize the long-term nature of the potential asset. The investment may be written off for tax purposes, but in terms of maximizing shareholder wealth, information technology is an investment with a long life.

The first step to managing an asset of this size and importance is to know how much is invested, where it is invested, and what are the assets, liabilities, and capabilities.

Information technology is no different from any other investment made by a firm—a return must be achieved, or the firm will eventually fail. The management of information technology requires no special treatment beyond the attention expected for an investment that often accounts for more capital than any other category of investment.

For convenience, we use the word *firm* throughout this book to describe the business enterprise. However, our comments relate equally to all enterprises, whether large, small, for profit, not for profit, or governmental. Our intention is to capture the imagination and to challenge the assumptions of managers in all industries, as no industry will remain unaffected by the new infrastructure.

How This Book
Is Organized

This book addresses these issues in three parts. Part 1 describes what strategies have worked (or failed), with a focus on creating value through information technology investments. Part 2 explains how to identify the information technology infrastructure capabilities that match a firm's strategic needs and presents a framework synthesized from the management approaches of successful firms. Part 3 outlines how successful firms manage and govern their information technology investments to maximize value, concluding with ten key leadership principles.

Those We Would
Like to Thank

IBM Consulting Group (IBMCG) provided significant research funding for our work on infrastructure in 54 businesses within 27 firms across seven countries (see appendix 1). The funding enabled us and our fellow researchers to spend significant time in each firm and to combine quantitative and qualitative evidence. Senior consultants from IBMCG encouraged us to expand our initial scope and engaged us in many stimulating conversations and symposiums. In particular, we wish to thank Don St. Clair, who worked with us throughout the project, who wrote papers with us, and with whom we had many thought-provoking conversations about directions, meanings, and the application of our findings. Don encouraged us to turn our insights into practical recommendations and contributed to the development of the Maxims and Deals framework. We would also like to acknowledge Al Barnes, Jerry Luftman (now at Stevens Institute of Technology), Joe Movizzo, and Scott Oldach, all of whom recognized the challenge of managing the information technology infrastructure and supported and contributed to the work.
In completing the work on infrastructure investments, we were joined by a talented group of international researchers who worked with us investigating firms in their regions. They all contributed

enormously in terms of conceptual development, inspiration, and sheer effort, and as wonderful colleagues working with us and the participating firms. We wish to thank

John Henderson and Christine Lentz, Boston University

Jim Short and Jeff Sampler, London Business School

Bob Tricker, John Whitman, and Ali Farhoomand, Hong Kong University

Peter Keen, International Center for Information Technologies

Jack Rockart, Jeanne Ross, and Judith Quillard, Massachusetts Institute of Technology

Neo Boon Siong and Christina Soh, Nanyang Technological University, Singapore

The Melbourne Business School (MBS) Foundation and Hewlett-Packard Australia financially supported the study of the implications of international business operations for the management of information technology. These sources provided funds for research assistance and travel to over 30 international sites.

Our MBS faculty colleagues from many disciplines have endured with us the progress of our research, and we thank them for their interest. We thank our director and dean, Professor John Rose, for the ongoing support and encouragement he has given us from the first day we started on this ambitious endeavor.

We thank Carey Butler and Tim O'Brien for the quality of their research assistance in completing site visits with us, writing case vignettes, and analyzing the data. We'd like to acknowledge Carey, Tim, and Dr. Paul Richardson, who contributed talent, energy, and good humor to the painstaking data analysis. Their careful and professional approach and their inquiring minds added greatly to the outcome.

For the past five years, we have been very fortunate to have Debi Chetcuti providing excellent administrative support. Debi has done everything, including compiling the text and creating all the diagrams and tables for this manuscript, producing the final versions of case studies, entering data, preparing course materials, administering our executive education programs, and running the administration of the Centre for Management of Information Technology. Her multiple talents are matched by an enthusiasm and commitment to work that we much appreciate. We thank you, Debi.

The benchmarks, the statistical analysis, and many of the vignettes in Part 1 are from 54 businesses that our research group studied and visited in seven countries. The work involved more than 250 hours of interviews with senior managers, and the collection and analysis of 622 data items of information on technology investment and performance in each firm over a five-year period. A complete listing of all the companies to which we owe our thanks can be found in Appendix 1.

We would like to thank and acknowledge our MBA students, who are our first testing ground and a fertile source of new ideas. Our students helped us generate, refine, and extend insights into creating business value from information technology, and they never let us get away with anything.

Kirsten Sandberg and her colleagues at Harvard Business School Press have been supportive and encouraging from our very first discussions. Kirsten provided wonderfully clear insights and many helpful suggestions on our first draft, which improved the book in many ways.

A Personal Note from Peter

I would like to thank Professor Jack Rockart, Director of the Center for Information Systems Research (CISR) at the Sloan School, MIT, and all the staff who hosted my 1992 sabbatical leave, when this work began. In 1992 Jack encouraged me to tackle the challenging issue of infrastructure and, during several visits since, to "make it interesting." Much of my part of the manuscript was written when I was a Distinguished Visiting Research Professor at Georgia State University in 1996. I would like to thank Professors Eph McLean and Dick Welke, the department, and the CIO Roundtable for providing a stimulating environment in which to work and test ideas.

I owe a significant intellectual debt to Peter Keen of the International Center for Information Technologies. His clarity of thought and quest for new insights have inspired and helped my work. I would also like to thank John Henderson, Hank Lucas, Margi Olson, John Sviokla, and Jon Turner, all of whom helped me grapple with information technology infrastructure.

My wife, Margi Olson, makes it all worthwhile. Margi never stops supporting, challenging my assumptions, understanding, and inspiring. I thank her and look forward to the future. Finally, I thank my parents, who have always encouraged me to learn.

A Personal Note
from Marianne

I would like to thank the Melbourne Business School for the opportunities provided to me as a faculty member from 1991 to 1997, particularly for the support to complete my industry research. In January 1998, I joined Gartner Group as director of its Information Technology Executive Program for Australia/New Zealand.

I would like to thank Professor John Henderson and the staff at the Systems Research Center at Boston University's School of Management for hosting the major part of my study leave from September 1995 through January 1996. This was a stimulating base from which to investigate North American firms and complete further work with participant firms in the infrastructure study. The insights of Christine Lentz on firm visits and her own concurrent work were much appreciated. In Singapore, the Information Management and Research Centre at the Nanyang Technological University, led by Professor Boon Siong Neo, provided valuable assistance and support in working with firms headquartered in Singapore. Professor Bob Tricker and John Whitman at the University of Hong Kong Business School provided a base for investigating Hong Kong firms. Professor Jiro Kokuryo and Japan's Keio Business School hosted my stay in Japan, while I worked with Japanese firms. In each case, our academic and industry colleagues assisted with education in local business conditions and facilitated contacts with major firms.

I would like to thank my children, David, Andrew, Patrick, and Katherine, for maintaining a healthy interest in whatever it was I was doing, for learning to cook and clean, and for erecting a permanent "Welcome Home Mum" sign. To other friends—you might now understand what has absorbed me over the past few years—and my parents, who always encouraged my curiosity. To my husband, Robert, thank you for the enduring love and companionship; for the space and encouragement to continue a crowded professional and personal life; and for insisting we maintain our regular theatergoing, dining out, and occasional holidays—no matter what the deadlines.

Finally . . .

We are very keen to hear about readers' experiences making decisions about and gaining value from the new infrastructure. Our aim is to provide an informed starting point for rethinking approaches to information technology investments and performance. We hope that you get as much enjoyment and challenge from reading and using the ideas in this book as we did researching and writing about them.

Creating Business Value through Information Technology

Part 1 of this book introduces the notion of the information technology portfolio and its four types of investment. We provide benchmarks for different information technology portfolios in different industries and examine the evidence to determine which investment strategies have worked and which have not. As more of a firm's cash flow is on-line, it is the longer-term decisions about information technology infrastructure investments that will differentiate competitive capabilities.

Chapter 1 provides an overview of the challenges firms face in maximizing business value from the new infrastructure and illustrates how successful firms face these challenges. Changing competitive environments have significant implications for the management and uses of information technology. Emerging technologies present firms with new realities, and electronic commerce is shifting the locus of competition. However, few senior managers are well equipped to make confident and competent decisions to implement the new infrastructure in their business. We explore how shifts in business and customer demands require rethinking from many perspectives: rethinking value from the customer's perspective, rethinking the nature of information technology investments, and rethinking the way a firm manages and governs that investment.

Chapter 2 introduces the investment portfolio as a new lens to rethink information technology management. In rethinking technology investments, we use concepts that are fundamentally those of business rather than of technology: portfolios, business value, investment, and alignment of resources with strategic goals. The objective of information technology investment is to provide business value through implementing current strategies and enabling new strategies. But, because several barriers exist, we need to rethink traditional alignment approaches. We explore new ways to drive business value through the notion of the information technology portfolio, balancing long- and short-term needs, as well as risk and return.

Generating business value from information technology infrastructure investments is a delicate balancing act. Chapter 3 provides the evidence for payoff from our research: which strategies have worked and the types of business value achieved in firms with different information technology portfolios. These patterns of business value identify the different risk-return characteristics of each type of information technology in the portfolio. The characteristics and actions of managers in firms that have achieved superior business value from their investments are also presented and analyzed. The evidence for payoff leads to a series of implications for maximizing value.

CHAPTER 1

Management Challenges of the New Infrastructure

InvestCo is a large firm with a broad product range. It faces severe competition from smaller, more agile firms offering a limited range of products to select demographic groups. InvestCo sees its future as developing long-term relationships with increasingly sophisticated consumers and providing them with a broad range of products. However, InvestCo has found it difficult to respond quickly and is beginning to lose market share. A major part of the problem lies in the difficulties of developing new products that cross InvestCo's traditional areas of responsibility and thus its business unit boundaries.

Until now the firm has operated as four largely independent business units whose senior managers are rewarded on business unit performance. The result has been very solid performance and a rising share price, but a high cost-to-income ratio relative to those of the firm's traditional competitors. The cost-to-income differential is even worse when compared to those new entrants who are offering similar products, such as loans, investment accounts, checking accounts, and insurance policies, over the phone and without InvestCo's large investment in a physical branch network.

One of the authors was asked to address InvestCo's newly formed Information Technology Council on the theme of how to generate business value from information technology investments.

The council comprises the chief executive officer (CEO), the chief financial officer (CFO), the chief information officer (CIO), the heads of the four business units, and the head of strategy. The CIO has worked, for two years, one on one with the senior executives to generate the necessary agreement to form this council, which will take a firmwide view of information technology.

Operating independently and entrepreneurially, each business unit has made large investments in information technology. To best meet its particular customers' needs, each business unit has implemented different systems, which has resulted in much duplication and incompatibility across the firm. Until now the CIO has been unable to convince the business unit heads to agree on a common approach to information technology infrastructure.

The air was thick with tension after the presentation benchmarking InvestCo against other firms operating in similar markets around the world. The eight officers looked around the table, wondering where this meeting would lead. The CEO began to speak, identifying several major problems in the information technology area. First, he said, InvestCo was spending far more than its competitors based on the recent benchmarking study of both information technology costs and business value. Worse still, the firm wasn't getting as much business value from its information technology investments as the average and far less than the leaders. The firm's vision of providing integrated financial services and leveraging the customer base by cross-selling was fast becoming a mirage. The CEO stressed that the firm's competitors were better at converting their information technology investments into business value. He gave a series of painful examples of competitors beating InvestCo to the market with new products at lower costs. Finally, he pointed out that the systems in each business unit were incompatible. For example, cross-selling an insurance policy to a customer with a mortgage was difficult. It was also almost impossible to determine the total business relationship that a customer had with the firm, certainly not while the customer was on the phone.

The CEO and CIO had come to the difficult realization that their approach to managing information technology was putting the firm's future at risk. In short, they weren't investing in information technology appropriately for their business objectives, and they weren't getting enough business value from those investments. The duplication of information technology investments had raised costs, which went straight to the bottom line and reduced profits. Even worse, incompatible technology investments limited the firm's strategic options.

The CEO described the Executive Choice package recently released by a major competitor. This attractive package offered a wide range of financial services for a single fee and provided the customer with a consolidated report.

The CEO didn't need to remind the group that InvestCo offered these same services, but that they were spread across the four business units. The cost of manually or electronically implementing this new offering to compete with Executive Choice was huge and probably would cause the firm to lose money on the package. However, without a similar offering, some customers were sure to defect to the competitor. InvestCo's senior managers hadn't realized that the value proposition they put to current and potential customers—a secure one-stop shop for financial services—was technically beyond their reach.

The CEO led several hours of tough discussion, during which the group agreed to a significant change in how InvestCo would invest and manage information technology. The heads of the business units left with mixed feelings. The logic of a shared information technology infrastructure made good business sense for the firm, but they didn't want to give up control of information technology in their businesses. They realized, too, that these discussions had wider ramifications for the way InvestCo was managing its people, its organization, and its business.

This book addresses the issues facing InvestCo and many other firms trying to leverage information technology investments to fulfill the firm's value proposition to customers. From our work with firms we have synthesized a practical management approach to the way market leaders leverage information technology. This approach draws on hard evidence of the market leaders' business value generation and includes extensive benchmarks for comparison.

Facing a New Reality

In this new era of competition in which firms find themselves, opportunities and threats abound. The merging of the computing, telecommunications, publishing, and entertainment industries, as well as the pervasiveness of the Internet and other vehicles for electronic commerce, present strategic opportunities and threats for every firm. Business and technology managers are anxious to make smart use of this powerful combination of business unit, firm, industry, and public infrastructures. However, like InvestCo, many firms struggle with their information technology investments, grappling with a multitude of technical and business choices, working to find the optimal balance of capabilities at corporate and business unit levels. Concurrently, managers must consider how their firm's technology infrastructure intersects with emerging industry and public infrastructures.

In the past there were fewer options and limited infrastructures providing channels to customers. Today there are many. As we move into the twenty-first century, when more and more of a firm's cash flow is on-line, the longer-term decisions about information technology infrastructure investments will differentiate competitive capabilities. The opportunities of the new electronic infrastructures will test many organizational decision-making processes. People will still be a firm's core asset, but the infrastructures they operate will be electronic. We will see the growing importance of the new electronic infrastructure and a declining importance of physical assets and location. Identifying how to benefit from the new infrastructures is a challenge for senior management, who must now take responsibility for these critical longer-term information technology decisions.

What Is the New Infrastructure?

Information technology has become pervasive within contemporary organizations, in order to do business electronically and to connect to customers, suppliers, regulators, and strategic partners. We define *information technology* as a firm's total investment in computing and communications technology. This includes hardware, software, telecommunications, the myriad of devices for collecting and representing data (such as supermarket point-of-sale and bank automatic teller machines), all electronically stored data, and the people dedicated to providing these services. It includes the information technology investments implemented by internal groups (insourced) and those outsourced by other providers, such as IBM Global Services or

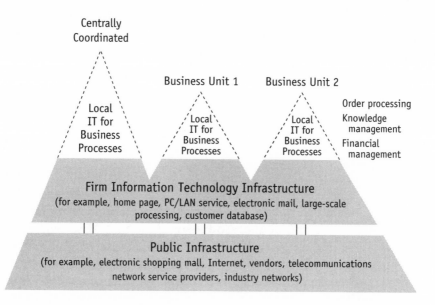

Figure 1.1 The New Infrastructure

EDS. We view the sum total of this investment as the information technology portfolio, which must be managed like a financial portfolio, balancing risk and return to meet management goals and strategies for customer and shareholder value.

The foundation of the information technology portfolio is the firm's longer-term information technology infrastructure, which is in turn linked to external industry infrastructures, such as bank payment systems, airline reservation systems, and automotive industry EDI networks, and to public infrastructures, such as the Internet and telecommunications providers. These infrastructures together enable firms to transact business by reaching customers and suppliers, and provide governments with cost-effective ways to deliver services to their communities. These technologies provide the basis for new organizational forms, new products, new markets, and many changed jobs. The combination of the firm's internal information technology infrastructure and the external public infrastructures make up the new infrastructure illustrated in Figure 1.1. This new infrastructure (depicted in Figure 1.1 as the entire shaded section) will be as important for enabling business processes in the future as the traditional physical infrastructure of roads, store fronts, bank branches, share certificates, delivery services, and product catalogs.

The new infrastructure, plus the information technology needed to perform business processes, make up the firm's information technology portfolio. The entire information technology portfolio represented by Figure 1.1 must be managed by a partnership of business and technical management to create business value.

Why Is the New Infrastructure Important?

In many organizations, information technology is the single largest capital expense. In the United States, more than 50 percent of all capital spending goes into information technology, accounting for more than one-third of the growth of the entire U.S. economy.[1] Senior managers clearly cannot afford to delegate or abdicate to technical personnel critical decisions about the new infrastructure. All managers need well-developed skills to deal confidently and competently with information technology issues so that these complex choices can take account of strategic, technical, competitive, financial, and organizational issues.

In the firms we studied over a five-year period, the average dollar investment in information technology rose by more than 12 percent each year (see Figure 1.2). The average firm invested 4.1 percent of revenues and 7.7 percent of expenses in information technology. Every year the ratio of information technology investment to expenses increased by 3 percent. So, every year, information technology accounted for over 3 percent more of the average firm's resources. In many firms, this increase was accompanied by a reduction in labor costs. Investments in information technology account for an ever-increasing percentage of a firm's discretionary investments and demand the attention of all senior managers.

The benchmarks in Figure 1.2 also illustrate variation by industry in the level of dependence on information technology. The finance industry (banking and insurance) depends most on information technology, followed by retail and process manufacturing. In service industries, such as banking, information technology is the engine that processes a huge number of transactions every day. Based on our study, a typical bank with assets of more than $100 billion will electronically process more than 530 million transactions, such as account withdrawals, every year. In the service sector, information technology *is* the production technology—the equivalent of the machine tools and production lines of manufacturing.

No. of firms	Finance 12		Manufacturing 10		Retail 5		All 27	
	5-yr.av.	Av%Δ	5-yr.av.	Av%Δ	5-yr.av.	Av%Δ	5-yr.av.	Av%Δ
Total IT (US$m)	146	+11.0	62.1	+4.4	41.4	+25.1	98.3	+11.7
IT % of Revenues	7.0	−0.6	1.7	−1.0	1.0	+16.4	4.1	+2.6
IT % of Expenses	14.2	−0.4	2.0	−0.2	1.1	+16.4	7.7	+3.0

Av%Δ = Average percentage change per year.

Figure 1.2   Information Technology Investment Benchmarks

Interestingly, the rate of increase was the largest in the retail sector, with huge recent investments in point-of-sale systems. Both large retail firms, such as Kmart and Wal-Mart, and smaller niche players, such as a chain of specialty music and electronic stores, have invested heavily. Their objectives were to determine exactly which items sold where and when, and to dramatically shorten the replenishment cycle. The value proposition of one department store chain we worked with was to ensure that its full range of stock was always available. This value proposition required rethinking the chain's information technology infrastructure to deliver the information- and transaction-processing power needed to manage the replenishment cycle from point of sale to ordering from suppliers, logistics for distribution, delivery to stores, and shelf restocking. The chain's information technology investment increased substantially to allow it to remain competitive and to deliver that value proposition to customers.

Retail executives want accurate data about what's selling and where it's selling and then work with suppliers to deliver store-ready quantities to distribution centers. Each step in the retail supply chain depends on receiving, manipulating, and sending data in a timely manner and in a form that can be readily used by buyers and suppliers. Each step is dependent on the new infrastructure, including the firm, its suppliers, and sometimes the entire retail industry. The business strategies of a quick-response initiative depend on a sophisticated communications infrastructure being in place to facilitate data capture and transfer.

Firms invest in many information technologies, from mainframe computers that process thousands of customer reservation transactions in airlines like Qantas and United, to pocket-size hand-held store management systems in Tokyo's 7-Eleven stores, which use infrared communication links to point-of-sale registers. These investments, whether led by business or technology managers, are made with the expectation of a positive return to the business. But too often, company boards and executive committees are asked to make large information technology investment decisions on a "trust me" basis.

Spectacular successes using information technology are legendary, including the American Airlines customer reservation system SABRE, which contributed $1.5 billion to the bottom line from 1977 to 1986.[2] Today SABRE utilizes the public infrastructure of the Internet for a direct channel to consumers. However, there are also huge failures, such as Australia's Westpac Bank, which reportedly wrote off more than $150 million in its Core Systems 90 project—originally designed to "catapult Westpac into a new era of retail banking products and services."[3] Experienced and, until that time, successful senior management teams made both decisions.

These types of decisions challenge the depth and nature of expertise of both business and information technology management. The thousands of small information technology investment decisions that are made every day in a large corporation are even harder to manage and coordinate. But if they aren't coordinated and managed, information technology can become a barrier, not an enabler.

For example, before implementing a firmwide standard, one large telecommunications company had 27 wide-area telecommunications networks (WANs) spanning its different geographic locations, business units, and functional groupings. Each network was sensibly justified in business terms by local managers but hindered the firmwide business goal of cost control. Each network required different support staff who understood the details of the network topography and standards, resulting in a huge overhead cost. Concurrently, the firm was rethinking its value proposition, which required a shift from account-based services to customer-centric services. Multiple, complex networks made it extremely difficult for different parts of the business to understand the firm's total relationship with each customer. After difficult organizational negotiations and technical considerations, the number of networks was reduced to two. Costs plummeted, and integration increased. The firm's strategy of customer-centric services wasn't achievable with the disparate infrastructure in place. Systems couldn't be linked, customer data couldn't be easily shared, and costs were too high. The new infrastructure was based on agreed-upon standards across multiple businesses. It gave each of the businesses a clear picture of each customer's relationship with the firm while minimizing costs.

Electronic Commerce

The importance of information technology decisions to a firm will only increase as we move closer to a world where electronic commerce prevails. Electronic banking, electronic catalogs, on-line distance education, Internet shopping malls, electronic stock trading, on-line car auctions, and on-line customized newspapers are a reality. Although some of these initiatives will fail, others will be wildly successful, changing the competitive landscape and creating new industries.

The Internet is a large, unregulated telecommunications network. Aside from adhering to the Internet's telecommunications and addressing standards, anything goes. Until now businesses and consumers have been concerned about security. For example, consumers have been wary of entering their credit card numbers into the Internet, fearing that personal data will be stolen. There have actually been surprisingly few reported cases of this type of theft. These security issues are being addressed by powerful consortia, including archrivals MasterCard and Visa. As the security issues are resolved, Internet financial transactions by individuals and companies will become commonplace. Meanwhile, security concerns have not deterred the emergence of major on-line businesses, such as bookseller Amazon.com and the travel service Expedia. The new on-line businesses are making aggressive use of the new infrastructure and will pose significant threats to businesses that fail to comprehend the realities of newly emerging channels. Agents, such as travel agents and mortgage agents, are at particular risk, as providers can access customers directly, and those customers will question what added value agents provide.

The first of the Internet-based banks, such as Security First Network Bank (SFNB) in Pineville, Kentucky, are now operational and geographically independent. It's no longer important where Pineville is, as the trade is electronic, not physical. SFNB offers a large range of services, including checking, loans, automatic teller access, bill paying, and many others. SFNB has Federal Deposit Insurance Corporation (FDIC) membership and is growing fast—and traditional banks are responding. Indeed, the Electronic Banking Resources Center, which has an interesting Internet site of its own, rates and provides direct links to the sites of more than 200 banks or credit unions represented on the Internet.[4]

Established banks have responded to new electronic competitors in several ways. First, they're forming networks of banks that will operate a secure platform for electronic banking and perhaps more general electronic commerce. For example, 15 North American banks and IBM have formed the Integrated Financial Network, which allows customers to bank and use other financial services via either IBM's proprietary Global Network or the Internet.[5] Second, they've looked to the capabilities of their own information technology investments, asking themselves: Do we have an integrated information technology infrastructure that will allow us to compete and have an integrated presence in the world of electronic commerce?

The financial services industry leads the way with electronic commerce, but many other sectors will follow. Electronic commerce generally lowers transaction costs.[6] For example, Booz•Allen & Hamilton[7] report that the cost of an average bank transaction completed via teller is $1.08; via telephone banking, $.54; and via the Internet, $.17. The economics are irresistible. Once a firm has captured the electronic channel to the customer, it can offer a broad range of its own and other firms' offerings electronically, including noncompeting and, eventually, competing products, for an appropriate fee. Point-of-sale systems in large retailers are of concern to many banks. These systems allow customers to use a wide variety of payment methods and easily withdraw cash from their accounts.

Leading retailers have captured the electronic channel and are now experimenting with offering traditional banking services (check deposits, car and housing loans) within supermarket walls. The executive management of a supermarket chain recently told us that more than 50 percent of its revenue is on-line and that, for the first time, last Christmas the firm had to truck cash in to its stores to accommodate customers using the point of sale as a cash withdrawal outlet from their bank.

The size of the investment in information technology, the strategic opportunities it brings, and the unstoppable move toward electronic commerce make the long-term information technology investment decisions about the new infrastructure critical. A firm's information technology infrastructure enables the performance of business activities such as transaction processing and the provision of management information. It has much in common with the public infrastructure of roads, schools, hospitals, and bridges, which must be centrally funded and put in place before the precise business needs are known.

There is convincing evidence that large investments in public infrastructures pay off.[8] In this book we present evidence for the payoff from firm-based information technology infrastructures.

In general, limited firmwide infrastructures are found in firms with stronger profits in the short term, whereas extensive infrastructures are found in more innovative firms with more revenue from new products and stronger revenue growth. The evidence provides guidance based on market leaders' strategies that work. Market leaders create a unique version of the new infrastructure, combining internal and external infrastructures, to enable their strategic goals.

The Capabilities of the New Infrastructure: A Matter of Strategic Choice

Firms take different views of the information technology infrastructure to arrive at different types of infrastructure capabilities. Consider the examples of these market leaders:

- The Hong Kong–based conglomerates Jardine Matheson and Hutchison Whampoa decided to make little firmwide investments in information technology infrastructure services.[9]

- Honda Motor Corporation, to reduce cycle time in new car production, developed a highly sophisticated communications network linking designers in Tokyo and Los Angeles.[10]

- The international paper and packaging manufacturer Amcor Ltd. provided *no* firmwide information technology services among its paper, packaging, and containers businesses.[11]

- Monsanto restructured from autonomous divisions to a series of strategic business units, to achieve greater business agility while putting more emphasis on shared business services, including selected information technology services.[12]

- Citibank Asia is centralizing and standardizing all backroom information technology processes for its Asian operations into one location, while its parent company, Citicorp, is forging ahead with higher levels of centralized and standardized infrastructure services throughout the world.[13]

Can each of these firms have made the right decisions? How did they make these very different decisions?

In each firm, executive management made deliberate and thoughtful decisions based on the firm's strategic context. The Hong Kong conglomerates regularly buy and sell businesses and would not wish to be constrained by information technology infrastructures that integrate business units. Some other firms take a utilitarian approach, focusing on only those infrastructure investments that promise clear cost savings. For still other firms, with strong local demands in their international operations, the emphasis is on maximizing local decision making. This can result in a decision for limited firmwide infrastructure in order to ensure maximum local agility.

At the other end of the spectrum, some firms view the new infrastructure as enabling centrally coordinated strategic flexibility. Their aim is to facilitate international agility and fast responses to change in the global marketplace. At Honda, the ability of designers in different locations to communicate and exchange designs is critical for reducing cycle time in new car production. The move toward some shared services at Monsanto was driven by the desire for greater competitiveness through more responsive, lower-cost, and higher-quality support.[14] Citibank Asia's business strategy drove an enabling view of infrastructure designed to deliver both agility and cost reduction.

The Role of Information Technology Architecture

An *architecture* is an integrated set of technical choices used to guide the organization in satisfying business needs. Pepsi-Cola International refers to the "art and science [of] architecting information technology solutions. . . . as with constructing a solid building, for each of our information technology components to work together smoothly there is a great deal of engineering—architecting—required."[15] In Pepsi-Cola International, converging "to a common set of best practices across the decentralized business operations is an art. Defining standard data definitions (i.e., chart of accounts, product codes, location codes) is more of a science. The science of architecture is what ensures a solid foundation. It also ensures that all parts 'fit together' as we add to and enhance our structure."

In taking an architectural approach to the challenge of providing technology support to the business, Pepsi-Cola International aims to ensure that information technology enables the integration of business processes, which can evolve over time, and maintains the proper balance of cost, performance, and scalability.

Information technology architecture[16] is a set of policies and rules that governs the use of information technology and plots a path to the way business will be done in the future. This architecture isn't set in concrete and must constantly be reviewed. In most firms it provides the technical guidelines rather than the rules for decision making. An architecture has to cope with both business uncertainty and technological change, making it one of the most difficult tasks for a firm.[17] A good architecture evolves over time, and is documented and accessible to all managers in the firm. Each architecture decision needs a sound business base, to encourage voluntary agreement and compliance across the business.

An agreed-upon architecture is necessary for a firmwide infrastructure to

- Achieve compatibility among various systems.

- Specify the policies and mechanics for delivering the information technology strategy.

- Describe the technological model of the organization.

- Cut through multivendor chaos and move toward vendor independence.

The combination of infrastructure plus architecture determines the practical range of applications that can be readily developed (or purchased) and installed.

Typical Information Technology Architectures

A typical architecture contains policies and guidance like these, for appropriate technical choices in five categories:

- *Computing (hardware and operating systems). For example, "For personal computers, Pentium Pro machines with at least 64 megabytes of memory and 4 gigabytes of storage running Windows 95."*

- *Communications/telecommunications networks. For example, "We will have only two networks, and both will be industry standards, X25 packet switching and TCP/IP."*

- *Data (data assets, use, storage, control). For example, "We will standardize all financial, customer, and product information but allow free definition of all other data by business units accessible via browsers." Data architecture defines all data elements and the relationship between them. Guidelines and definitions for the way the data will be accessed, used, stored, and controlled are then indicated. For shared data, all business and functional groups should use the same definitions and follow the same guidelines. If not, hard-to-maintain mechanisms, such as translation tables, are required to integrate different data standards in an application.*

- *Applications (their functions, the relationships between applications, and how they will be installed or developed). For example, "We will standardize on an agreed-upon set of packaged solutions for all financial applications; each new application dealing with customers must be consistent and integrated with existing applications. We will use a standard methodology to develop all applications for consistency in work practices, to share expertise, and so that the progress of developments can be carefully monitored."*

- *Work (standard processes, measures of success, and work policies). Although not technically part of the information technology architecture, the work architecture is the basis for technology decisions. A work architecture involves the specification of a high-level map of the major business processes and is the essential starting place for the other parts of the architecture.*

The technical policies of an architecture often lead organizations to recommend or require that all parts of the firm purchase from a specific set of information technology components to ensure compatibility, consistency, and economies of scale. For example, the multibusiness manufacturing firm Southcorp Holdings aimed to gain economies of scale across its diverse businesses, which include wines, packaging, home appliances, and water heaters.[18] Southcorp operates with a largely decentralized information systems structure, where each business is responsible for its own systems. The small corporate information systems group works closely with senior business managers, business-based user representatives, and information systems managers in a policy and facilitation role to develop overall information systems policy, key information systems strategies, and recommendations for information technology architecture.

As an acquisitive company, Southcorp inherited a diverse range of technologies and information systems, which made economies of scale difficult to achieve. With guidance from the corporate information systems group, each business adopted the policy of open common systems, based on an agreed-upon architecture. The businesses then agreed to standardize on a specific set of products, which included Hewlett-Packard hardware, Unix operating systems, Oracle databases, and transmission control protocol/Internet protocol (TCP/IP) communications. Relationships with vendors are now based on partnership models, and all negotiations take place through the corporate information systems group. This has both improved vendor relationships and reduced costs; less information technology staffing is required to support compatible systems from a small range of vendors.

Setting the governance structure for these decisions on information technology infrastructure and architecture required an informed top management team working with information technology management.

How Well Equipped Is Top Management?

The size of the investment alone makes information technology the prerogative of senior management. But it is the strategic opportunities that information technology offers, or the strategic limitations of poor choices, that will most challenge the talents of top management teams. Top management is often inadequately prepared for this challenge. Few of today's senior management career paths have included responsibility for the information technology group. Indeed, few top managers have taken responsibility for information technology investments in areas they have managed, such as marketing, operations, or finance.

Managers have often delegated or abdicated decisions to information technology professionals. Technology professionals vary in their orientation. Some are very business focused and inform all their technical decisions with business drivers. Others are real "techies," far more influenced by technical elegance than by business relevance. A friend of ours rather unfairly calls these people "propeller heads." We need the expertise of "propeller heads" to make the technology work, but not as the prime business decision makers for the new infrastructure.

In most businesses, deciding on information technology capabilities is far too important a strategic decision to be left to the technical people or, worse, to the outsourcer with its own business objectives and need to make a profit. The firm's information technology capabilities are a top management responsibility. Certainly the technical people determine the implementation of a particular information technology capability, and outsourcers may provide it. But, as in InvestCo, top management must question and understand the technology implications of the value proposition and then decide on capabilities and funding priorities. On evaluating advice from the Information Technology Council, InvestCo's executive management must authorize the organizational changes and information technology investments needed to move toward a common information technology infrastructure for enabling cross-selling and lower costs. When executive management determines the information technology capability required and authorizes the expenditure to develop the capability, the implementation becomes the responsibility of technical specialists inside or outside the firm, working in partnership with business managers. The role of the CIO at InvestCo is to help the Information Technology Council understand what is technically possible and the resulting opportunities for the business.

Changing Strategy, Changing Technology

Changing business environments and competitive demands, like those experienced by InvestCo, shift the underlying strategic assumptions on which many firms compete. These strategic assumptions in turn have significant implications for the management and uses of information technology.

Johnson & Johnson: Changing Business Demands New Services

Early in 1995, Johnson & Johnson (J & J),[19] the world's largest manufacturer of health care products, established Johnson & Johnson Health Care Systems (HCS) to market the products of its existing companies to large customers. Dennis Longstreet, chairman of Johnson & Johnson HCS, explained that the pressures to focus on the economics of health care were changing the industry itself and that J & J had to respond: "What's happened is that stand-alone hospitals and physicians, who had been our primary customers for health care products, are no longer the sole decision-makers. It's become an integrated delivery system, where the doctor and the hospital and the payor and the insurance company are all becoming more connected to focus on delivering cost-effective quality health care."

J & J established the Johnson & Johnson Customer Support Center to sell its consumer products to large U.S. retailers, such as Wal-Mart and Kmart. Jim Litts, president of the Customer Support Center, noted that his efforts to work closely with different Johnson & Johnson operating companies represented a countercultural approach: "Johnson & Johnson has over 100 years of history authorizing operating companies to manage all business facets to maximize their brands' P&Ls. Today, we are learning how difficult it is to break those paradigms and work together to leverage the strength of the firm with larger retail customers."

HCS and the Customer Support Center departed from J & J's usual independent operating company model. To Longstreet and Litts they represented how the firm would operate in the future. Johnson & Johnson needed to form long-term relationships with customers, particularly large customers. The new value proposition to large customers demanded cooperation and coordination to deliver customer information that could be shared and communicated across J & J companies. Concurrently, the firm needed a new organizational model with significant implications for Johnson & Johnson's culture. The firm's strategy, value proposition, emerging organizational model, and information technology infrastructure requirements are intimately linked.

Johnson & Johnson: The Information Technology Implications

For J & J the shift in strategy and value proposition meant significant changes in direction in the firm's information technology investments. The shift meant investing in infrastructure in the form of shared information technology services across previously autonomous businesses. Like InvestCo, J & J had to rethink its information technology infrastructure capability and investments in order to achieve major strategic changes and a new operating model. This process involved a new set of principles for the management of information technology, driven by the new strategy. The result was an increased emphasis on shared information and information technology infrastructure, balancing cost, synergies, and local agility.

In the three parts of this book, we draw on the experiences of Johnson & Johnson and other market leaders to describe how executives can specify and manage their information technology portfolios to achieve their business objectives.

Overview of This Book

In Part 1 we address how information technology creates business value. We introduce a new lens for viewing the firm's information technology as an investment portfolio in Chapter 2. Like any investment portfolio, the information technology portfolio must be aligned with strategic goals and balanced for risk and return. Different business strategies require different information technology portfolios with different capabilities. A series of information technology investment benchmarks is provided to help identify a firm's relative position.

The evidence of payoff from five years of information technology investment in 54 businesses is presented in Chapter 3. The payoff and risk vary across the different parts of the portfolio, so we discuss the need for identifying the appropriate mix of investments. Because some firms achieve better business value than others from their information technology investments, we identify the characteristics and management practices of these successful firms. The outsourcing of information technology services has been heralded as an effective approach, and in this chapter we provide evidence showing the mixed success of outsourcing to date.

Part 2 identifies how market leaders use information technology opportunities to create business value. Such leaders understand the nature of information technology infrastructure investments and have clear management processes for making judicious decisions. In Chapter 4 we describe four different approaches to investments in information technology infrastructure. Each approach has different objectives, investment levels, and capabilities, and results in different types of business value. To allow for comparisons, we present benchmarks of investment and infrastructure capability, and examples of firms taking these different approaches. Understanding the dimensions of infrastructure capabilities is central to making investment decisions. In Chapter 5 we look in more detail at patterns of infrastructure capability in firms and ways to describe them in business terms. In particular, we identify the business-oriented indicators of a firm's need for higher or lower levels of information technology capability.

In Chapter 6 we explain further how these capabilities are linked to strategic choices. There we outline how successful firms underpin their strategic positioning and value proposition to customers through executive-led thinking and decision making about the new infrastructure. These processes are overt and convert information investments into business value for the firm. We call this process "Management by Maxim," in which firms identify both business and information technology maxims. These maxims are short, sharp strategic statements that encapsulate the future concerns of the whole firm. Using this process, top managers can make the best decisions for their strategic context—from no infrastructure at all through to the extensive capabilities of the new infrastructure, linking the extended enterprise and leading the industry in information technology–based business value.

But not all firms are ready or able to take this top-down firmwide approach. In Chapter 7 we contrast different management processes for the new infrastructure. About half the firms studied took a "Management by Deals" approach, in which information technology infrastructure decisions were a deal-making process based on the more immediate needs of each business. The deal-making process does not generally result in extensive firmwide infrastructure capabilities. Until the Information Technology Council meeting described earlier, InvestCo adopted a deal-making process because it lacked a strong business rationale and executive mandate for firmwide investments.

The new competitive environment meant that it had to shift to Management by Maxims to deliver its value proposition to customers.

In Part 3 we examine how to manage the information technology portfolio to maximize business value. We review the new infrastructure requirements of different types of business transformations in Chapter 8. Implementing business process redesign, competing with electronic commerce, extending international business operations, and managing knowledge all make new demands on the information technology portfolio. In Chapter 9 we describe the particular nature of information technology investments and illustrate how firms can appraise potential investments. We review how managers can assess the health of their portfolio to provide an informed basis for decision making, including both infrastructure and applications.

In Chapter 10 we consider a range of governance approaches aimed at linking business and technology decision making and management. We discuss the characteristics of firms that are better able to convert their investments into business value. How can other firms adopt these characteristics? What's the role of information politics in facilitating or hindering return on information technology investments? How do successful firms sustain informed expectations by executive management about information technology investments, and by information technology management about changing business requirements?

We clarify the necessary roles and responsibilities of senior management for maximum business value from the information technology portfolio. In the final section of Chapter 10, we present our Top Ten Leadership Principles for senior managers who want to drive business value from their information technology investments.

CHAPTER 2

Rethinking Technology Investments: The Information Technology Portfolio

Information technology is an investment like any other we make to create business value. When you strip away all the technical mumbo jumbo we are trying to achieve a few basic business objectives. We need to look at it like a series of investments which on balance must meet our objectives and make a return or will go broke.

Managing Director,
Major Business Unit,
Large Manufacturing Firm

Firms invest in a bewildering array of information technologies: local area networks, point-of-sale devices, image-processing systems, personal computers, scanners, databases, Internet home pages, security cameras, word processing software, and integrated applications suites. Investment in this technology can have many different management objectives, such as cost reduction or providing real-time information to senior management. Thousands of management decisions contribute to this portfolio of investments. Like any investment portfolio, this one needs to be actively managed to meet the goals of the firm. Like any investment portfolio, it is made up of investments with different objectives—each with different risk-return profiles to be balanced to meet the goals of the firm.

The information technology portfolio of an organization is its entire investment in information technology, including all the people dedicated to providing information technology services, whether centralized, decentralized, distributed, or outsourced. The investments include all computers, telecommunications networks, data, software, training, programmers, support personnel, point-of-sale systems, databases, and fax machines, whether integrated or standalone. The resulting systems range from the on-line order-processing systems used by telesales agents at companies like L. L. Bean and Victoria's Secret, to personal computers for desktop publishing.

So, firms have portfolios of information technology investments, just as investors have portfolios of financial investments. Individuals make different decisions about personal investments based on their commitments, aspirations, experiences, values, and attitude to risk. Managers make decisions about information technology investments based on a cluster of factors, including capabilities required now and in the future, the role of technology in the industry, the level of investment, the clarity with which technology investments are viewed, and the role and history of information technology in the firm.

The concepts fundamental to managing information technology are those of business, not of technology: portfolios, business value, investment, and alignment of resources with strategic goals. The objective of information technology investments is to provide business value in two related ways: to successfully implement current strategies and to use the technology to enable new strategies. The application of information technology strategies is often flawed by a "one size fits all" approach. Instead, the objective should be to tailor the information technology portfolio to the firm's unique strategic context.

In this chapter we explore different types of business strategies and the different types of information technology portfolios they require and provide a set of benchmarks for comparison. The foundation of each portfolio is the infrastructure: the enabling information technology investments, which are large, have long lives, are shared by multiple business areas, and support many applications. As the managing director at the beginning of this chapter points out, the composition of the portfolio must be driven by the demands of business strategy. However, aligning the information technology portfolio and strategy is tough, as they have fundamentally different characteristics. Firms often have multiple strategic goals and strategies that are fluid, constantly adapting to shifts in the business environment. Information technology infrastructures necessarily take time to develop and technical discipline to put in place and integrate. Although the new infrastructure is as important to firms as their traditional physical infrastructure of buildings, plant, and location, it has proved harder to conceptualize and manage. We discuss the ongoing difficulties of aligning business and technology strategies, and the importance of viewing information technology investments through the lens of an investment portfolio.

The investment portfolio is a strong, business-oriented lens familiar to executives. The information technology investment portfolio approach is based on the well-understood approach to managing financial portfolios—by balancing risk and return for a particular strategic objective. Appendix 2 contains a simple diagnostic for assessing the extent to which a firm's strategy and information technology are currently aligned to provide business value.

Why Do Firms Invest in Information Technology?

Firms invest in information technology to achieve four fundamentally different management objectives: transactional, infrastructure, informational, and strategic. These management objectives then lead to informational, transactional, infrastructure, and strategic systems, which make up the information technology investment portfolio. Figure 2.1 depicts these different management objectives and their interrelationships as they form the information technology portfolio.

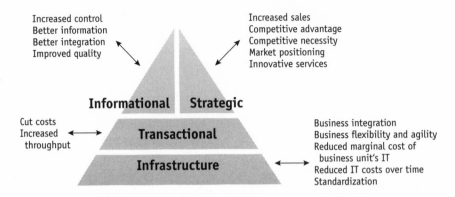

Figure 2.1   Management Objectives for the Information Technology Portfolio

Infrastructure Technology Objectives

At the base of the information technology portfolio is the infrastructure capability. Infrastructure, the foundation of information technology capability, is delivered as reliable services shared throughout the firm and coordinated centrally, usually by the information systems group. The infrastructure capability includes both the technical and the managerial expertise required to provide reliable services. For example, information technology infrastructure services in a firm often include firmwide communication network services, provision and management of large-scale computing, the management of shared customer databases, firmwide intranet capability, and research and development expertise aimed at applying emerging technologies to the business. The information technology investment, which uses and sits on top of this infrastructure, is made up of the applications that actually perform the business processes. The infrastructure services are standardized and shared by multiple business areas and are typically used by several different applications. Having the required infrastructure services in place significantly increases the speed with which new applications can be implemented to meet new strategies, thus increasing the firm's strategic agility and flexibility.

Transactional Technology Objectives

The next level of the information technology portfolio is the transactional information technology that processes and automates the basic, repetitive transactions of the firm. These include systems that support order processing, inventory control, bank cash withdrawal, statement production, accounts receivable, accounts payable, and other transactional processing. Transactional systems aim to cut costs by substituting capital for labor or to handle higher volumes of transactions with greater speed and less unit cost. Transactional systems build on and depend on a reliable infrastructure capability. Transactional systems, such as an order-processing system for a catalog sales firm, use several different infrastructure services, including the telecommunications network, the product database, the customer database, the local area network, and large-scale processing. Having the necessary infrastructure services significantly reduces the time and cost of building an order-processing system.

The apex of the information technology portfolio contains the informational and strategic uses of information technology, which rely on and are supported by the infrastructure and transactional systems. Usually both infrastructure and transactional systems must be in place before informational or strategic systems are feasible.

Informational Technology Objectives

Informational technology provides the information for managing and controlling the firm. Systems in this category typically support management control, decision making, planning, communication, and accounting. The total quality movement has resulted in large investments in informational technology, through systems that summarize and report the firm's product and process performance across a wide range of areas. Another example of an informational system is the Executive Information System (EIS) in a large international bank, which summarizes all the daily transactions in all the business units and branches and provides a picture, on the personal computer of each senior manager, of the firm's exposure and financial position. The EIS uses both the infrastructure and the transactional systems. The EIS uses infrastructure services such as the telecommunications network and the desktop local area network. The data come from summaries of the transactional systems, such as the account ledgers, and from external data services on the industry, competitors, and economy. The product of informational systems is a combination of data, information, and knowledge as an input to decision making and control.

Part of the firm's informational investments are the systems that support its knowledge management initiatives. The consulting firm Bain & Company leverages its knowledge base by providing quick identification of people within the company to contact for expertise and experience in certain situations. The system BRAVA (*Bain Resources Access for Value Addition*) contains critical information that enables consultants to tap these key people.[1] Ford Australia's Product Development Group initiated an Electronic Corporate Memory to capture lessons learned in developing new models. This knowledge is applied to new car projects, resulting in a shorter product cycle and more efficient use of staff time and resources.

Strategic Technology Objectives

The objective of strategic technology investments is quite different from those of the other parts of the portfolio. Strategic investments are made to gain competitive advantage or to position the firm in the marketplace, most often by increasing market share or sales. Firms with successful strategic information technology initiatives have usually found a new use of information technology for an industry at a particular point in time. An example is the first finance company to provide immediate 24-hour, seven-day-a-week loan approvals in car dealerships using expert systems technology; immediate loan approvals changed the way cars were sold.

The best way to determine a successful strategic information technology initiative is to check for competitors' responses to it. Successful systems will generate competitive responses aimed at copying or improving on the initiative. The speed with which a competitor can respond will depend significantly on the strength and flexibility of its own information technology infrastructure. Automatic teller machines (ATMs) were a very successful strategic use of information technology in the 1980s. Citibank pioneered the first large-scale use of ATMs in New York City and changed banking forever. For Citibank, this strategy was brilliant. Provide customers 24-hour access to their funds while asking them to perform the data entry themselves. The strategy was very successful and, coupled with Citibank's other initiatives, led to an increase in market share from 4 percent to 13 percent.[2] The impact in the marketplace forced other banks to respond quickly and begin building ATM networks at great expense. Competitors often found it necessary to build or acquire the infrastructure capability first, thus delaying their response. After most of the banks followed, what began as a strategic system then became transactional for the industry—a way to reduce the cost of a transaction through automation. Indeed, a major bank published that their average transaction cost via teller was between $1.50 and $3.00, compared to between $.50 and $1.20 via ATM. ATMs were no longer a way to differentiate and grow market share, but a way for each bank to reduce costs.

In recent years, ATMs have evolved further, to become infrastructures for the industry; that is, shared services. Now the typical ATM accepts cards from dozens of banks. Initially, this was a free service, but now banks often charge each other for the service. The Wachovia Bank ATMs in Atlanta charge Citibank customers a fee of $1.00 per ATM transaction. What was once strategic then became transactional and is now shared infrastructure, complete with a system of chargebacks between institutions. This type of shared infrastructure is bound to appear in other industries in an effort to increase connectivity and lower costs by reducing redundancy within the industry.

Multiple Objectives

A significant new investment may have just one management objective or all four. For example, Sun Life of Canada's Shared Health Net (SHN) enables drugstores and dental offices to directly submit claims electronically to insurers.[3] This reduces the time taken to submit and process a claim as well as the volume of paper involved. Sun Life's management objectives for this system probably contain elements of all four objectives: strategic objectives to increase sales through more satisfied clients (providing clients with easy ways to deal with Sun Life), some transactional (reducing the cost of processing a claim), some shared infrastructure (communications systems that support SHN), and informational, which facilitate monitoring of the process and customer information.

If investments in information technology are closely aligned with business strategies, there is good evidence of better payoff.[4] However, like the impact of lifestyle changes on personal investment portfolios, strategies shift and change, making alignment with the information technology portfolio temporary at best. Before presenting benchmarks on how much firms invest in information technology and for which management objectives, a discussion of the dynamics of strategy will clarify how aspects of strategic context affect different parts of the information technology portfolio.

The Dynamics of Business Strategy

The key objective of managing information technology investments as a total portfolio is to meet the changing needs of business strategies at both firm and business-unit levels. Like personal investment portfolios, longer- and shorter-term business strategies have different implications for the information technology portfolio, often requiring trade-offs in objectives. Managing the information technology portfolio is about the sort of choices and trade-offs that go to the very heart of strategy. As in managing a financial portfolio, if a firm's strategy is different from those of its competitors, its information technology portfolio must also be different—trading off short-term goals such as cost reduction with long-term goals such as agility and flexibility.

Strategies are derived and emerge from the firm's complex set of business, competitive, organizational, and environmental circumstances and are often not clearly articulated or universally agreed upon in a firm. The term *strategy* has become one of the most overused and broadly defined words in the business lexicon. We suggest a more practical perspective on strategy as a basis for developing a sound and well-aligned information technology portfolio.

Michael Porter neatly sums up the concept of strategy as emerging to help managers transform the daily chaos of events and decisions into an orderly way of sizing up a firm's position in its environment.[5] In this way, useful strategies make trade-offs and choices, and provide guidance for decision making throughout the firm.[6] The strategy is the firm's collective intention, according to Henry Mintzberg, where strategy formulation and implementation merge in a fluid process through which creative strategies evolve.[7] Strategies continually change, and John Kay convincingly argues that the strategy of successful firms is opportunistic and adaptive.[8]

Given this perspective, strategies must be sufficiently specified, articulated, and communicated to develop and allocate resources appropriately. But is this usually the case? For a sobering exercise, ask the staff interacting with your customers about the firm's approach to doing business—your strategy. In many firms, the wide variety of replies will be astounding and disturbing.

The constructs and processes of strategy have to be simple and flexible—and clearly articulated. We've seen many strategic planning processes flounder in a morass of bureaucratic requirements. This results in processes so complex and expensive that they strip the firm of the enthusiasm and commitment necessary to generate and implement new ideas. Such processes hinder strategic thinking, often resulting in paralysis by analysis and several volumes of wonderful material that nobody ever reads or acts on.

To work through how to support and stimulate strategy with the firm's information technology portfolio, we need a clear sense of direction for the long term and specific strategies for the shorter term.

Strategic Context

To achieve the delicate balance between articulating strategic objectives and overwhelming managers with demotivating processes, we use three constructs to help inform the information technology portfolio's needs: strategic intent, current strategy, and business goals. Together, these three constructs form critical components of a firm's strategic context.

The strategic context of the firm combines the long- and short-term strategies and the business goals. The strategic context is the essence of the firm's desired position in its environment. The situation of the Royal Automobile Club of Victoria (RACV), an Australian, membership-based insurance and roadside services firm headquartered in the state of Victoria, illustrates these concepts.[9]

Strategic Intent

The strategic intent of a firm specifies its long-term, stable goals[10]— a worthwhile destination for where a firm desires to go. The destination should require a stretch for the firm. RACV's strategic intent is for membership to be essential for all Victorians. Currently more than 60 percent of Victorian drivers are members of RACV for basic roadside services. But not all of those members use RACV's other products and services, where the market share is 40 percent of drivers. RACV aims to provide a total range of motoring, insurance, finance, and assistance products and services, which makes it easy for their 1.5 million roadside members to meet all their motoring and insurance needs with one organization.

Current Strategy

Current strategy specifies how the firm will do business today. What is the combination of products and services offered, to which customers, through what channels, at what price and quality levels? Current strategies have relatively short lives, and many firms have new current strategies every 12 months.

RACV has entered into a new era of competition. Until now, RACV and its counterparts in other states focused regionally and faced little competition. But now the equivalent organization in a neighboring state extended its base into Victoria, resulting in increased competition. RACV's current strategy now involves a strong focus on membership acquisition and customer needs. This focus is coupled with offering innovative products and services utilizing its extensive cross-selling opportunities to increase each roadside member's business with RACV.

For example, recently the RACV introduced Aussie Assist, an add-on to car insurance that provides insured customers with access to a range of additional benefits, including return transportation from the accident/breakdown site, lodging, towing, medical assistance, ambulance, and other support services. Aussie Assist was a very successful differentiator, yielding a 14 percent increase in new vehicle policies in its first year. The initiative invoked a competitor response, and similar products soon followed Aussie Assist into the marketplace. The Aussie Assist product was extended to home insurance and had a similarly dramatic effect on increasing the number of policies in home insurance.

RACV's strategic intent and current strategies shifted when its competitive environment changed. Current strategies were redeveloped, requiring significant changes to RACV's information technology portfolio. The implementation of the strategic initiative, Aussie Assist, required the implementation of a strategic system to support it. The new emphasis on cross-selling meant changes to the information technology infrastructure of RACV, so that transactions could be processed and information shared across business units.

Business Goals

The business goals of RACV, which flowed from its strategic intent and current strategies, include quantitative and qualitative business targets, with measures to determine progress. Robert Kaplan and David Norton's idea of the balanced scorecard is very useful here, to ensure goals and measures that balance short-term and long-term success.[11] A balanced scorecard includes measures of current performance, such as profit and return on equity, all of which are lagging indicators. In other words, these measures are generally end-of-period indicators that lag the business activities and describe past performance. The scorecard also includes medium-term indicators, such as customer satisfaction, and longer-term indicators, such as the number of new product innovations or revenues from new products. These are both leading indicators of future financial performance. Each firm requires a balance of leading and lagging indicators driven by its strategic intent. For example, a firm focusing on longer-term growth will put more emphasis on the leading indicators. In a large resources firm we studied, the list of performance measures in the firm's balanced scorecard was used as the specification for their new informational system to measure and consolidate business-unit performance. The inaccessibility of data for these measures and the inability for the information technology infrastructure to support this level of integration were motivations to rethink the firmwide infrastructure capability.

The balanced scorecard is useful in evaluating all investments, including information technology. In the investment process there is a temptation to focus on short-term profits at the expense of investment that will lead to future revenue streams, perhaps from new products. Firms with this focus struggle to invest in long-term information technology, such as infrastructure. A balanced scorecard approach encourages a firm to change the balance in good times and bad, just like bull and bear markets for financial investment. In tough times, tilt the balance toward the short-term profit goal. However, as with personal investment portfolios, even in the tough times of a bear market, a little needs to be invested with a longer-term perspective, to balance the scorecard and maintain a well-balanced portfolio.

The key question is whether a firm's investment in information technology is in harmony with its strategic objectives (intent, current strategy, and business goals) and thus building the capabilities necessary to deliver business value. This state of harmony is referred to as "alignment." It is complex, multifaceted, and never completely achieved. It is about continuing to move in the right direction and being better aligned than competitors. Alignment between strategic objectives and the information technology portfolio requires planned and purposeful management processes, within both business and information technology disciplines. Complete alignment can never be achieved, as the demands of business, competitive activity, management needs, and technology choices are constantly changing. It often takes firms many years to build or substantially change their information technology portfolio, making alignment over any period of time very challenging. As a consequence, non-alignment is the natural state of firms. The key consideration is: Are we heading in the right direction to align the portfolio with business needs, and are we better aligned than our competitors?

Alignment and the Information Technology Portfolio

The information technology portfolios of well-aligned firms often look different from one another. Each unique strategic context leads to different strategic objectives and different types of information technology portfolios. Two firms in Figure 2.2, CabinetCo and Ace Rentals, demonstrate the use of the information technology portfolio to assess the alignment of information technology with business strategy. Both are single-business-unit firms with strong alignment of their information technology portfolios and business strategy.

CabinetCo has a strong growth strategy and values flexibility and responsiveness to marketplace changes. This strategic context leads to an information technology portfolio with a flexible and extensive national infrastructure and strategic applications that position the firm as an innovative leader in the marketplace. Ace Rentals' strategic context is all about low cost. Ace focuses on the vacationer market, uses "preloved" cars, and has outlets just outside airports and in the cheaper, slightly more seedy side of town. Ace Rentals has a low-cost, no-frills approach and a limited, inflexible infrastructure that supports applications for processing transactions and providing cost and control information. Ace Rentals spends less on information technology as a percentage of revenues (and expenses) and less of the portfolio on infrastructure. Ace's informational technology is geared to controlling costs, with a heavy bias toward transactional investments and minimal infrastructure.

CabinetCo relies on and invests more in information technology. CabinetCo invests in strategic information technology to differentiate itself as a leader by offering in-store 3-D perspective drawings of custom-designed cabinets with on-the-spot quotations with a confirmed delivery date. Less of the cabinetmaker's portfo-

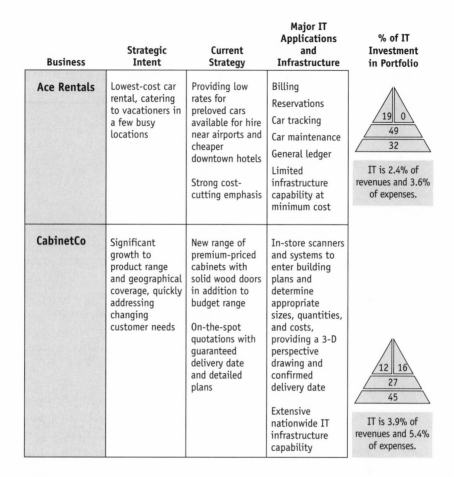

Business	Strategic Intent	Current Strategy	Major IT Applications and Infrastructure	% of IT Investment in Portfolio
Ace Rentals	Lowest-cost car rental, catering to vacationers in a few busy locations	Providing low rates for preloved cars available for hire near airports and cheaper downtown hotels Strong cost-cutting emphasis	Billing Reservations Car tracking Car maintenance General ledger Limited infrastructure capability at minimum cost	19 0 49 32 IT is 2.4% of revenues and 3.6% of expenses.
CabinetCo	Significant growth to product range and geographical coverage, quickly addressing changing customer needs	New range of premium-priced cabinets with solid wood doors in addition to budget range On-the-spot quotations with guaranteed delivery date and detailed plans	In-store scanners and systems to enter building plans and determine appropriate sizes, quantities, and costs, providing a 3-D perspective drawing and confirmed delivery date Extensive nationwide IT infrastructure capability	12 16 27 45 IT is 3.9% of revenues and 5.4% of expenses.

Figure 2.2 Comparing Information Technology Portfolios in Two Firms

lio is dedicated to cost reduction. CabinetCo spends more than the industry average on information technology, whereas Ace Rentals spends less. The strategic context of each firm drives both the level and the mix of investments in the information technology portfolio. Using the lens of the information technology portfolio and benchmarks, the senior managers of each firm are confidently able to assess and manage their investments and work with their information technology management to improve alignment. If either firm had the information technology portfolio of the other, poor alignment between information technology and strategy would result, leading to lower business value.

Many firms comprise more than one business or business unit. The management of their information technology portfolios is more complex than at CabinetCo and Ace Rentals. We now look at the portfolio patterns of multibusiness-unit firms and present a series of benchmarks for comparison.

Multibusiness-Unit Firms and Information Technology Portfolios

The notion of management objectives and the information technology portfolio can be extended to multibusiness-unit firms as well. Figure 2.3 depicts a multibusiness-unit firm with multiple information technology portfolios: one centrally coordinated and others within each business unit. The services required by the entire firm are provided by a combination of public and firmwide infrastructure, whereas business-unit infrastructures are more tailored to specific needs. These business-unit infrastructures should fit as "plug-ins" to the firmwide infrastructure.

For example, a large process manufacturing firm with eight business units provides some information technology infrastructure services (such as large-scale processing and telecommunications networks) centrally. All business units are encouraged to use these centrally shared services and to develop more customized local infrastructures if needed. One business unit, the biggest and most powerful business unit in the firm, has no local infrastructure and uses only the central services. Other business units use a few centrally provided services and have their own business unit–specific infrastructures. A small but growing business unit broke away altogether, citing poor service and its unique needs. At the moment there is no pertinent reason to bring that business unit into the centralized infrastructure. However, if the need arises, it will be time consuming and expensive, as the standards and systems in use are now different and not readily compatible.

We now look at how much firms invest in their information technology portfolios, comparisons across different industries, trends in these investments, and their distribution between centrally coordinated and business units. This information provides useful benchmarks for comparison and leads to further insights into why it remains a challenge to gain business value from these investments.

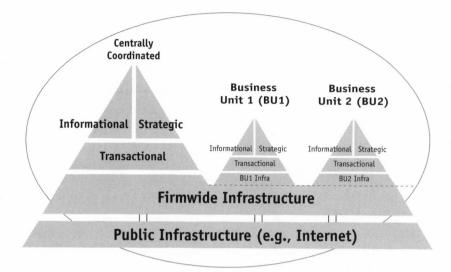

Figure 2.3   Information Technology Portfolios in a Multibusiness-Unit Firm

How Much Do
Firms Invest?

Firms invest differently in their information technology portfolios in terms of both the amount and the spread of investment. These differences arise from a combination of the different industries, strategic objectives, and diverse perspectives on the business contribution of information technology. In our study of the role and value of information technology infrastructure, we collected information technology investment data from 54 businesses in 27 companies in seven countries. The companies were in three industries: finance (banking and insurance), process manufacturing, and retail. Five years' benchmarking data, which may be used to understand the scope and spread of information technology investments and to benchmark a particular firm, are presented in Figure 2.4.

The benchmarking data illustrate how intensively each of the industries invests in information technology. Overall, firms invested 4.1 percent of revenues and 7.7 percent of expenses each year in

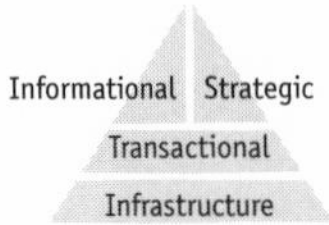

Five-Year Averages

	Finance	Manufacturing	Retail	All	All Av%Δ
No. of firms	12	10	5	27	
Firmwide $IT as % of Revenues	7.0	1.7	1.0	4.1	+2.6
Firmwide $IT as % of Expenses	14.2	2.0	1.1	7.7	+3.0
Corporate IT as % of Total IT	73	52	66	64	+4.4
Corporate IT Investment	14% / 9% / 8% / 69%	20% / 9% / 7% / 64%	1% / 6% / 11% / 82%	14% / 8% / 8% / 70%	−5% / −14% / −18% / +8%
Business Unit IT Investment (average 2 BUs per firm)	12% / 25% / 25% / 38%	24% / 20% / 16% / 40%	17% / 31% / 19% / 33%	18% / 24% / 20% / 38%	+9% / +18% / +19% / +11%
% of Total IT Outsourced	5.9	17.0	7.6	9.7	+8.2

Av%Δ = Average percentage change per year.

Figure 2.4   Information Technology Portfolio Pyramids in Different Industries

their information technology portfolios. The two lines of pyramids represent the firmwide and business-unit information technology portfolios for the three industries and overall. On average, 64 percent of the information technology portfolio is centrally coordinated and provided (often by a Corporate Information Technology group). The centrally coordinated portfolio can be a mix of firmwide information technology infrastructure and applications.

The three industries differed in their dependence on information technology and in how they allocated resources within the portfolio. The finance industry is typical of service industries where information technology *is* the production technology. Over five years, information technology accounted for 7.0 percent of revenues and 14.2 percent of expenses there. Although information technology accounts for only 1.0 percent of revenues in retail firms, this is a very significant amount of discretionary investment, given the large percentage of revenue accounted for by the cost of goods sold. The retail sector had by far the fastest increase in dependence on information technology in the five years studied, with a strong trend toward centralized infrastructure.

Several key trends are apparent over the five years' data in Figures 1.2 and 2.4. Firms are

- Increasing their dependence on information technology at 12 percent per year in dollars and more than 3 percent per year as a percentage of expenses.

- Increasing central coordination and sharing infrastructure investments but reducing centrally coordinated applications.

- Increasing their business unit's strategic and transactional investments in information technology at more than 18 percent and 19 percent per year, respectively.

- Outsourcing an average of 10 percent of their information technology investment and increasing at more than 8 percent per year.

Firms are increasingly placing their strategic information technology investments at the level of the business unit. This is sensible, as such systems need to be managed as close as possible, organizationally, to the products and services of which they are a part and as close as possible to the customers they serve. The more interlocked the strategic information technology is with the activities of the business unit, the more difficult it is to imitate and the more sustainable the advantage.[12]

Combining the corporate and business-unit investments reveals the total information technology investment: 58 percent in infrastructure, 14 percent in strategic, 16 percent in informational, and 12 percent in transactional systems. The 58 percent in shared and standard infrastructure underscores the significance of infrastructure investments and the necessity for senior management involvement in such investment decisions.

The key questions to ask while considering the last three and the next two years of investment, and while benchmarking a firm, are

- How much is invested in your portfolio?

- What is the balance of your firm's information technology portfolio in terms of transactional, infrastructure, informational, and strategic investment?

- How balanced and aligned with your strategic context is your portfolio?

- Is your portfolio helping your firm to meet its strategic objectives?

We now propose a framework for considering these questions.

The Challenge
of Alignment

It is sensible and desirable for management to focus on aligning the information technology portfolio with the business strategy. However, this will always be difficult to achieve. In the following pages we explain why, by describing traditional approaches and identifying the barriers that management often encounters.

The four ingredients of the traditional approach to alignment are depicted in the four boxes in Figure 2.5: strategic context, environment, information technology strategy, and the information technology portfolio. Complete alignment is usually nonsustainable because strategic context constantly changes and because information technology portfolios are assets that take a long time and significant investment and expertise to develop. The environment changes, competitive strategies shift, customers change profiles, and the firm's current strategies will evolve both in anticipation of and in response to the market situation. Alignment is dynamic—a change in any one of the ingredients usually requires another shift elsewhere. The goal is for information technology investments and the portfolio to be heading in the right direction to maximize the value of those investments to the business.

The arrows in Figure 2.5 indicate the major links required between the four components to achieve better alignment. The strategic context of the firm drives information technology strategy, which in turn strives to achieve better alignment of the information technology portfolio. The environment influences the process in two ways. First, opportunities, threats, constraints of regulations, and competitors influence the strategic context. Second, the impact of emerging technological developments, such as lower costs of processing power or the evolution of the Internet, influence the potential and the economics of the information technology portfolio.

The information technology portfolio can also influence the strategic context in two ways. First, the information technology portfolio provides information about how the firm is performing. Second, if well designed, the portfolio enables new current strategies to emerge, consistent with strategic intent.

The elements of the strategic context that are important to this process are strategic intent and current strategy. The strategic intent

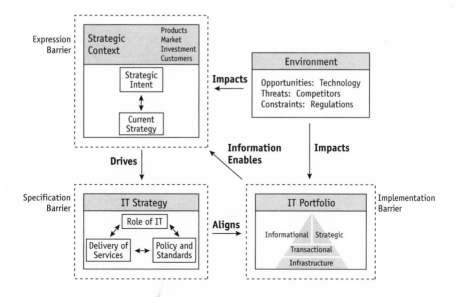

Figure 2.5   Aligning Business Strategy and Information Technology

drives long-term investments in the information technology portfolio; that is, the infrastructure component. Both strategic intent and the infrastructure component of the information technology portfolio are relatively stable over time. The current strategy in turn drives the applications—that is, the strategic, transactional, and informational parts of the portfolio—and is expected to change regularly as customer needs change.

The information technology strategy must balance and reinforce the strategic context in several important ways: the perceived role of information technology in the firm (core or support), the way information services are delivered (centralized, decentralized, outsourced versus insourced), and technology policies and standards. In a firm with a well-aligned information technology portfolio, the right amount is invested in information technology; the mix of investments is appropriate for the firm's strategy; the information technology investments are successfully converted into business value; and the information technology portfolio facilitates the family of current strategies likely to be implemented within the firm's strategic intent. But in most firms, things hardly ever work that smoothly.

Why Is Alignment So Difficult?

Using the four elements of the traditional alignment approach as a general framework, let's look at the major difficulties firms experience in aligning business strategy, technology strategy, and the information technology portfolio. Three types of barriers are commonly encountered: those of expression, specification, and implementation. These barriers, represented as broken-line boxes in Figure 2.5, prevent links between the four alignment elements, reducing the likelihood of alignment and hindering better return on investment and shareholder value.

The first group of barriers is *expression barriers*, which result in insufficient understanding of and commitment to the firm's strategic focus by operational management. They arise from the firm's strategic context and from senior management behavior—including lack of direction in business strategy, changing strategic intents, and insufficient top management awareness of information technology.

The second group of barriers is *specification barriers*, in which business and information technology strategies are set in isolation and are not adequately related. These arise from the circumstances of the firm's information technology strategy. There is lack of information technology involvement in strategy development, business and technology management conduct two independent monologues, and information technology ends up being uncoordinated across the firm.

The nature of the firm's current information technology portfolio creates the third set of barriers—*implementation barriers*—which arise when there are technical, political, or financial constraints on the current infrastructure. Perhaps the acquisition of a business has resulted in multiple diverse portfolios which are hard to change in the business time frame required. Often the portfolios contain "legacy systems" that are difficult to integrate into a firmwide infrastructure. The changes required to improve alignment may be too large an investment for the firm, based on the way business cases are currently approved.

Seven common examples of barriers, covering each of the three types of barriers, follow.

Expression Barriers

Lack of Direction in Business Strategy

Clear and well-articulated strategic intents and current strategies are necessary in improving alignment. These provide the directions and bases for developing the information technology portfolio. Poor specification of strategic objectives often leads to the information technology group setting an information technology strategy in isolation from the business.

The CEO of a welfare agency we worked with was concerned that insufficient business value was being generated from the agency's substantial information technology investments. On visiting the information technology group, we found a very impressive operation with a well-developed infrastructure but few business applications. The information technology group benchmarked well in technical terms.

In response to questions about his approach, the information technology manager was adamant that there had been no articulated business strategy in the organization for years. His response was to produce a very flexible information technology infrastructure that could respond quickly to "any new business strategy they come up with." Were his actions responsible? Surely not. But equally to blame for this situation were the CEO and the executive committee, who did not clearly articulate and communicate the agency's strategic objectives. Yet they approved the information technology budgets year after year!

In a situation where there is an insufficiently articulated business strategy, information technology investments, particularly infrastructure, should be minimized until good direction is attained.

Changing Strategic Intents

Strategic intents, the long-term stable goals of the firm, are usually stable over time. Strategic intent provides a basis for information technology infrastructure decisions and for the family of business needs, and thus applications that are required. Current strategies and business goals change regularly, are articulated, and evolve throughout the implementation process. If appropriately designed, the information technology infrastructure provides support for the introduction of a wide range of new products with minimal further investment. A poorly crafted infrastructure won't cope well with frequently changing current strategies. However, almost no information technology infrastructure will readily accommodate strategic intents that change regularly.

Insufficient Awareness of Information Technology

Many top managers are aware of the importance of information technology in their industry and their business. But top management awareness isn't enough. Top management must set the vision for how the technology will be used, particularly the business capabilities required of infrastructure investments. Too often this vision setting is abdicated or delegated to the information technology manager or the chief financial officer. The result is often a technical or financial vision for information technology use that restricts business opportunities and doesn't optimize business value.

Specification Barriers

Lack of Information Technology Involvement

Many firms don't seriously consider the impact of information technology industry developments in their strategy-setting processes. They appear not to be alert to the potential impact of electronic commerce or the Internet on their current strategies. Top management needs to ensure that the capabilities of information technology to deliver the product differently (as in phone banking and electronic shopping) or to control inventory more effectively (as in point-of-sale systems) are identified. This requires management processes that integrate information technology input from the internal information technology group, consultants, or vendors.

Two Independent Monologues

Information technology professionals usually have very strong technical backgrounds. They like technology, are fascinated by emerging technologies, and believe in technical solutions. They are inherently optimistic about technology's ability to deliver value. Information technology professionals are very important to firms, particularly those firms that have identified information technology as a core competence. But if there isn't a strong business focus among information technology managers, then problems often emerge.

Peter Keen[13] describes the conversation between the average business manager and information technology professionals as consisting of two independent monologues. Many of us have observed business and technology managers talking at cross-purposes and in nonproductive settings where each is using a different set of jargon. Information technology managers need to be hybrids: They need to have good technical skills *and* a practical understanding of the firm's business issues and directions. On the other hand, business managers need to take responsibility for informed decision making about the technical capabilities of their business. Only in this way will the two monologues become a dialogue, so that investments will be well made.

Uncoordinated Information Technology

In some firms, the investment in information technology is uncoordinated across the firm. Funds for information technology investments often come from several different budgets. Some firms we studied couldn't initially tell us how much they invested, where, by whom, and on what. In such a situation, aligning information technology with strategic intent is even more problematic. Where business units have common customers, products, processes, or suppliers, there are usually opportunities for synergies and a need to consider information technology investments across the firm or at least across several business units. Even without synergies, there are often opportunities to cut information technology costs by sharing expensive resources such as data centers. To make appropriate investment decisions, top management must at least have an overview of the firm's total information technology portfolio and its relationship to strategic objectives.

Implementation Barrier

But We're Different

Implementation barriers occur where there is the will and vision to form the appropriate information technology portfolios, but the task cannot be completed. A common barrier to implementing a shared infrastructure, such as a customer database, are the heartfelt concerns of different business units in a firm that "We're different, and the shared infrastructure won't meet our needs."

In the process manufacturing firm with eight business units mentioned earlier in this chapter, one business unit opted out of using the shared infrastructure. The problem was that the corporate information technology group imposed a series of technical standards on the soon-to-be-renegade business unit without any convincing firmwide business drivers as justification. The business unit, which was highly profitable and thus powerful, said no, thank you, or less polite words to that effect. Without a convincing trail of evidence linking the firm's strategic context to a firmwide business need, and then to the necessary firmwide information technology initiative, the business unit opted out.

CHAPTER 3

The Evidence for Business Value

The chairman of a $5 billion supermarket chain was visiting a leading business school and had just delivered an inspiring address to the MBA students. The address touched on the firm's innovative uses of information technology, including the "digital supermarket" pilot program, in which customers in remote communities may select groceries for delivery from product images of a fully stocked supermarket. After a few questions on retail profitability, target marketing, and personal time scheduling, one student asked, "How do you determine payoff of your firm's information technology investments?" The chairman answered, "I am certain half our information technology investment doesn't pay off—the problem is I really don't know which half." The chairman went on to explain the supermarkets' different types of information technology investments and the postimplementation information needed to manage each investment.

The chairman was trying to come to terms with the value the supermarkets were getting from their information technology investments and to use the payoff experience as a guide for making future investments. Unfortunately, there is little reliable information about the payoff of information technology investments in any firm or group of firms. Partly for this reason, large information technology investments are often made on faith, rather than on solid evidence for a real return.

This chapter presents evidence for the business value achieved—or not achieved—by firms investing in information technology in different ways. The evidence is based primarily on our studies but also draws on the growing literature in the area. The four types of information technology investment in the portfolio—strategic, informational, transactional, and infrastructure—have different impacts on business value and thus have different risk-return profiles and are effectively different investment classes. Successful firms can achieve significant premiums over the average by managing and converting their information technology investments more effectively. Senior management is in a much better position to make informed decisions when armed with information technology investment benchmarks, historical risk-return information of the different types of information technology, and the characteristics of more successful converters of the investment.

The evidence for business value is captured in three critical questions addressed in this chapter:

- What is the evidence for payoff from the firm's information technology portfolio?

- What is the nature of the payoff from different parts of the information technology portfolio?

- Why do some firms get relatively more business value from their information technology investments than their competitors?

The answers to these questions have significant implications for managing the information technology portfolio. As with financial portfolio management, knowing the historical performance patterns can yield insights into current and future investment and management decisions. Although new technologies are available to add to the portfolio every day, the mix of technologies in sizable firms changes slowly, so the relationships found in studies of the recent past are likely to hold true for several years. If a particular information technology investment strategy hasn't been associated with superior performance, this doesn't mean that the strategy should be avoided. It does mean that the strategy is more risky and requires vigilance and discipline for successful implementation and delivery of business value.

What Is Business Value?

In our executive programs on the management of information technology, we often ask groups of 40 or more senior managers: What is business value to you? The variety of responses is astounding, ranging from revenue growth to building systems faster. Business value is strongly dependent on the firm's context and objectives. In assessing the business value of information technology, we've adopted a broad base of measures to encompass this variety and use a four-level hierarchy of business value. Figure 3.1 presents this hierarchy and provides sample measures of business value at each of the four levels.

Very successful investments in information technology will have a positive impact on all four levels of the business value hierarchy over time. Less successful investments may show a positive impact at the lower levels but are not sufficiently strong to touch the higher levels. The effect of information technology can also be diluted or swamped by other factors.

The first level of business value is provided by the firmwide information technology infrastructure, with measures such as infrastructure availability (for instance, percentage of downtime) and cost per transaction and workstation. The second level of business value is provided by business-unit information technology performance, with measures such as time and cost to implement new applications. The third level is provided by the operational performance of the business, with measures such as quality and time to market for new products. The top and most important level is the financial performance of the firm, with measures such as return on assets (ROA) and revenue growth.

The financial measures at the top of the hierarchy are typically lagging measures of business value. They are available only after the events have occurred, and they measure only past performance. The measures of operational performance are leading indicators of business value, which will partially predict future financial performance. The measures of information technology performance and information technology infrastructure performance specifically track the efficiency of using information technology assets.

Investments in information technology are made at the bottom two levels in the hierarchy by both information systems departments and line managers. Measuring the information technology investments at the bottom two levels and performance at all four levels is key to

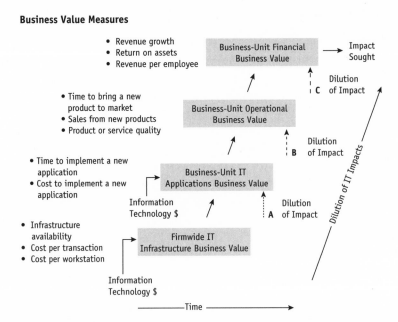

Figure 3.1   Hierarchy of Impact of Information Technology Investments

assessing business value. Then we can track the impact of information technology investments up this hierarchy of business value, providing solid evidence and insight into how value is or is not created.

As the impact moves up the levels, the dilution of that impact increases with the influence of other factors (represented by the dashed arrows *A*, *B*, and *C*), such as pricing decisions and competitor moves. Measuring the impact of an information technology investment will be much easier at the bottom of the hierarchy (at point *A*) than at the top, where many other factors dilute the effect. In determining the impact of information technology, the sequence (and dilution) of impact moving up from bottom to top must be taken into account. It is only by understanding how the investment affects each level that one can build a coherent picture of the payoff of information technology investment.

The Payoff from the Firm's Portfolio

After the completion of many careful studies, the evidence for the payoff from a firm's total investment in information technology investments is mixed. Some studies find that firms that invest more in information technology also perform better, whereas others find no statistical relationship.[1] Paul Strassmann, former CIO of Xerox, argues convincingly that there is little correlation between a firm's total investment in information technology and firm profitability. However, Eric Brynjolfsson and Lorin Hitt of the Sloan School at MIT have statistically demonstrated that there is a spectacular payoff.[2]

Given the mixed evidence, there must be other factors, apart from the size of investment, influencing the relationship between information technology investment and business value. Two such factors are the balance between different parts of the information technology portfolio and the ability of the firm to convert these investments into business value. We address the first of these next and the second later in this chapter.

The Payoff from Different Parts of the Portfolio

Each of the four types of investment in the information technology portfolio have different characteristics and influence business value in different ways. They are effectively different investment classes but are also dependent on one another. Figure 3.2 presents a summary of the relationships between the different types of information technology investment and business value.[3] All of the relationships described in Figure 3.2 and in the remainder of this chapter are statistically significant; therefore, it is very unlikely they were due to chance.[4] Identifying and recognizing the existence of these relationships is very helpful in making future decisions. It is the ability to take the evidence and apply it to the future that will distinguish the top-performing firms.

Transactional Technology Investments

Transactional investments provide the information technology to process the basic, repetitive transactions of the firm. These include systems that support order processing, inventory control, claims processing for insurance firms, accounts receivable, accounts payable, bank withdrawals, billing, and other transactional processing, such as ATMs. Transactional systems are developed to cut costs, often by substituting capital for labor, or to make it possible to handle higher volumes of transactions.

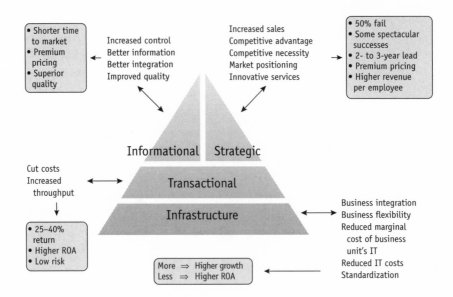

Figure 3.2   Information Technology Portfolio and Business Value

Colonial Life & Accident Insurance Company, part of UNUM Life Insurance Company of America, is the leader in payroll-deducted, voluntary employee benefits offered to employees at their work sites.[5] Colonial sells its products to employees and employers in large commercial organizations, public sector organizations, and smaller commercial organizations. Colonial sends bills to smaller employers and receives bulk information transfers from large employers, who deduct the premium amounts from each employee's paycheck each pay period.

Colonial relies heavily on its information technology for fast, reliable processing of millions of transactions per month, with an average policy premium of $28. Both the billing and the enrollment systems are complex, and the processing requirements are equally intensive and voluminous. Colonial receives 15,000 to 20,000 new applications each week. Operating effectiveness and reducing the costs of a transaction are among Colonial's core competencies, and the customer is at the heart of that strategy. Customers can call a single 800 number for answers to all their questions. A customer service representative retrieves the appropriate customer file from the mainframe database, downloads it to his or her personal computer, and makes any necessary changes or updates while the customer is on the phone. The system's response time is less than 3 seconds. At the conclusion of the phone call, the updated customer file is uploaded to the mainframe.

In our five-year study, transactional investment represented 8 percent of centrally coordinated information technology investment and 20 percent of business-unit investment, accounting for 12 percent of the firm's total information technology portfolio over five years. There is very good evidence that transactional information technology investment pays off at the top of the performance hierarchy in measures of profit, such as ROA. The impact can be tracked up the hierarchy through significantly better operational performance measures, such as labor productivity and the ability to profitably charge lower prices. The statistical analysis indicates an average return of between 25 and 40 percent on each dollar of transactional information technology.

Transactional information technology is only one of four types of information technology investment where more investment was consistently associated with more business value and superior financial performance. The effect on performance (ROA) was equally strong with a one-year, two-year, and three-year lag between investment and performance. So transactional investments made in 1993 were still measurable as positively related to performance in 1996. Simply put, the more of the information technology portfolio dedicated to transactional information technology, the stronger the impact on performance. Also, the more money invested in transactional information technology as a percentage of the firm's revenues or expenses, the stronger the impact on performance. For example, in our study of American valve manufacturers, increasing transactional investment as a percentage of revenues by one percentage point (say, from 2 to 3 percent) was associated with an increase in ROA of 0.7 percent.[6] It is likely that at some point investing more in transactional information technology will no longer produce positive business value, but none of the firms studied had reached that level of investment.

This is strong evidence that investments in information technology that support streamlined processes and that automate transactions with the objective of cutting costs are successful in creating business value. The key differentiation is that the management objective for business value in this case is to cut costs.

Interestingly, firms that invested more in transactional information technology also had lower revenue growth. The lower revenue growth was probably due to a focus on cost reduction in the firm as a whole, leading to an information technology portfolio with a strong transactional focus.

Transactional information technology is relatively low risk, with evidence of solid if not spectacular returns. Transactional investments are like the cash management accounts, bonds, and blue chip equity investments of a financial portfolio. They are an essential part of a balanced information technology portfolio.

Informational Technology Investments

Informational technology provides the information for managing and controlling the organization. Systems in this category typically support management and financial control, decision making, planning, communication, and accounting. Over the five years studied, informational investment represented 14 percent of centrally coordinated information technology investment and 18 percent of business-unit investment, accounting for 16 percent of the average firm's total information technology portfolio over five years. Firms whose strategies are highly dependent on information are heavy investors in this type of information technology. These include firms that focus on

- Marketing to highly specific customer segments.
- Knowledge management by codifying and making organizational knowledge available.
- Carefully monitoring product and process quality.
- A strong cost control discipline with detailed information on expenditures.
- Scouring environmental trends for new product and service opportunities.

Information has little value in its own right. It is the application of information to decisions that leads to business value. For example, one large business bank had an excellent economic forecasting group that tracked the bank's investment and customer profiles very carefully. However, the information was rarely used, or used well, by management. There was a misguided belief that, because the information was gathered, it was used in decision making. This wasn't the case, and the bank suffered a disastrous period of real estate loan defaults in the early 1990s as a result.

Having too much information or the wrong information is also likely to have a negative impact. Our findings on the payoff of informational technology investment reflect this delicate balance.

Firms investing more of their portfolios in informational information technology have a number of desirable performance characteristics. They have a shorter time to market for new products, superior product quality, and the ability to charge higher prices than competitors.

In general, firms with more of the information technology portfolio in informational systems have significantly better operational performance measures at level *C* in Figure 3.1. This is particularly true for operational measures that are highly information intensive, such as quality and time to market.

There is compelling evidence that informational investments are significantly more effective in improving operational performance when they are made at the level of the business unit rather than firmwide. Informational investments are more effective when specified and managed closer to or by the managers making the decisions. The closer to the affected managers, the more focused the investment is and the more likely it is to reduce information overload.

However, we couldn't find any consistent impact on financial measures of performance, such as ROA or revenue growth. More information appears to affect operational performance, but not sufficiently strongly to influence the bottom line. The dilution of other factors washes out any measurable effect before it reaches the financial indicators.

Firms making large investments in informational technology include

- A large financial services firm using a data warehouse to consolidate information from different systems in order to obtain one view of the total relationship with each customer.

- An executive information system in a global multibusiness-unit manufacturing conglomerate that summarizes key performance data daily for senior executives of the 50 operating units.

- A department store's buyer support system that summarizes the transactions of the past 81 weeks at the stock-keeping-unit (SKU) level, as a basis for forecasting and ordering supplies of nonbasic stock.

But having more and better information isn't sufficient to generate financial business value. Management must be able to act decisively and consistently on the information. Some firms are better at using their information than others. The difference is having clear business drivers and management processes in place to use the information. Therefore, informational investment is higher risk than transactional information technology. Managers must carefully understand and improve the business and management processes to use this information across the firm. Simply adding more information will not affect the bottom line.

Strategic Technology Investments

Strategic investments in information technology are made to gain competitive advantage or to position the firm in the marketplace, most often by increasing market share or sales. Firms with successful strategic information technology initiatives are usually involved with a use of information technology that is new for an industry at a particular point in time, and thus inherently risky. Over the five years we studied, strategic investment represented 8 percent of centrally coordinated information technology investment and 24 percent of business-unit investment, accounting for 14 percent of the total portfolio.

Competitive advantage is always difficult to sustain, and competitive advantage through information technology is no different. There is evidence of some spectacular successes in the use of strategic information technology in each industry. It's easy to recognize a success, as competitors quickly follow with their own version or perhaps join forces with the leader. However, the high risks of strategic information technology initiatives also lead to a high failure rate. We found that approximately 50 percent of strategic information technology initiatives failed, with a negative net present value for the project five years later. Aside from a select number of very successful investments, the rest of the strategic information technology projects broke even and retained competitive position rather than delivered a sustained advantage.

On average, successful strategic information technology initiatives retain competitive advantage for two to three years before the competition is able, or chooses, to follow. Followers who copy or improve on the initiative dilute the leader's dominant position. What was strategic now becomes transactional for the industry, and every firm has to make that investment to compete.

One of the barriers to firm's following a competitor's strategic information technology initiative is the lack of a well-developed firmwide infrastructure. For example, American Hospital Supply implemented its pioneering use of information technology to allow customers to order and check inventories and prices on-line. Competitors took several years to offer the same service, as they were structured in separate business units with separate ordering systems on separate infrastructures, preventing a one-stop order point. Many firms today continue to have infrastructures that would not support proactive or reactive strategic information technology initiatives across business units or among product groups.

Strategic uses of information technology were significantly more common in the finance industry but were increasing at a faster rate in manufacturing. This trend is likely to continue as more information is embedded in manufactured products. Indeed, the opportunities for competitive advantage from strategic information technology are higher in industries like process manufacturing, where the information technology infrastructures of competitors are often less developed and not usually a core competence.

Firms that invested more in strategic information technology had higher labor costs in the short term and positive impacts on ROA in the third year after the investments. In general, firms that invested more of their information technology portfolio or more of their expenses in strategic information technology had significantly faster time to market, were able to charge premium prices, were perceived to have higher-quality products, and had higher revenues per employee.

From these results emerges a pattern of firms that rely more on strategic uses of information technology. They operate at the premium end of their market and are more innovative and more agile with new products. These firms are generally more reliant on information technology than their competitors and generate more revenue per employee.

Strategic information technology initiatives were also more effective when implemented at the business-unit level. These investments require an intimacy with customer needs that is more likely present when managed by the business unit, which is closer to the customer. The major exception to this principle arose where the objective was to provide firmwide customer access to products offered by different business units.

Some strategic information technology initiatives include

- Laptops for salespeople of a valve manufacturing firm, to allow on-site custom design, quotation, and guaranteed delivery dates in the customer's office.

- Pacific Pride's turning the commodity business of supplying fuel to commercial clients into a value-added service. Pacific Pride, a fuel company operating in the U.S. Northwest, provides management reports to customers on fuel purchases by vehicle each month, including engine efficiency details. Pacific Pride was able charge up to an eight-cent premium per gallon for this service.

- Home banking on personal computers in the 1980s, such as Chemical Bank's Pronto system.[7] This is an example of a failed strategic information technology initiative. A number of banks are relaunching this product, expecting that the penetration of the Internet and PCs means that the time has now come for home banking.

Strategic information technology is the high-risk and high-return part of the portfolio, having much in common with the financial investment class of equity investments in emerging markets, or call and put options.

Infrastructure Technology Investments

By their very nature, information technology infrastructure investments are large and long term and have no real value on their own. Infrastructure's value lies in its ability to quickly and economically enable the implementation of new applications, often across business units or the firm, which in turn generate business value. One of the strengths of a more extensive infrastructure is the standardization of services, such as one integrated telecommunications network or a unified customer database. This standardization allows easier integration and information access across business units. For example, we found that firms seeking more synergies and cross-selling between separate business units have significantly more infrastructure investment and capability. However, this extensive infrastructure capability costs more up front, and these costs, as well as the benefits, are reflected in the relationships to the business value of the firm. Over the five years we studied infrastructure, investments represented 70 percent of centrally coordinated information technology investment and 38 percent of business-unit investment, accounting for 58 percent of the average firm's total portfolio.

The issues of investing in and managing information technology infrastructure are very similar to those of managing the public infrastructure of roads, bridges, hospitals, and schools. Both types of infra-

	Less or Decreasing Infrastructure	**More or Increasing Infrastructure**
Business-Unit (BU) Financial Performance	• Lower growth in revenue per employee • Higher return on assets (ROA) • Lower revenue growth* • Lower revenue per employee	• Higher growth in revenue per employee • Lower ROA • Higher revenue growth* • Higher revenue per employee
BU Operational Performance	• Fewer sales from new products • Slower time to market	• More sales from new products • Faster time to market
BU IT Performance	• Shorter time to build new applications • No difference in cost to build new applications	• Longer time to build new applications • No difference in cost to build new applications
Firmwide Infrastructure Performance	• Less processing power per dollar • No difference in costs per workstation • Less system availability	• More processing power per dollar • No difference in costs per workstation • More system availability

Note: These relationships are all statistically significant after controlling for industry differences.
*In the finance sector.

Figure 3.3 Evidence for Business Value of Information Technology Infrastructure

structures are centrally provided and funded out of transfers from the eventual user groups. Standards must be set centrally to ensure compatibility (rules for the development of buildings or software applications that use the infrastructure services). Perhaps the most difficult challenge is that the infrastructure services must be sized and put in place before the precise business requirements are known.

To build a convincing case for determining the relationship of information technology infrastructure to business value, we track the impact up the hierarchy from Figure 3.1. An intricate set of relationships unfolds, revealing a delicate balance between the costs and benefits of extensive infrastructure capability. The relationships[8] to the hierarchy of performance measures of having more or increasing infrastructure are summarized in Figure 3.3.

Firms with increasing infrastructure had a faster growth in revenue per employee, and firms with more infrastructure had higher revenues per employee. Firms with increasing infrastructure also had stronger overall revenue growth. The effect on overall revenue growth was found in industries with a strong reliance on information flows, such as banking and insurance. Firms with more infrastructure also had significantly more sales from new products and a faster time to market for new products. Firms with more infrastructure had more integrated firmwide infrastructures, allowing easier cross-selling of products between business units and faster introduction of new products. The faster delivery of new products appears to increase sales from new products, which in turn increases revenue growth.

The time to market was particularly sensitive to the extent of infrastructure. Firms with more extensive infrastructures linked business units and integrated different business processes, as well as reached beyond the firm electronically to customers and suppliers. These firms had faster times to market. Firms with extensive, tailored business-unit infrastructures were also more agile in bringing new products to market faster. The extensive integration and communication across business units required for products and processes with a firmwide focus, such as cross-selling, was enabled by more extensive infrastructure. The extensively tailored business units' infrastructures enabled an electronic platform integrating the various functional areas that are necessary for fast time to market, such as marketing, product development, management accounting, and project management.

Sales from new products were also particularly sensitive to an extensive business-unit infrastructure tailored to the strategy of the particular business but fitted like a "plug-in" with firmwide infrastructure.

Firms with more extensive infrastructures, either at firmwide or business-unit levels, require a significantly longer time to build or integrate new applications. These firmwide infrastructures are complex, and any new application must interface with existing infrastructure services and applications. This level of integration and testing takes longer than building or acquiring new applications on stand-alone infrastructures not requiring such extensive integration. In addition, extensive infrastructures inevitably contain a combination of technologies from different eras of computing and different vendors. These differences combine to contribute to the longer time to integrate. Costs to build new applications were also higher where more infrastructure was found at the business level rather than firmwide. The provision of more tailored business-unit infrastructures contributes positively to business value but adds costs to produce applications.

The positive influences on business value of more infrastructure also appear to come at a cost. Although firms with less infrastructure have lower revenue per employee or revenue growth, they also have significantly higher profitability (as measured by return on assets), particularly in the short term. Firms with less infrastructure also have less sales from new products and take longer to bring new products to market. They will find it more difficult to cross-sell products between business units.

Firms with less integrated infrastructures can build new applications more quickly and at lower cost, as less effort is required for integration. Interestingly, although the applications are built faster and for less money, these applications generate fewer sales from new products. Therefore, these new applications are unlikely to be strategic applications or those associated with new products.

In terms of firmwide information technology costs and performance, there was no difference in response times to screen commands and recovery times from failures for firms with more or less firmwide infrastructures. However, firms with increasing firmwide infrastructures have significant economies of scale in their ability to provide more processing power at a significantly cheaper cost. Interestingly, these economies don't extend to the cost per workstation. There was no difference in cost per workstation between firms with less or more firmwide information technology infrastructure.

In summary, firms with less extensive infrastructures have fewer resources tied up in infrastructure and are more profitable. However, these firms have lower sales from new products and take more time to reach the market with those new products. This means that, although firms with less infrastructure may currently be performing profitably, they aren't as agile in reacting to shifts in market needs affecting the whole firm as firms with a more extensive, firmwide infrastructure capability. Firms with less infrastructure have lower revenues per employee, with a lower rate of increase as well as lower revenue growth. This less extensive approach to infrastructure is well suited to firms that compete predominantly on cost.

Firms with more extensive infrastructures have more resources tied up in infrastructure, but have more sales from new products with a faster time to market. These firms also have faster-increasing revenues per employee and stronger revenue growth, but lower profits.

Thus a delicate balance exists between short-term profitability and revenue growth. Less extensive infrastructures require less investment, but these firms are slower to produce new products and they get fewer sales from them. These firms also increase revenue per employees at a slower rate and have lower overall revenue growth.

The decision of how much infrastructure capability to put in place depends heavily on the strategic goals of the firm and the measures of performance that are of the highest priority. Firms with goals including revenue growth and fast response to market shifts are better served by more infrastructure—particularly firmwide infrastructure if cross-selling is desired. Firms with a focus on shorter-term profitability are better served with less infrastructure, both in terms of investment dollars and as a proportion of the information technology portfolio. A prudent strategy to maximize short-term profit is to minimize infrastructure investments and focus on transactional uses of information technology. In Part 2 of the book we describe how firms link the infrastructure capability to their strategic contexts.

Balancing the Portfolio for Risk and Return

The four types of information technology investment in the portfolio have different risk-return profiles. Like any investment portfolio, the information technology portfolio must be managed to balance risk and return while maintaining the appropriate level of investment to meet strategic goals. The strategic context of the firm, like the long-term aims of an individual investor, must drive these decisions.

Strategic information technology is the high-risk, high-return part of the portfolio. The failure rate is high, but the potential pay-off is great. There are strategies to reduce the risk. Firms adopting a fast follower strategy attempt to reduce risk of strategic information technology initiatives by learning from the leader. The fast follower misses the advantage of being first entrant to a successful market but reduces the risk of failure. However, a successful fast follower response usually requires extensive infrastructure capability to be in place as a platform for new initiatives.

Transactional information technology is generally a reliable investment. The returns are solid, and the risk is low. Firms new to information technology or those that don't see information technology as a core competence should bias their information technology portfolios toward transactional investment.

Firms wishing to gain cost reduction economies from information technology, rather than strategic positioning, will have minimal infrastructure and a portfolio heavily loaded with transactional investments. They will have minimal strategic investment, and their informational investment will be focused on information to control costs. Their total investment in information technology will be below the industry average.

Firms wishing to balance a cost-reduction strategy with agility will invest in information technology at around the industry average, with substantial infrastructure and a balance among strategic, informational, and transactional investment. The economies will come from significant use of transactional information technology and some sharing through a substantial infrastructure.

Firms seeking to gain competitive advantage through agility, such as faster time to market, and to cash in on economies from sharing information technology will have a different portfolio. They will invest above the average of their competitors in information technology and have more substantial infrastructure capability and proportionally larger strategic investments. Their more extensive infrastructure capabilities provide agility through flexibility and integration, as well as some economies through reduced duplication. Typical information technology portfolios for firms following each of these three business strategies are presented in Figure 3.4.

Outsourcing Information Technology

There has been much interest in recent years in outsourcing part or all of the provision of the information technology portfolio. Outsourcing isn't new. The computer industry was founded on service bureaus with mainframe computers leasing out processing time and other services to many customers. The service providers operating today, such as IBM Global Services, CSC, and EDS, are much more sophisticated and provide a large range of information technology services.

In our study, we found that outsourcing averaged 9.7 percent of the total information technology investment and was increasing at an average rate of 8.2 percent per year over five years. The performance characteristics of firms that outsource more of their information technology provide an informative picture about different types of business value.

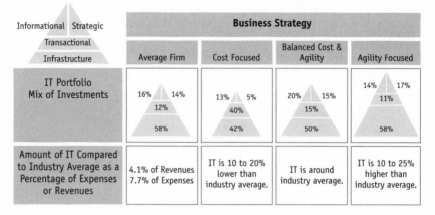

Figure 3.4   Typical Information Technology Portfolios

Again, the patterns below are statistically significant and thus aren't likely to be due to chance. Relative to other firms, those that outsourced their information technology portfolio at a faster rate in the last five years had

- A significant increase in transactions per dollar of corporate information technology investment.

- Lower cost per unit of large-scale processing power.

- Lower cost to provide an infrastructure of comparable capability.

- Lower cost to develop new applications, but no difference in time to develop.

- Significantly increasing information systems staff turnover.

- Strategies involving lower pricing and lower perceived product or service quality than their competitors.

- Longer times to market for new products.

- A slower rate of increase in revenue per employee and return on assets than firms that increased outsourcing at a slower pace.

Firms that outsourced more were often in industries like process manufacturing, where information technology is less likely to be a core competence and a source of competitive advantage. In industries like retailing, where information technology is becoming more of a core competence, we saw a significant reduction in the amount of outsourcing.

There is a lot of debate about the pros and cons of outsourcing. Based on this evidence, the benefits are mixed and depend heavily on the strategy of the firm. More outsourcing isn't necessarily good or bad. There are some significant cost-reduction benefits to outsourcing, which suit firms with low-cost strategies. Again, we need to consider how the firm wishes to compete. Firms requiring faster time to market and growth, and that see information technology as a core competence, are better served by less outsourcing. These firms will still outsource, but only well-understood commodities like telecommunications network services, large-scale processing, or desktop maintenance. Bendigo Bank, a regional Australian bank, recently decided to bring information technology back in house. Vicky Kelly, Bendigo Bank's CIO, explains: "In banking now, the lines between the business of banking and IT are becoming blurred. We need the IT knowledge within our organization so we can use it to help the business and we want immediate access so we can change direction at a moment's notice. Outsourcing doesn't provide that."[9] Decisions about the extent of outsourcing are secondary to establishing the nature of the information technology capabilities required. Once the capabilities of the information technology portfolio have been determined, then it is appropriate to decide how they should be sourced.

Why Some Firms Achieve More Business Value

Some firms consistently achieve more business value for their information technology investments. Our research shows that these firms have five characteristics in common.[10] The evidence is strong that being excellent or even above average in these five areas results in better payoff. These five characteristics are representative of a strong information technology management culture, which has a mature and deliberate approach to generating maximum value. The competitor that has the same level of information technology investment but is below average in these areas gets less value for its information technology investment. These five characteristics can be managed to improve a firm's capability. We call the process of getting more value from information technology investment "conversion effectiveness." These five characteristics indicative of better conversion effectiveness are

1. More top management commitment to information technology.

2. Less political turbulence.

3. More satisfied users of systems.

4. More integrated business and information technology planning.

5. More experience with information technology.

Strategic and infrastructure investments are particularly sensitive to conversion effectiveness. The long-term nature and the complexity of these two types of information technology increase the positive impact of conversion effectiveness.

Top Management Commitment to Information Technology

As with every firm initiative, such as total quality management, reengineering, or knowledge management, top management's commitment to the effective use of information technology is critical. This commitment is evident in many areas, including attention given to the business rationale for information technology and willingness to attend meetings on information technology issues. The reporting level of the most senior information technology manager is another indicator of top management's commitment.

It isn't only the commitment perceived by top managers themselves; it's the perception of this commitment by others in the firm—such as those who deal directly with customers and those who build or implement the systems—that is important. Some senior managers are surprised at how their heartfelt, but poorly communicated support for information technology isn't generally recognized in the firm.

We recall the experience of one manufacturing firm where, after we completed an analysis of conversion effectiveness, the time came to present the findings to top management. The firm had scored high on self-perceived top management commitment. However, the front-line people reported perceiving a very low top management commitment to information technology. Top management was surprised and frustrated by the result. The CEO asked, "Why don't they get it?" The simple answer was that implementation of information technology decisions was poor and there wasn't enough top management attention to the issues. Top management hadn't passed on its enthusiasm for the use of the technology to the rest of the firm and didn't follow through to ensure careful implementation. Most important, there was no reflection of this commitment in the reward systems of those involved.

Senior managers with high commitment to information technology take the following types of actions. They

- Attend information technology council meetings themselves and don't send a delegate.

- Work with the information technology group to specify the required infrastructure in business terms.

- Require carefully considered business cases for investments, identifying measures and responsibilities.

- Support the strategic uses of information technology by providing seed funding that doesn't require traditional net present value financial justifications.

- Encourage postimplementation reviews which are not witch hunts and facilitate the gathering and dissemination of the lessons learned.

- Encourage, fund, and actively support training in the use of information technology.

Less Political Turbulence

Information technology is inherently integrative. It links different parts of the firm and promotes sharing of information. Political turbulence, such as a high level of internal competition rather than cooperation, reduces the likelihood of payoff from information technology investments.

A medium-sized valve manufacturer was implementing its new laptop system for salespeople. The system allowed each salesperson to connect back to the firm's production scheduling system by telephone from the customer's office. Customers were particularly impressed by the salesperson's ability to actually slot their custom order into the schedule and provide a firm delivery date. When the firm first implemented the system, however, the production manager was mortified. "No flaky salesperson is going to touch my production schedule" was his comment. In this case, the order entry system outlived the production manager, who was asked to retire. Political turbulence is a powerful force, often much more subtle, subversive, and insidious than the reaction of this particular production manager.

Firms with less political turbulence have managers who take the following actions. They

- Exhibit a strong sense of community, a feeling of shared interests, purpose, and cooperation among managers. This is reinforced with reward systems and incentives that are based on a balance of firmwide and local measures.

- Capture relevant data in one business area and willingly share it across the firm. Cross-functional and business opportunities to improve service and reduce costs are actively sought.

- Encourage cooperation via cross-functional teams, temporary transfers, and movement of personnel.

More Satisfied Users

Firms with more satisfied people using their systems also get more business value from their investments in information technology. Lack of satisfaction is created by a number of factors, including

- Lack of confidence in the reliability and completeness of information in the systems.

- Lack of a sense of relevance and accuracy of the information in the systems.

- A poor level of support provided to those using the systems. Particular problem areas are slow or less-than-helpful help desks and slow or ill-prepared visits from technical personnel.

- Limited user understanding, often stemming from inadequate or poor training.

- Users' feeling that the attitude and responsiveness of those who provide support for systems is begrudging and unprofessional. One information technology support group we visited had a whiteboard listing the key systems users with such creative nicknames as "Master of Nothing," "O Demanding One," "Clueless," and "Phony Freddie." It's not surprising that this firm's user community is frustrated.

Firms with above-average user satisfaction have managers who take the following actions. The information technology groups use regular surveys to track the satisfaction of different systems' users over time. The results are also integrated into the reward structure of the systems providers and support personnel, whether the systems are provided by an internal information systems group or an outsourcer. Given the importance of user satisfaction in getting value from an information technology investment, best practice is to have these types of incentives integrated into the management of information systems groups. In one impressive organization, the year-end bonuses of the information systems staff were tied 50 percent to the financial performance of the business and 50 percent to the satisfaction of their internal clients. The satisfaction levels were identified through a series of measures such as response time for problem solving and system reliability.

Integrated Business Information Technology and Planning

Firms with tight coupling of information technology planning and business planning also get more value from their information technology investment.

We compared the business and technology strategy formation processes in the banking industry[11] and found that the bank that led the industry in effective use of technology had the most well developed strategy formation processes. These processes included

- Executive management consideration of the information and technology implications of their business strategies.

- Regular high-level briefings on the implications of information technology industry developments for financial services.

- Clear and well-documented accountabilities for achieving strategies.

- Articulation of the respective roles and responsibilities of business and information technology management in achieving effective and efficient systems and in delivering business benefits. Managers were named and held accountable.

This leading bank spent less on information technology than some major competitors and generated less documentation in its planning processes. The difference was the level and sharpness of its focus, high-level integration of technology issues, and clear lines of accountability. The bank continues to lead its industry in its chosen market areas.

One way to improve the integration of business and technology planning is to insist that all business plans have an information technology component written by the business managers with assistance from information technology management. The trend in many firms to put a great deal of effort into information technology planning is a concern.[12] This can be a very technology-oriented exercise and tends to separate information technology from the business issues. Technology plans have a tendency to become an end in themselves rather than a means to create business value. This problem is accentuated by the different time frames of business and technology changes. Changes in current strategy often occur yearly or more often in businesses. In contrast, the building of a large information technology infrastructure is necessarily slow and painstaking, and making changes to one is time consuming, too. The business and technology perspectives and time frames must be brought together, not in the isolation and sterile environment of the information systems group, but in the more volatile setting of a practical business plan.

More Experience

Experience in the field of information technology is expensive. Just ask a CIO how much it costs to hire an expert in the newest technology. At the moment, expertise in implementing the newest integrated software package or in developing creative and effective home pages for the Internet is in short supply and expensive. Analysis of firms that get more business value from their information technology investment shows that they are also more experienced in their use of the technology.

Successful firms have been using the technology longer in areas that are critical to the business. For example, firms that have good experience with transactional systems, such as order processing, have a higher success rate with strategic uses of information technology. The skills for managing systems that must reliably process thousands of transactions every day of the year are a good base for managing the more risky and often customer-sensitive strategic systems.

Taking advantage of their experience, information systems groups and line managers in these firms take the following types of actions:

- Redesign, simplify, or reengineer business processes before a cent is spent on information systems.

- Maximize the reuse of business process and information systems components.

- For every new information technology project that is not infrastructure, have a businessperson as champion, with clearly identified deliverables and responsibilities to the business and technology provider.

- Treat infrastructure investments separately from investments in applications, to take into account their shared nature and long life.

- Ensure that innovative use of information technology in the business units is encouraged by the information systems group, even if firmwide standards aren't always followed. Integration can be achieved later if the uses prove successful.

Outsourcing is one way to acquire expertise. Outsourcing of well-understood processes is a sound strategy, as long as a careful set of guidelines is given to an outsourcer from a well-developed marketplace with several providers. However, in areas where information technology is a core competence and part of the firm's engine for growth, outsourcing is less attractive. Cosourcing is an attractive option here, in which the customer and the provider share the risk and the rewards of the project. Whether or not the information technology service is insourced, outsourced, or cosourced, firms with more experience in managing the technology achieve greater payoff from their investments. This is particularly true for the more risky parts of the information technology portfolio: the strategic and infrastructure investments.

Achieving Competitive Advantage through Conversion Effectiveness

A good business strategy is much easier to formulate than to implement. This is also true in managing information technology. It isn't surprising, then, that firms that get more business value from their information technology have the preceding five characteristics. Successful firms relentlessly focus on improving their conversion of information technology investments into business value. These five characteristics are representative of strong firmwide, business-relevant information technology cultures. Such cultures will have other desirable features, such as strong project management disciplines and a consistent approach to technology justification.

The ability of firms to convert their information technology investment into business value varies significantly. For example, when comparing two firms in the same industry that spend the same percentage of revenues on information technology infrastructure, we found that one had better conversion effectiveness. This firm achieved a more extensive infrastructure capability at a lower cost. The firm with better conversion effectiveness produced systems faster and more cheaply and had better operational and financial performance. The management skills necessary to convert information technology into business value are the same as those needed to convert any other business investment effectively. These companies are just better at managing their assets.

Implications for the Management of Information Technology

Each senior management team must decide how much it should invest in information technology. The team must decide on the management objectives for the investment, which will determine the size and makeup of the portfolio. The portfolio must be balanced for risk and return, taking into account the different risk and return characteristics of the four types of information technology portfolios. Senior managers must also decide on the managerial processes to make this investment decision and to maximize the business value achieved from the investment.

Below is a checklist of important issues and general principles, drawn from our evidence for payoff, to consider in managing the information technology portfolio.

Issues for Senior Management

❑ How much should we invest in information technology in dollars and relative to competitors?

❑ How do we balance the information technology portfolio for risk and return?

❑ How do we handle the justification process?

❑ How do we alter our management practices to improve the effectiveness of converting information technology investments into business value?

❑ What measures and incentives are necessary?

General Principles for Managing the Portfolio

❑ Size the information technology portfolio relative to strategic needs and benchmarks.

❑ Balance the portfolio for risk and return. Consider each type of information technology as a different investment class, as listed in Figure 3.5. In general, the order of increasing risk is from bottom to top. Transactional information technology is low risk and has a solid return. Strategic information technology investment is high risk and high return. Infrastructure and informational investments have moderate risk and moderate return, with infrastructure the higher risk because of its long life.

❑ Senior management should encourage business units to manage their own transactional information technology and not sponsor firmwide transactional systems.

❑ If there are no other compelling factors, senior management should centrally coordinate some infrastructure services. Centrally coordinating the basic infrastructure

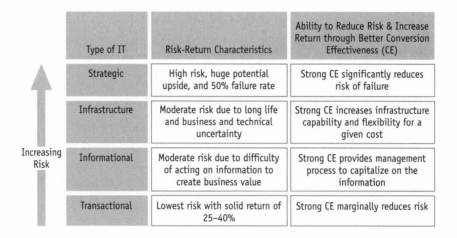

Type of IT	Risk-Return Characteristics	Ability to Reduce Risk & Increase Return through Better Conversion Effectiveness (CE)
Strategic	High risk, huge potential upside, and 50% failure rate	Strong CE significantly reduces risk of failure
Infrastructure	Moderate risk due to long life and business and technical uncertainty	Strong CE increases infrastructure capability and flexibility for a given cost
Informational	Moderate risk due to difficulty of acting on information to create business value	Strong CE provides management process to capitalize on the information
Transactional	Lowest risk with solid return of 25–40%	Strong CE marginally reduces risk

Increasing Risk

Figure 3.5   Risk-Return Profiles in the Information Technology Portfolio

capability and services will generally pay off with cost reductions through shared expertise and through economies of scale and scope. Centrally coordinating extensive infrastructure capability and services is more expensive initially, but better in the long run, when revenue growth, sales from new products, and cross-selling are the major focus.

❏ Where the aim is to improve operational performance measures that are information intensive (for example, quality, knowledge management, sales per customer), allocate more of the information technology portfolio to informational systems.

❏ Senior management should encourage informational investments, such as management reporting, to be made at the business-unit level.

❏ In industries where competitors have less-developed information technology infrastructures, look for opportunities for longer-term competitive advantage from strategic information technology.

❏ As in any investment, the portfolio should have some high risk–high return strategic investments. Where strategic information technology investments are consistent with strategic goals and the firm has proven conversion effectiveness, invest more in this potentially high-payoff area.

❏ Recognize and manage factors that influence conversion effectiveness. In general, these can significantly increase the return for a given level of information technology investment (see Figure 3.5 for details). Each of the five characteristics of conversion effectiveness is important and can actively be managed by looking to the action items listed previously under each characteristic. Good conversion effectiveness is all about relentlessly pursuing a few key principles for each of the five characteristics. The way firms achieved excellent conversion effectiveness for a particular service can be summed up by a simple formula for best practice. This formula is equally relevant whether the service was provided by an internal information systems group or an outsourcer:

Effective Information Systems Management = Specification + Service Level Agreements (SLAs) + Incentives

Best-practice information systems management requires a clear specification of what is required in a system or service in business terms; a service-level agreement with measures for the provision of the specified requirements; and a set of incentives for both parties to the agreement.

PART 2

Identifying Opportunities to Create Value

Many firms face similar challenges, but the specific situation of each firm is different. Each executive management team needs to make choices to shape a unique and sustainable response to suit its specific circumstances.

In Part 2 we explain different types of information technology infrastructure views and capabilities, and how to identify which capabilities are necessary to match the strategic needs of a particular firm. Different strategic needs arise through the combination of the firm's value propositions to its customers, its investment climate, the nature of its products and services, the firm's history, the capabilities of its people, and the markets in which it chooses to compete. These differences lead to varying requirements for capabilities, particularly the depth and spread of the new infrastructure to deliver business value.

Chapter 4 focuses on the infrastructure component of the information technology portfolio. The chapter opens with examples of three firms that differ significantly in their approach to the new infrastructure: Citibank Asia, Telstra, and Keppel Corporation. We then examine information technology infrastructure carefully from a business perspective. What is it? How much does it cost? How does one measure it? What are its capabilities? How can one compare infrastructures across firms? We conceive of infrastructure capability as a combination of a set of services and the "Reach and Range" of those services.

Four different approaches to information technology infrastructure are identified, with different levels of investment resulting in different information technology capabilities. These four distinct approaches are driven by different benefit expectations, lead to different performance outcomes, and reflect clear strategic choices that firms must make. The characteristics of the four approaches are explored, with tables of benchmarks presented for comparison.

Each of the four views of infrastructure has different implications for infrastructure capabilities. In Chapter 5 we specify the types of infrastructure capabilities that match each of the views—from no capabilities to extensive capabilities. We look at the patterns of infrastructure capability in firms, as well as business indicators of high and low levels of infrastructure. These indicators provide pointers to the infrastructure profile that would suit a specific firm.

Decision making about infrastructure requires a purposeful process with a particular focus on linking the firm's strategic context and value propositions with infrastructure capability. We have synthesized the way market leaders make informed information technology infrastructure decisions in the "Management by Maxim" framework. The goal is to create a visible chain of evidence connecting what the firm aims to achieve, its positioning in the marketplace, and the necessary information technology infrastructure investments to support those aspirations.

In Chapter 6 we describe the key components of Management by Maxim, from strategic context to setting maxims, clarifying an infrastructure view and implementing infrastructure capabilities. We start with strategic intent and current strategies at firmwide and business-unit levels, along with the nature and extent of synergies among business units. We explore the notion of value disciplines for different types of infrastructure services and the implications of diverse value disciplines. We lead from strategic context to the articulation of business maxims, short statements that encapsulate firmwide strategic directions and priorities.

The combination of a firm's business maxims leads to a series of IT maxims, which are principles for firmwide information technology investments. The combination of business and IT maxims and the future infrastructure view determines the level and nature of information technology infrastructure capabilities required for the firm to achieve its strategic objectives.

In Chapter 7 we use examples from firms such as Johnson & Johnson to illustrate how maxims can be used to drive change. Shifts in business and customer demands require rethinking value from the customer's perspective, rethinking information technology investments, and rethinking the way a firm manages and governs those investments. Management by Maxim is an iterative, strategy-led process. However, the maxims route assumes that both business and information technology managers are willing and able to take a firmwide view. We found that this situation exists in about half the firms we studied. The other half used a deal-making process focusing on the more immediate needs of each of the businesses. We compare the maxims and deals processes, and illustrate how a financial services firm changed from the deal-making route to the maxim route. We discuss the conditions under which each is appropriate and explain how expression, specification, and implementation barriers can be overcome.

Four Approaches to Information Technology Infrastructure Investment

Citibank Asia has centralized and standardized back room processing across five countries in Asia. The driver for this change is "Citibanking"—"combining relationship banking with technology that enables the customer to exercise greater control over his or her funds."[1] The technology enables the Citibanking vision in two major ways: (1) with one-stop paperless account opening, instant card and check issuance, and instant account availability; and (2) with a customer relationship database that supports cross-product relationships, creation of customized products, and relationship pricing that more closely matches the value of the service provided to the customer. The Citicard is the key to such Citibanking services as checking, money market, and bank card accounts. In addition, the centralization of card processing operations for ten countries reduced costs per card to less than one-third of what they had been and enabled a 24-fold increase in productivity.

Firms approach information technology infrastructure investments differently depending on their strategic goals for cost savings through economies of scale, synergies across businesses, or longer-term requirements for flexibility and agility. Citibank centralized its information technology infrastructure to deliver on its Citibanking strategy and achieved synergies between business units as well as cost savings. The nature of a firm's information technology portfolio can be tailored to firm-specific needs, just as a personal financial portfolio can be related to an individual's lifestyle, aspirations, and resources. The platform of a sound information technology portfolio is the infrastructure—the enabling foundation of reliable services.

In this chapter we focus on the infrastructure component of the information technology portfolio and introduce four different views of information technology infrastructure that firms take. Each view is driven by different strategic objectives, has different levels of up-front investment, and results in different capabilities with different benefit expectations.

Why Information Technology Infrastructure Is a Strategic Issue

Investing in information technology infrastructure involves difficult decisions for senior managers. These are large investments with long-term business implications, which nevertheless must be made before precise business needs are known. Infrastructure investments are significant, accounting for more than 58 percent of information technology dollars. Infrastructure as a percentage of the information technology portfolio has increased at the rate of 9 percent per year for over five years in the firms we studied. The purpose of building information technology infrastructures is to enable the sharing of information and expensive resources, the execution of business processes, and connecting to customers and suppliers as part of the extended enterprise. This sharing can create cross-unit or cross-functional integration that allows the firm to benefit from a combination of economies of scale, synergies, and flexibility. The combination of objectives is a senior management decision informed by business drivers. Having separate and incompatible infrastructures limits the firm's strategic options and is often an impediment to quick response to competitor initiatives.

To put information technology infrastructure in context, let's look at two more market leaders who made different infrastructure decisions driven by their distinct strategic contexts.

Telstra's Firmwide Standard Operating Environment

In an industry in transition, many telecommunications firms have undergone radical change in the past five years. In 1992, prior to complete deregulation in 1997, Australia's telecommunications provider, Telstra,[2] lost its monopoly position to a duopoly with Optus Communications. The situation was summarized by Telstra's CEO, Frank Blount:

> Rapidly developing new technologies, new markets, fierce competition and higher customer expectations are combining to generate change on a scale never experienced in the Australian telecommunications industry. . . . The changes we have made deal with the very structure of our organization and with all of our systems: management, financial, operating and product/service development.[3]

Telstra's competitive situation changed dramatically. Customers now have a choice, leading to a new set of business imperatives that emphasize customer service and value. This customer emphasis in turn demands that managers of formerly separate business units with disparate operational systems reconsider the nature of their customer information and transaction processing.

In the early to mid-1990s Telstra identified an integrated information technology infrastructure as an enabling platform to achieve business growth through the development of new markets in Australia and internationally. The first step was the implementation of a standardized set of technology policies, referred to as an Overall Systems Architecture (OSA), to provide the basis for integrating business processes across multiple business units.

The OSA provided the building blocks of information technology capability to be exploited in the introduction of new products, processes, and work practices. "What we ended up with," explained the CIO, "is an amazing corporate asset. We have the most standard corporate desktop in the world in terms of user numbers (over 40,000 PCs and terminals in use), probably the third or fourth largest electronic mail network in the world, and a very, very large network taking over from twenty or thirty competing wide area networks that had built up over the years."[4] Telstra now has the information and functionality required to service customer needs immediately at the customer service point. New products are being introduced much more quickly and easily than was possible with the previous approach to infrastructure.

No Firmwide Infrastructure at Keppel

The Keppel Corporation is a conglomerate headquartered in Singapore, with businesses in shipbuilding and ship repair; offshore and specialized shipbuilding; property, banking, and financial services; logistics; telecommunications; and engineering. Revenues increased more than 50 percent between 1993 and 1995 to more than $1.9 billion, with profits increasing more than 30 percent.[5] Keppel's range of businesses buffers the group during cyclical changes in any one industry, while a "common vision draws together the different strands. Each business activity adds to the whole." While the corporation continues on its path of diversification, the "Keppel Group progresses as one . . . tapping on each other's expertise, resources, and network, with members of the group lending strength to one another."

Whereas Keppel's firmwide business infrastructure includes corporate planning, public affairs, personnel, and financial and legal services, there is a minimum of firmwide information technology infrastructure services. The diversity of the Keppel Corporation businesses led to the development of separate information technology portfolios to ensure maximum flexibility for each separate business unit to compete effectively.

Citibank Asia, Telstra, and Keppel Corporation are successful market leaders who have made appropriate but different decisions about the information technology infrastructure. The decisions were informed by different combinations of business drivers to

- Capture synergies between business units, such as cross-selling.

- Realize potential economies of scale.

- Provide agility to lead competitors in quickly developing products and services to meet customer needs.

- Provide local autonomy and flexibility, and forgo any potential economies of scale or synergies.

For Citibank Asia and Telstra, the drivers were a combination of synergies, economies, and agility, with different weightings in the two firms determined by their strategic context. For Keppel Corporation, choosing to provide flexibility at the business-unit level to meet changing competitive demands acknowledges the diversity of information technology requirements in different businesses.

In these firms, the decision to pursue a particular information technology infrastructure capability was a senior management business decision. Certainly the technology specialists decided how to implement the decisions, but the drivers for the decisions were strategic, not technical. For senior management to make such decisions requires understanding, in business terms, of what information technology infrastructure is and how it creates business value.

The Structure of Information Technology Infrastructure

The various elements of information technology infrastructure are presented in Figure 4.1, with the remaining parts of the portfolio depicted above as "Local Application." At the base of this framework[6] are the technology components, such as computers, printers, database software packages, operating systems, and scanners. These devices are commodities and readily available in the marketplace. The second layer comprises a set of shared information technology services. The technology components are converted into useful shared services by a human information technology infrastructure composed of knowledge, skills, standards, and experience. This human infrastructure binds the technology components into reliable services that form the firm's information technology infrastructure.

The infrastructure services in a firm often include telecommunications network services, management and provision of large-scale computing (such as mainframes), the management of shared customer databases, and research and development expertise aimed at identifying the usefulness of emerging technologies to the business. An increasing number of firms have an additional layer of shared and standard infrastructure applications used by all business units. These often include firmwide applications that support shared services in functional and support areas, such as accounting, human resources management, and budgeting.

The set of infrastructure services required by a firm is usually relatively stable over time. Generally, similar services are required from year to year, with gradual improvements over time to take advantage of new technologies and efficiencies. Occasionally, new services are required to support a new initiative.

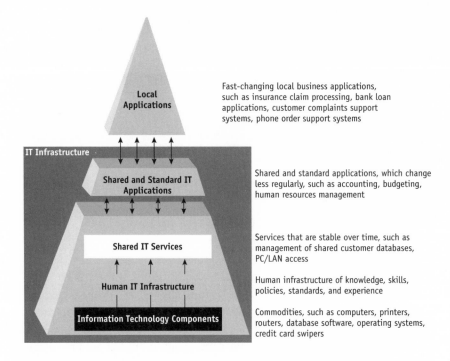

Fast-changing local business applications, such as insurance claim processing, bank loan applications, customer complaints support systems, phone order support systems

Shared and standard applications, which change less regularly, such as accounting, budgeting, human resources management

Services that are stable over time, such as management of shared customer databases, PC/LAN access

Human infrastructure of knowledge, skills, policies, standards, and experience

Commodities, such as computers, printers, routers, database software, operating systems, credit card swipers

Figure 4.1 The Structure of Information Technology Infrastructure

In contrast, the information technology required for business processes (applications) changes more frequently, often annually, as business processes are altered to better suit customer needs or in response to competitor activity. The information technology for business processes utilizes the infrastructure services necessary for the particular application. For example, in building a new order-processing system, a particular process manufacturing firm will use the information technology infrastructure services of mainframe processing, customer databases, personal computers, and local area and national communications networks. Having those infrastructure services in place will significantly reduce the time and cost to build the order-processing system.

Infrastructure capability is a firm resource[7] that is difficult to imitate, as it is created through the fusion of technology and human assets. It is these types of capabilities, with long lead times (five to seven years) to emulate, that can provide a source of competitive advantage. We know from our research (see Figure 3.3) that firms with more infrastructure have faster times to market and more sales from new products. Building an infrastructure tailored to a firm's strategic context takes considerable time and expertise. Although the components are commodities, the management processes to implement the best mix of infrastructure capabilities to suit a specific firm are a much more scarce resource.

Shared infrastructure applications have traditionally accounted for a small proportion (less than 5 percent) of a firm's information technology portfolio but are rapidly increasing. However, implementation of a particular shared infrastructure application requires agreement on and standardization of that business process across the firm.

The nature of infrastructure capability can be described from a business perspective using two useful concepts: information technology infrastructure services and the infrastructure "Reach and Range." Services describe the business functions provided by the infrastructure, and Reach and Range describes its business dimensions.

Services: Business Functions of the Infrastructure

The services notion of information technology infrastructure is very powerful. The concept emerged from our discussions with business managers grappling with what they were actually getting for their information technology investments. Business managers told us they have great difficulty valuing the technology components, such as a midrange computer (for example, a Unix box) or a database package. New information technology staff appointments are also difficult to value. However, business managers can more readily value a service, such as the provision of a fully maintained PC with access to all firm systems and the Internet. These services can be specified and measured, and their costs controlled. Perhaps most important, managers can price services in the marketplace for comparison. Thinking of infrastructure as services places the consumer—the business manager—in charge, rather than the provider, such as the information systems group or outsourcer. The notion of a service also gives the provider much more certainty as to its responsibilities and allows more precise planning.

Innovative business processes can be delayed by the lack of information technology infrastructure services. For example, a firm selling hospital products wishes to offer electronic purchasing facilities to customers so that they can order directly and determine stock availability. Several of the required infrastructure services are in place, such as a customer database and a communications network. However, the security services are not in place. The firm must postpone launching the new initiative until the security services are ready.

5 Core IT Infrastructure Services in Firms	Percent of Firms
1. Manage firmwide communications network services	100
2. Manage groupwide or firmwide messaging services	100
3. Recommend standards for at least one component of IT architecture (e.g., hardware, operating systems, data, communications)	100
4. Provide security, disaster planning, and business recovery services for firmwide installations and applications	100
5. Provide technology advice and support services	100
20 Additional IT Infrastructure Services	**Percent of Firms**
6. Manage, maintain, support large-scale data-processing facilities (e.g., mainframe operations)	96
7. Manage firmwide or business-unit applications and databases	96
8. Perform IS project management	88
9. Provide data management advice and consultancy services	84
10. Perform IS planning for business units	80
11. Enforce IT architecture and standards	76
12. Manage firmwide or business-unit workstation networks (e.g., LANs, POS)	76
13. Manage and negotiate with suppliers and outsourcers	76
14. Identify and test new technologies for business purposes	72
15. Develop business-unit–specific applications (usually on a chargeback or contractual basis)	68
16. Implement security, disaster planning, and recovery for business units	60
17. Provide management information electronically (e.g., EIS)	56
18. Manage business-unit–specific applications	56
19. Manage firmwide or business-unit data, including standards	52
20. Develop and manage electronic linkages to suppliers or customers	52
21. Develop a common systems development environment	52
22. Provide technology education services (e.g., training)	36
23. Provide multimedia operations and development (e.g., videoconferencing)	16
24. Provide firmwide intranet capability (e.g., information access, multiple system access)	↑
25. Provide firmwide electronic support for groups (e.g., Lotus Notes)	↑

↑= service that is just emerging and soon will be widespread.

Figure 4.2   Firmwide Information Technology Infrastructure Services

An application allowing a customer (or any other party) direct access wasn't considered in the initial design of the infrastructure services.

Based on our work with firms listed in Appendix 1, we identified the infrastructure services typically provided on a firmwide basis. These are presented in detail in Figure 4.2.[8] All of the firms studied that had any firmwide information technology infrastructure services had all 5 of the core services. The remaining services were provided to varying degrees, depending on the strategic context of each firm. For example, one of the banks provided the 5 core and 12 additional services, whereas a manufacturer provided the 5 core and 3 others centrally. The right-hand column in Figure 4.2 indicates the percentage of firms that provided each of the services.

We found that firms had distinct patterns of information technology infrastructure services. Those firms with considerable synergies among their business units offered more firmwide services in the areas of communications, applications, the use of standards, and the management of information technology than those with more limited synergies. Whereas communications provide a basic technical capacity, the other three areas focus more on the application of human expertise. Information technology infrastructure services can be provided at several levels in the firm, such as firmwide, at the business-unit level or confined to a geographic area. The firmwide infrastructure across all the business units provides the basis on which business units have more tailored infrastructures. These in turn support specific applications. The business-unit infrastructures fit like plug-ins into the firmwide infrastructure. This plug-compatible fit requires agreement on an information technology architecture, as outlined in Chapter 1, covering technical standards and information technology relevant to firmwide services.

A process manufacturing firm, ChemCo, has three business units. The Plastic Products business unit developed a new order-processing system that utilized both firmwide and business-unit–level infrastructure services. The firmwide services included the communications network (Figure 4.2, service 1) and security and disaster planning (service 3). At the business-unit level, the order-processing systems utilized a customer database, one of the business-unit–specific infrastructure services. These services are transparent to business managers in Plastic Products, who see only the order-processing system.

Typically, where the business unit has different customers, products, and processes, the amount of shared infrastructure is small. This is often the situation in a conglomerate like Keppel Corporation. Where there is considerable synergy of customers, products, and processes among business units, as at Telstra, the amount of shared infrastructure is larger. Given the tailoring required, the infrastructure services in place sometimes do not suit newer or acquired businesses, which tend to develop their own local business-unit infrastructure.

Each service can be offered at different levels from selective through extensive. A selective level of service implies selectivity in one of three ways:

1. Only a basic level of the service is provided in terms of functionality.

2. The service is not available across all international locations.

3. The service is not mandatory across the firm.

An extensive level of service indicates that this service has extensive functionality and is offered across all business units or that its use is

Service 1 Manage firmwide communications network services	Service 3 Recommend standards for at least one component of IT architecture	Service 23 Provide multimedia operations and development
Selective Development of a wide area network (WAN) linking domestic and international operations, with day-to-day management of the WAN undertaken by the one business unit for which the group receives a management fee	**Selective** Development of selected IT standards to support the implementation of enterprise- wide information architectures, which include data and voice telecommunications, electronic mail, document interchange format, and videoconferencing	**Selective** Provision of video- conferencing facilities
Extensive Management of all communi- cations networks within the firm, including headquarters and the 226 branches through- out Malaysia Development and management of the corporate communi- cations network for all Australian, New Zealand, and international operations	**Extensive** The development of an integrated set of information, applications, and technology architectures to ensure timely and usable business data, protect IT investments, minimize costs, and deliver solutions more quickly	**Extensive** The development and management of multimedia applications to support high-bandwidth technical information and human communication across countries

Figure 4.3   Examples of Selective and Extensive Services

mandatory. Two examples of the infrastructure service "Manage firmwide or business-unit applications and databases" illustrate selective and extensive levels of service. Times Publishing in Singapore implements and maintains selected applications at the firmwide level, consistent with the use of information technology in the publishing industry. Responsibility for the development of business applications rests with the business or functional level. However, the Development Bank of Singapore competes with integrated financial products and provides an extensive level of service. The corporate information systems group takes responsibility for managing all the bank applications and databases in a consistent and "plug-compatible" way. Figure 4.3 presents examples of three of the services, indicating different depths of each.

The number of infrastructure services offered by a firm, together with the depth of these services, indicates different degrees of business functionality offered through the firm or business-unit infrastructures. Together, the services and Reach and Range define an infrastructure's capability.

Reach and Range: Business Scope of the Infrastructure

The concept of Reach and Range, first proposed by Peter Keen,[9] describes the business scope of the firm's infrastructure—what types of messages can be sent and transactions processed between employees, suppliers, and customers (see Figure 4.4).

Reach refers to the locations and people the infrastructure is capable of connecting. Reach can extend from within a single business unit to the ultimate level of connecting to anyone, anywhere. *Range* refers to functionality in terms of the business activities that can be completed and shared automatically and seamlessly across each level of Reach.

A large Reach and Range means that a firm is able to simultaneously perform transactions on multiple applications, updating all databases across different business units—be they located in the home country, such as the United States, or in other countries as well (see Figure 4.4, point *A*). In a Chicago-based firm with the *A* level of Reach and Range, a business unit located in Madrid could take an order and process it through inventory, production, scheduling, and eventually accounts receivable—and automatically update the centralized executive information system back in Chicago. A small Reach and Range, indicated by point *B* in Figure 4.4, supports sending standard messages within a single-business-unit location.

The Internet has added another dimension to the Reach and Range of many firms. The shaded area in Figure 4.5 shows the Reach and Range of an insurance firm we call UnionCo, which has a number of business units. UnionCo can send a memo electronically to people across a large Reach—all the way from within a single-business-unit location to customers and suppliers regardless of their information technology base. Using this infrastructure capability, the firm can send new product announcements to all customers and agents who have computer-based systems. UnionCo achieves this level of integration simply by connecting its internal mail system to the Internet. Its customers also access the Internet to send mail to and receive mail from UnionCo.

UnionCo can access stored data across different business units located in its domestic country base. For example, a manager with the appropriate security clearance in the automobile insurance business unit can electronically check the credit rating of a customer of the life insurance business unit when that customer inquires about automobile insurance.

Using the infrastructure's ability to process simple transactions, the firm can provide the customer with a quotation, take and con-

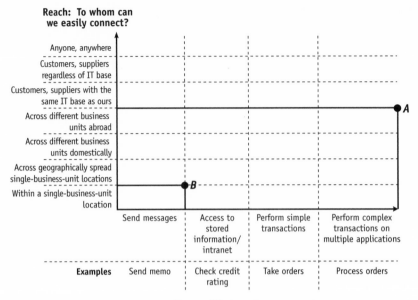

Figure 4.4   Infrastructure Reach and Range

Source: Reprinted with permission of Harvard Business School Press. Adapted from *Shaping the Future: Business Design through Information Technology,* by Peter G. W. Keen. Boston, Mass. 1991, p. 180. Copyright © 1991 Peter G. W. Keen. All rights reserved.

firm the customer's order for automobile insurance, and confirm this to the customer. When the customer responds positively with his or her credit card number, the infrastructure's ability to process complex transactions (accessing several different systems and databases) is used in processing the order for insurance. The details of the customer are retrieved from the life insurance business unit. The new insurance policy is generated, and the general ledger is updated to include the payment. UnionCo's overall portfolio risk management systems are updated to take account of the new insurance policy. The transaction processing is conducted by telephone with the credit card firm. UnionCo's infrastructure doesn't provide the capability to connect to customers and business partners when processing a complex transaction. UnionCo cannot electronically and automatically send the credit card company the details and receive a confirmation.

A good way to use the Reach and Range framework is to identify typical business activities for each subdivision of Range. The current functionality can then be compared to what is required to execute any planned strategies. Often there is a significant gap between the actual

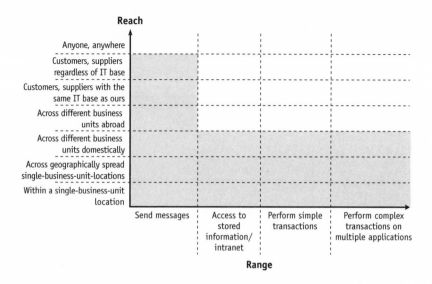

Figure 4.5   Infrastructure Reach and Range Using the Internet

Reach and Range and that desired by senior management to implement new initiatives. When there is a good dialogue between business and information technology management, this gap can be identified. Technology managers can then assess the cost, time, and difficulty of the required increase in Reach and Range. This provides business managers with valuable information about the challenges they face in implementing specific business strategies. Without real dialogue, business managers often don't even realize that there is a gap until it's too late. Strategies cannot be implemented, new products and services are delayed, and both business and technology managers are frustrated in trying to achieve the best outcomes for their firm and customers.

Assessing a firm's investments and infrastructure capabilities presents significant challenges but is essential in clarifying industry positioning and the ability to make best use of the new infrastructure.

Industry Benchmarks for Information Technology Investments

To provide a basis for comparison, we present a series of benchmarks of information technology investment and infrastructure

Five-Year Averages

No. of firms	Finance 12	Manufacturing 10	Retail 5	All 27	All Av%Δ
1. IT % of Revenues	7.0	1.7	1.0	4.1	2.6
2. IT % of Expenses	14.2	2.0	1.1	7.7	3.0
3. Centrally Coordinated IT as % of Total IT	73	52	66	64	4.4
4. % Infrastructure of Centrally Coordinated IT	69	64	82	70	8.0
5. % Centrally Coordinated Infrastructure of Total IT	49	34	52	45	11.0
6. Number of Services (0–25)	17	14	18	16	
7. Reach and Range (0–100)	38	32	32	35	
8. % of IT Outsourcing	5.9	17.0	7.6	9.7	8.2

Av%Δ = Average percentage change per year.

Figure 4.6   Benchmarks of Information Technology Investments by Industry

capability by industry in Figure 4.6. The benchmarks are from firms in the finance, process manufacturing, and retail sectors that we studied over a five-year period. We then classify firms by their strategic view of information technology infrastructure investment, and benchmark again.

The first two lines show how extensively the firms use information technology. The third line ("Centrally Coordinated IT as % of Total IT") describes the level of information technology resources coordinated at the corporate level. Line 4 ("% Infrastructure of Centrally Coordinated IT") is the percentage of the centrally coordinated information technology investment that is infrastructure. Line 5 ("% Centrally Coordinated Infrastructure of Total IT") describes the percentage of the firm's total information technology investment in firmwide shared infrastructure.

Line 6 ("Number of Services") identifies, on average, how many of the 25 services were coordinated and provided centrally. Line 7 ("Reach and Range") presents the scope of the typical infrastructure, using the Reach and Range framework. We explain how this was calculated on a scale from 0 to 100 in Appendix 3 at the end of this book. Line 8 presents the percentage of the firm's total information technology that was outsourced. The right-hand column ("Av%Δ") is the average percentage change in the figure per year over the five years.

Lines 4 and 5 tell us how much of the firm's information technology resources are used to provide the infrastructure, whereas lines 6 and 7 tell us about the capability of the infrastructure the firm has achieved for its investment.

Some interesting conclusions emerge from the data:

1. Centralized information technology infrastructure is increasing at a rate faster than that for investment in information technology as a whole. Thus firms are tending to centralize a larger proportion of their infrastructure to capture economies and synergies.

2. Firms in manufacturing generally have less firmwide information technology infrastructure than finance or retail firms in terms of their Reach and Range, number of services, and investment levels.

3. Having the information technology services provided from outside the firm, through outsourcing accounts for about 10 percent of the information technology investment and is growing at 8 percent per year.

The benchmarks by industry are useful but tend to mask the different perspectives on infrastructure. The next section describes how firms view infrastructure, with very different strategic objectives resulting in significantly different investment levels, capabilities, and performance impacts.

Information Technology Infrastructure Investment Views

During our research, we identified and statistically confirmed[10] four approaches to information technology infrastructure investments.[11] We call these approaches to infrastructure investment strategic *views* of information technology infrastructure. One of four views of information technology infrastructure predominated in each firm:

View	None	Utility	Dependent	Enabling
	• Independent business units • No synergies	• Often not a strategic resource • Utility service at lowest cost • Administrative expense	• Response to particular current strategy • Derived from business plans • Business expense	• Integrated with strategic process • Enables new strategies • Influenced by strategies • Business investment to achieve agility
Management Objective	Independence Forgoing any Economies of Scale	Cost Savings Via Economies of Scale	Life-of-Strategy Business Benefits	Current and Future Flexibility

Figure 4.7   Different Views of Information Technology Infrastructure

1. **None:** No firmwide information technology infrastructure.

2. **Utility view:** Employ firmwide infrastructure where clear cost savings are achieved.

3. **Dependent view:** Infrastructure capability driven by a current business strategy, such as customer service.

4. **Enabling view:** Infrastructure is a core competence, and extensive capability is provided to increase strategic options.

The four views involve different levels of up-front infrastructure investment, with different approaches to cost justification and different benefit profiles. Figure 4.7 describes the features of the four views. The lower row of boxes identifies the benefit expectations of each view.

In moving from None to Utility to Dependent to Enabling, the extent and level of top management attention to information technology infrastructure increases, as does the investment and capability in the form of extent of infrastructure services provided and the Reach and Range.

None of these views is superior across all firms. A particular view of infrastructure is best suited to each firm for a particular period of time in a firm's strategic life. Firms can move slowly from one view to another, depending on their current strategic contexts. Information technology infrastructure investments are large and often occur in bursts. Changing views is typically a slow and deliberate process.

"None" View of Infrastructure

A "none" view of infrastructure implies that the firm has no firm-wide information technology infrastructure. The firm usually has independent business units with few synergies. This type of firm usually operates with a minimum of mandates from headquarters. Each business unit is encouraged to invest independently in information technology as in other assets. In taking this view, the firm forgoes any potential economies of scale or business synergies from the sharing of information technology infrastructure.

Ralston Purina Company: No Infrastructure

Ralston Purina, a very successful $8 billion, U.S.-based firm has several large business units. The Ralston Purina Company is the world's leading producer of dry dog food and dry and soft-moist cat foods, marketed under the Purina brand name. Ralston Purina is also the world's largest manufacturer of dry-cell battery products, including Eveready and Energizer brand products, and a major producer of dietary soy protein, fiber food ingredients, and polymer products. Information technology is dispersed to the divisions of Ralston Purina, and there is no corporate information systems group or firmwide information technology infrastructure. Information technology infrastructure decisions are made at the divisional level in conjunction with the operational and strategic needs of the unit. This is consistent with other business functions. The decision is consistent with the company's strategic intent to achieve alignment with markets in each business in which it competes.[12]

Utility View

A utility view of infrastructure implies that expenditures on information technology infrastructure are made primarily to achieve cost savings through economies of scale. The infrastructure is not a strategic resource, but rather a utility that incurs administrative expenses and is a necessary and unavoidable service. The management thrust is to minimize the expense for a desired level of utility service. The two major drivers are

1. Consolidation of multiple sites, perhaps in different states or regions or from two firms that have merged.

2. Decreases in the cost of technology, which allow replacement and modernization of existing services at significant cost savings.

Carlton & United Breweries: Utility View

Carlton & United Breweries (CUB)[13] has made the transition from local brewer to Australia's largest and most successful brewer with approximately 50 percent market share nationally and more than $1.5 billion annual revenue. Its brands, Foster's Lager, Foster's Light, Foster's Special Bitter, Victoria Bitter, Carlton Genuine Draught, Carlton Light, and Crown Lager, are household names today throughout Australia and in many parts of the world.

In the early 1990s, CUB aimed to be Australia's leading brewer by "maximizing returns through the dominance of the Australian beer market and minimizing of costs." CUB aimed to be the lowest-cost producer in all markets. CUB is viewed as the cash generator of the Fosters Brewing Group, and its aim is to maintain revenue growth from the lowest cost platform possible. To fit its strategy of the early 1990s, CUB took a utility view of infrastructure. Information technology investment has been used to reduce costs and to take advantage of economies of scale. Recently, CUB has embarked on project Genesis, a major business process and information technology review and investment program, including a master plan of how to do business in the future.

Utility-view firms focus on achieving cost savings, such as through standardization of systems and consolidating data centers. Nolan Norton and Co. studied the economics of data center consolidation and reported an average annual saving of 26 to 48 percent depending on the firm's cost base.[14] The potential for these types of savings are likely to occur in large firms at regular intervals of five to seven years, as mergers occur and technology prices drop. Capturing these potential savings requires senior management attention to focus the firm's information technology infrastructure investment on relentlessly pursuing cost savings.

Dependent View

A dependent view of infrastructure implies that the infrastructure investments are primarily for and in response to well-articulated business strategies. Dependent infrastructure investments are derived from business plans that specify strategic objectives, including strategic intent, current strategies, and business goals. These objectives lead to or imply information technology needs. Thus planning for infrastructure is undertaken after current business strategies have been articulated. For example, a bank might invest heavily by consolidating previously independent databases into an integrated customer relationship database. This infrastructure investment is dependent on a current strategy of differentiating customer service through relationship banking. Previously the bank could not determine its full relationship with a customer, as the different account information was spread over a series of data files that had been developed at different times and linked to different account types.

Maybank: Dependent View

Maybank was established in the early 1960s by the Malaysian government to provide local banking facilities for the average citizen.[15] *In the mid-1990s, Maybank provided multiple financial and banking services, had 22 percent of the industry's domestic loan market, held more than 4 million deposit accounts, and was the largest bank domiciled in Malaysia. Maybank's vision is "to be a quality organization—one characterized by sustainable growth with good performance indices such as respectable return on capital and on assets and earnings per share." However, the bank is careful to note that profitability is not to be the only indicator of its success. Maybank's comparative advantage lies in its extensive branch network, capitalization, a wide range of financial services, and an information technology infrastructure of telecommunications network and application systems. In the late 1990s, the bank is looking beyond the shores of Malaysia and Singapore, with the aim of becoming a major regional player through overseas expansion.*

To accomplish its goals, Maybank aims to reach out to target customers through the most effective and efficient delivery channels and to optimize synergies by harnessing resources. Underpinning and supporting these aims is the commitment to using information technology for competitive advantage in a cost-effective way.

Maybank has a dependent view of information technology infrastructure, where investments are made in response to current business plans. Senior banking and information technology managers work together on aligning information technology and business goals, and on generating strategic thrusts for information technology. The role of technology is to enable the bank to achieve competitiveness in five areas: improvement of customer service, increased productivity, product innovation, provision of management information for informed decision making, and risk management. Specific strategies for achieving each of these have been identified; these include the use of customer self-service delivery channels.

Nearly 40 percent of the firms studied took a dependent view of infrastructure. Senior management of firms with a dependent view invest and manage to provide the capability to balance the objectives of low-cost operation and strategic flexibility.

Enabling View

An enabling view of infrastructure implies that infrastructure capability is a core competence and strongly integrated with the strategic context. An enabling infrastructure provides extensive infrastructure capability, thus increasing strategic options and agility. Enabling infrastructures are often created by expanding the Reach and/or Range of a dependent infrastructure and increasing services beyond the current requirements of the business. In this way the infrastructure provides future options for implementing current strategies consistent with the strategic intent. The flexibility of the infrastructure permits a number of as-yet-unspecified business strategies to be implemented more rapidly than in firms with a dependent or utility view of infrastructure. To take an enabling view, senior managers must perceive a flexible infrastructure as an asset of the firm which provides a competitive advantage and thus overinvest in infrastructure based on current needs. This view also implies that the firm values this future flexibility during the project justification process.

Commonwealth Bank of Australia: Enabling View

Commonwealth Bank[16] is divided into business units, including Retail Banking, Institutional Banking, Development Bank, and Financial Services. Retail and Institutional Banking together form the largest profit contributors. The bank's mission statement is to "strive to be the leading provider of banking and other services in its domestic markets, with compatible presence overseas." Commonwealth Bank has had a competitive advantage in personal banking and the small business market. Future directions focus more on product innovation and on offering customers a full range of support facilities. Future developments are linked to the growth of the Asia Pacific region and to a recognition that Commonwealth Bank will achieve an enhanced presence in this region.

There is a general acceptance that information and information technology will be critical to future growth in a manner that will minimize risk. Early warning signals of problems, customer trading patterns, predictive tools, and other information systems will all be crucial to the bank's future.

Commonwealth Bank exhibits an enabling view of information technology. Technology investments are based on a two-way flow of influence between technology and the business strategy. Information technology investments must meet the strategic requirements of the business. However, as the business environment has

*become increasingly volatile, it is more difficult to pre-
dict future requirements. In order to cope with high levels of uncertainty, the infrastructure must be flexible and
able to cope with changes in strategic direction. Meeting
the needs of the current strategy is the minimum performance criterion. The recognition of the infrastructure's
ability to influence the business strategy is supported by
the appointment of a general manager of information
services who comes from a branch management position
with a business focus, rather than from an information
technology background.*

Where greater flexibility and agility in using firmwide resources
are part of the firm's strategic intent, an enabling rather than a utility view of the role of infrastructure provides a higher level of alignment between information technology and business strategy. Where
cost competition and cost savings dominate a firm's strategic intent,
a utility view is usually appropriate.

In any one firm over a period of several years, it is likely that different projects will be undertaken that will cover the full range of
views. For example, an enabling telecommunications network might
be installed, and then a utility approach to data center location
might occur in the same firm. However, one view tends to dominate
the information technology portfolio.

No One View Is Best for All

Infrastructure capability is a strategic choice, and no single view
of infrastructure suits all firms. However, a particular view is best
suited to a firm at any point in time. The different views have different impacts on firm performance. For example, in Chapter 3
(Figure 3.3) we show that on average higher levels of current
profitability were found in firms with lower investments in
firmwide infrastructure. On the other hand, firms with higher levels of infrastructure investments had higher rates of growth in
revenue and sales from new products. Senior managers must
ensure a fit of their information technology infrastructure investment with their strategic goals, while understanding the performance impacts of each view.

Measuring and Comparing Views

To manage information technology infrastructure and compare firms we must have measures. We combined five items to create a robust measure of a company's view for information technology infrastructure.

1. Firmwide information technology infrastructure investment as a proportion of the firm's total information technology investment (measured as a percentage averaged over five years)

2. Firmwide information technology infrastructure investment as a proportion of revenue (averaged over five years)

3. Approach to the justification for firmwide information technology infrastructure investment, ranging from a focus only on cost savings (score of 1) to only providing flexibility (score of 5). The seven questions used to determine a firm's approach are included in Appendix 3 and are averaged to create a measure of the firm's approach to justification.

4. The Reach and Range of the firmwide information technology infrastructure (from a minimum of 0 to a maximum of 100). Details of how this measure is calculated are in Appendix 3.

5. The number of firmwide infrastructure services (from 0 to 23).

Figure 4.8 presents the views and their information technology benchmarks.[17] In moving from no infrastructure to an enabling view, the relative level of infrastructure investment increases as a percentage of the entire information technology portfolio, as do resources dedicated to infrastructure as a percentage of revenue. As investment increases, so does infrastructure capability in the form of Reach and Range and the number of services. For firms that take a "None" view of infrastructure, there is no firmwide investment or justification, and thus no services provided. Firms taking a "none" view typically have a small Reach and Range, which supports doing business electronically only within a business unit.

Firms that take a utility view focus on investing in information technology infrastructure primarily where cost savings are achieved. Because the motivation is financial rather than strategic, the investment is relatively low, but not insignificant, at 0.4 percent of revenue.

No. of firms	None 1	Utility 8	Dependent 10	Enabling 8	All 27
% Centrally Coordinated Infrastructure of Total IT	0.0	29.0	50.0	59.0	45.0
% Centrally Coordinated Infrastructure of Revenue	0.0	0.4	1.9	3.1	1.8
Justification (1 = cost, 5 = flexibilty)	n/a	3.2	3.5	3.6	3.4
Reach and Range (0–100)	9	27	33	48	35
No. of Services (0–25)	0	14	16	20	16
View of Infrastructure*	16.7	43.0	51.0	59.0	50.0

*none = 0 to <25; utility = 25 to < 45; dependent = 45 to < 55; enabling = 55+.

Figure 4.8   View and Information Technology Benchmarks

Firms with a dependent view provide an infrastructure to deliver a particular strategy (for instance, branch banking), often balancing the competing tensions of cost reduction and the strategic agility to bring new products to market quickly. Firms with an enabling view will focus more heavily on flexibility and are prepared to pay a higher up-front cost to put the infrastructure in place to enable agility, as in the rapid development of new products.

To identify a firm's current view, gather the five items of information and compare your firm's results to the benchmarks for each view in Figure 4.8. Check each measure and then assess which of the four views represents your firm's current position. The first three measures identify what and how the funds are invested, and the last two identify the capabilities achieved. Many firms will fit neatly into one of the views. However, there are effects of good or poor management. One very well managed firm achieved the level of capability of an enabling infrastructure, with 21 services and a Reach and Range of 78, but spent the amount typical of a dependent firm. Another had the capabilities of a dependent view but spent like an enabling view.

A very useful way to use this information is to compare where your firm is now and what view you should take to meet your firm's strategic context. The benchmark data can also show what it costs the average firm to take a particular view and achieve the associated capability. This profile can then be compared to the firm's current view, investment, and infrastructure capability.

The characteristics of each view are summarized in Figure 4.9. A firm taking an enabling view, for example, will lead its industry in

Characteristics				
Investment in IT Infrastructure as % of Firm's Total IT Investment	**Investment in Firmwide IT Infrastructure as % of Revenue**	**Approach to Justification**	**Reach and Range**	**Number of Infrastructure Services**
None — Lowest	None	No attempt	Within BUs	None
Utility — Low	Lower than average (37% of total IT)	Cost focus	Within and between BUs for data and simple transactions	Basic (13 of the 25 services in Figure 4.2)
Dependent — Average	Just above average (45% of total IT)	Balance cost and flexiblity	Within and between BUs; Some complex transactions, some customers	Basic plus a few services that are strategic (16)
Enabling — Highest	Well above average (50% of total IT)	Flexibility focus	Within and between BUs, complex transactions; any customer	Extensive (20)

View of Infrastructure

Figure 4.9   Characteristics of the Four Views of Infrastructure

infrastructure investment level and provide an extensive set of infrastructure services centrally. Firms with an enabling view will also focus primarily on strategic flexibility in the justification process and provide an infrastructure with extensive Reach and Range between business units, with the potential to link to any customer and to perform complex transactions electronically. These firms typically have more sales from new products and faster time to market with faster revenue growth. In contrast, firms taking a utility view will have a lower-than-average firmwide information technology infrastructure investment and provide a few basic infrastructure services centrally. Firms with a utility view will primarily take a cost-reduction focus during the justification process and have infrastructures with a more limited Reach and Range between business units, focusing on simple transactions. Firms with a utility view typically have fewer assets tied up in technology, and have higher profitability and return on assets—particularly in the short to medium term.

Firms with a dependent view will attempt to balance cost and flexibility in the justification process, which results in an average investment in information technology infrastructure for their industry. Firms with a dependent view provide the basic infrastructure services centrally, plus several that are key to their strategic objectives—for example, a shared customer database. We identified the following patterns from our analysis.

Firms are more likely to take a utility[18] view if they

1. Operate in less information-based industries, such as manufacturing.

2. Focus on the cost savings that shared infrastructure can provide.

3. Don't require an electronic platform to enable cross-selling or synergies between business units.

4. Are larger firms with more business units.

Firms are more likely to take an enabling view if they

1. Operate in an information-based industry, such as finance or retailing.

2. Desire the firmwide strategic flexibility and agility that an extensive infrastructure can provide.

3. Wish to exploit greater synergies and cross-selling between business units.

4. Are smaller firms with fewer business units. It is organizationally and politically easier to integrate electronically with a firmwide infrastructure in smaller firms.

5. Have integrated the process for determining the information and information technology needs more fully into business planning processes.

Barriers to Increasing Infrastructure Capability

Barriers to increasing information technology infrastructure capability in a multibusiness-unit firm include

1. The incompatibility of different computers, telecommunications standards, and operating systems supplied by different vendors and in some cases the same vendor.

2. Different data definitions, such as how customer information is stored and accessed, and different technical standards

used in several applications in various parts of the firm, making systems incompatible.

3. Politics and power issues across different areas within the firm, such that managers are reluctant to share information or allow other areas to connect to their systems.

4. The reluctance of senior management to provide the substantial up-front dollars required to invest in an extensive infrastructure.

Creating a firmwide infrastructure from several business-unit infrastructures that were developed independently is difficult. Consider the example of an insurance company with four business units—Property and Casualty, Health, Life, and Investment products—where each business unit was managed autonomously. The business units had their own information technology infrastructures, developed at different times and with largely incompatible technology. Due to a shift in the strategic context, the firm wanted to cross-sell, for example, investment products to health insurance customers. The process of creating a firmwide information technology infrastructure was particularly expensive and took several years.

Fortunately, technology has evolved to significantly reduce the problems described in points 1 and 2 above. With the emergence of the TCP/IP telecommunications standard, much of the difficulty of increasing infrastructure Reach goes away. With the continued development of browser technologies, it is much easier to access previously incompatible systems and databases. It is still early, but there are indications that many of the incompatibility barriers will disappear, still leaving the political, financial, security, and organizational barriers.

The role of senior management in the insurance company was to recognize that integration would be necessary and to work with information technology management to make it happen. Decisions about the nature and extent of the capability of the firmwide information technology infrastructure are the responsibility of senior management. Successful decision making involves business and technology management working together. We explain how market leaders achieve this in the following chapters.

CHAPTER 5

Matching Views with Infrastructure Capabilities

When senior managers make major business decisions, there are almost always implications for the firm's information technology capabilities. Just as a major shift in a business and competitive environment requires fundamental rethinking of strategy, shifts in strategy demand a serious review of the firm's information technology portfolio.

Recall the Royal Automobile Club of Victoria (RACV), the membership-based insurance and roadside services firm described in Chapter 2. Due to a significant shift in competitor strategy, the RACV faced greatly increased competition, leading to major changes in its strategic intent, current strategies, and business objectives. These changes involved utilizing cross-selling opportunities to the loyal customer base. For any firm, the basic requirements of cross-selling are a technology platform and infrastructure capabilities that span business units to identify and share information about customers and develop a new range of products. This change often means transforming the infrastructure view and infrastructure capabilities from a cost-focused utility view to an enabling view, with higher investment levels in information technology infrastructure. To meet this higher need for integration, firms like the RACV expand their infrastructure capabilities both in functionality—through the number and depth of infrastructure services available—and in scope, through much more extensive Reach and Range.

Strategic contexts have implications for a firm's view of the information technology infrastructure. Each of the four views of infrastructure leads to different infrastructure capabilities. In this chapter we specify the types of capabilities required for each of the views in terms of a Reach and Range, and the number and depth of the infrastructure services implemented across the firm.

Reach, Range, and Infrastructure View

The extent of Reach and Range varies with the view of infrastructure. Figure 5.1 presents typical examples of how Reach and Range vary across four firms that represent each of the four views of infrastructure: none, utility, dependent, and enabling. We've measured and benchmarked the infrastructure capabilities of all four firms, and each has a Reach and Range that suits its strategic intent.

Firm A is an international conglomerate with minimal synergies between its businesses and the desire not to interlink the businesses, as they could be sold at any time and other businesses bought. Firm A has a "None" view of infrastructure, similar to Ralston Purina or some Hong Kong conglomerates, and almost no firmwide infrastructure in place. This firm has the smallest Reach and Range: the ability to send messages and access data within domestic business units.

The next level of Reach and Range is for firm B, a process manufacturing firm that took a utility firmwide view of infrastructure and encouraged each business unit to have a tailored infrastructure. This basic level of Reach and Range supports interbusiness-unit messaging and interbusiness-unit queries of stored data, such as checking inventory levels across multiple sites. Transactions such as processing an order can be completed electronically only within one site. This Reach and Range may become a limitation if the strategy shifts toward more global operations, requiring connectivity across multisite business units.

The consumer products manufacturer with a strategy requiring a degree of connectivity between different business units has a more extensive Reach and Range (firm C). The infrastructure, driven

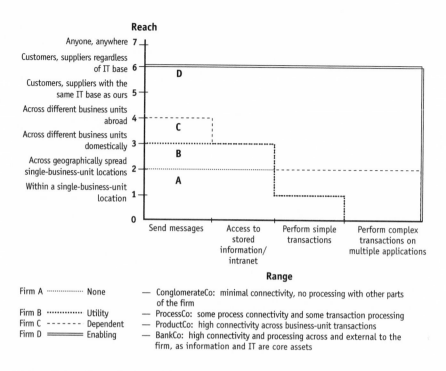

Figure 5.1 How Reach and Range Vary

from a dependent view, enables the sending of messages across business units both abroad and domestically, as well as access to stored data, such as customer buying patterns across domestic business units. Within a multisite business unit, this firm can process complex transactions across different computers and applications, updating all databases. For example, the firm can take a large order in Tokyo, check and allocate inventory in the Hong Kong warehouse, and list the required goods for manufacture in its factory on the outskirts of Kuala Lumpur.

A bank, firm D, with information technology management as a core competence, has an extensive Reach and Range. The firm's business and information technology planning are so integrated that they are indistinguishable. Firm D takes an enabling view and has produced an extensive infrastructure integrating all the business units and their different types of computer hardware, software, and data. The bank's strategy requires electronic links to large customers and some other financial institutions such as stockbrokers. The bank continues to invest above the industry average for information technology. The value of future flexibility is often acknowledged by senior business managers in business cases for information technology investments.

Reach and Range provide very powerful tools helping senior business and information technology management to work together with a common framework.[1] Reach and Range are useful as workshop tools to turn the two monologues into a dialogue. Business and information technology managers meet to discuss the required Reach and Range, starting with the firm's current Reach and Range. To assess the current Reach and Range, they determine the achievable Reach for a number of standard business activities for each level of Range. For example, within the "Send messages" level of Range, to whom can they readily and seamlessly send a memo or advertising message? Then they discuss the firm's future plans and goals for products and services, and the known or anticipated activities and capabilities of competitors. Will the current Range limit the firm's strategic flexibility? What changes are needed? Where changes are needed, information technology management can estimate the cost and time required to expand the Reach and Range. This process is often iterative, with trade-offs made among the firm's strategic desires, its actual capabilities, the expansion required, technical realities (such as to what extent the current architectures represent barriers), and what is achievable and realistic, taking budgetary constraints and time pressures into account.

Infrastructure Services and View

The second major component of a firm's infrastructure capability is the nature and depth of its infrastructure services. As with Reach and Range, the business functionality needed for its strategic contexts will determine the extent of these services. Those with the "None" view of infrastructure, such as Ralston Purina, don't offer any firmwide infrastructure services. To illustrate the business functionality of infrastructure services, three firms are profiled here. EnergyCo (a regional resource firm under the parent organization Energy International), Sun Life of Canada, and Commonwealth

Bank of Australia have taken the utility, dependent, and enabling views, respectively.

Utility View: Deciding on Basic Services

Firms with business drivers focusing on cost savings and economies of scale tend to take a utility view of infrastructure and offer fewer services. The average for a firm with a utility view is 13 of the 25 (see Figure 4.2) services, often provided selectively rather than comprehensively. EnergyCo has taken a utility view of information technology infrastructure, and information technology is a support function. EnergyCo's strategic vision focuses on delivering superior performance in its chosen markets, using a two-pronged strategy: first, that of total cost leadership, recognizing that oil is a commodity. The only way to generate greater profits is by controlling costs and minimizing the impact of poor economic conditions. The second strategy is the creation and management of "advantaged assets." Such assets have the capacity for generating products or services with distinguishable core competencies. "Disadvantaged assets" are sold off.

EnergyCo's infrastructure services include

- Provision of centralized large-scale processing for core systems.

- Management of firmwide applications that provide invoicing and sales tracking capabilities.

- Management of some business-unit applications.

- Assistance with information systems planning to business units.

Most of the firm's infrastructure services are offered at a selective, rather than a comprehensive, level. For example, information systems planning assistance is available to the business units on request, and the development of business-unit–specific applications involves introduction and support for personal computer packages.

The primary drivers for the operation of shared services in EnergyCo have been cost savings and efficiencies. The firm's orientation toward growth in market share and the need for greater emphasis on integrated, electronically based consumer retail systems are moving the group toward a more dependent view of infrastructure and further services. Concurrently, Energy International views itself as a global organization with a global value chain and aims to standardize certain information technology infrastructure services throughout all regions. EnergyCo plans to adjust its infrastructure services to complement and be compatible with Energy International.

Dependent View: Deciding on Competitive Services

Firms with a dependent view of infrastructure have a more extensive information technology infrastructure capability than utility firms. On average, dependent-view firms have 16 of the 25 infrastructure services and a higher level of investment than those with a utility view. Sun Life of Canada is a leading multinational life insurance and financial services organization with more than 4 million customers in Canada, the United States, Britain, Ireland, the Philippines, Hong Kong, and Bermuda.[2] Sun Life is a largely decentralized organization, with strong country or regionally based management teams in national offices in Canada, the United States, the United Kingdom, and Manila (Asia Pacific).

The competitiveness of Sun Life is based on a strong asset base, experience, reputation for integrity, local field agents, and a strong focus on information technology. Sun Life balances strong local knowledge with interconnections to a worldwide organization. In the insurance industry, each country is a different market with a different regulatory environment, where local factors strongly influence the products offered. Each national office operates essentially independently but relies on the Toronto headquarters for input regarding new processes, products, and know-how.

Sun Life's strong commitment to technology-based initiatives and to synergies such as expertise resulted in a dependent view of information technology infrastructure investments, heading toward an enabling view. Although business and information technology strategies influence each other, infrastructure investments must meet defined and measurable business needs and are monitored for the value they provide. As with all parts of Sun Life, the cost and quality of information systems are ongoing concerns.

Sun Life's Canadian National Office, together with the corporate central services division, offers both basic and strategically focused infrastructure services, including

- The operation, maintenance, and support of mainframe computing facilities (encompassing the scheduling and running of applications).

- Data administration.

- Planning and support of voice and data communications.

- Negotiations with information technology suppliers.

- Universal file access.

- A series of shared applications.

- E-mail and voice mail.

- Videoconferencing.

Some of these services are offered at a selective level, whereas others are comprehensive. For example, multimedia operations and development are offered selectively with the provision of videoconferencing facilities. But relationships with vendors are handled at a high level and coordinated across the firm. Sun Life regularly enters into joint ventures with vendors (and sometimes with other insurance firms) to develop new strategic applications, resulting in many successful initiatives. Sun Life has average Reach, with a high level of connectivity to customers and suppliers, and a moderate level of Range to perform simple transactions.

Enabling View: Deciding on Extensive Services

Firms with an enabling view of infrastructure usually provide an extensive set of infrastructure services, consistent with a high level of infrastructure capability. On average, enabling-view firms have 20 of the 25 infrastructure services and consequently the highest level of investment of all the views.

Commonwealth Bank of Australia (CBA) has a high degree of synergy among its businesses and an enabling view of infrastructure.[3] CBA has extensive firmwide infrastructure capability, including

- Management of all large-scale data processing facilities, including maintenance and support of mainframe, midrange, and local area network (LAN) computing facilities, as well as 24-hour, seven-day running of applications

and maintenance of all hardware located in two central
sites and distributed to more than 1,500 locations.

- Communications network services, encompassing planning,
  implementation, and support of domestic and international
  voice and data networks.

- Planning and budgetary control for all corporate technology
  expenditures.

- Security of all electronic information.

- Development and maintenance of applications to meet
  business-unit needs.

- Provision of corporate technology standards.

- Evaluation of new technologies.

- Research and development of new concepts and products.

- Planning for future infrastructure requirements.

- Planning and support for disaster recovery services.

- Training services for technology skills.

- Maintenance of the bank's printing and distribution function.

- Check processing and interbank settlement functions.

These infrastructure services provide the capability to meet the
bank's business strategies, which are based on having available at the
point of contact all the information needed to service any customer.
The customer contact point information is critical to the bank's
strategic goal to "continuously improve the quality of relationships
with customers" in an increasingly crowded and competitive market.
The extent of these services reflects the bank's two-way flow of influence between business and information technology strategies. In the
words of Commonwealth's general manager of information services,
"The bank and information technology are inseparable." Information technology investments must meet the strategic requirements of
the business. However, as the business environment becomes more
volatile, it becomes more difficult to predict future requirements, so
the information technology infrastructure must be flexible enough to
cope with changes in strategic direction.

CBA recently formed a strategic partnership with the outsourcing firm EDS Australia.[4] CBA is outsourcing its entire processing

operation to EDS at a cost of $400 million per year for 10 years. In turn, the bank is taking a 35 percent equity stake in EDS Australia to offset risks and to benefit from rapid growth in the outsourcing industry. CBA expects the arrangement to result in reduced costs, improved productivity, and faster introduction of new technology, while the equity arrangement with EDS minimizes risk.

Patterns of Infrastructure Capabilities

To understand the patterns of infrastructure capabilities in firms with different strategic contexts, we studied and benchmarked a set of firms. Using Reach and Range and the number and focus of infrastructure services,[5] we looked for patterns in the firms' strategies. Figure 5.2 provides a summary and overview of our findings,[6] linking aspects of the strategic context of firms with the extent of information technology infrastructure capabilities. Where the words *more, fewer,* or *higher* appear, we found a statistically significant relationship.

Our research indicates that higher levels of infrastructure capability are found and are generally desirable in firms where

- Products change quickly.

- Attempts are made to identify and capture synergies across business units.

- There is greater integration of information and technology needs as part of planning processes.

- There is greater emphasis on tracking the implementation of long-term strategy.

Lower levels of infrastructure capability are found in firms

- In the manufacturing industry, where the level of information intensity of the products created or the services offered are less than in finance and retail.

- Where resource decisions are based on current rather than future needs.

	Number of Services	Reach and Range
Industry		
Finance firms	-	-
Retail firms	-	-
Manufacturing firms	Fewer	-
Marketplace Volatility		
Firms that value organizational flexibility	-	-
Firms that base resource decisions on current needs	-	-
Firms that need to change products quickly	More	-
BU Synergy		
Firms that document how a BU contributes to achievement of firm strategic intent	-	-
Firms that identify cooperation between BUs	More	Higher
Strategy Formation Processes		
Firms that integrate information and IT needs into the overall process	More	Higher
Firms that report progress toward the achievement of firm strategic intent	More	Higher
Firms that name those responsible for tracking achievement toward firm strategic intent	More	Higher
Firms that describe how to measure achievement toward firm strategic intent	More	-

Figure 5.2   Firm Characteristics, Infrastructure Services, and Reach and Range

The Depth and Focus of Services

Although the five core services in Figure 4.2 are evident in all the firms with firmwide infrastructure that we've studied, the depth of each differs. For example, the most pervasive infrastructure service is management of the corporate communications network. The network becomes increasingly important for firms with a dependent or enabling view of infrastructure. Firms with a utility view often use the network for business activities of limited depth; for example, using the network for electronic messaging rather than as part of inter- or intraorganizational systems for executing business processes. In firms with an enabling view, such networks are used extensively for business transactions and business processes both within and between firms and their customers and suppliers, indicating more extensive depth in specific service areas.

To better understand their patterns, we grouped the infrastructure services into 8 management clusters by functionality, and the complete list of all 25 can be found in Appendix 4. Figure 5.3 shows which clusters of services were particularly important to firms with different characteristics.

	IT Infrastructure Services Clusters							
	Applications Management	Communications Management	Data Management	IT Education	IT Services Management	IT R&D	Security	Standards Management
Industry								
Finance firms	-	-	-	-	-	-	-	-
Retail firms	-	-	-	-	-	More	-	-
Manufacturing firms	Fewer	Fewer	-	-	Fewer	Fewer	Fewer	-
Marketplace Volatility								
Firms that value organizational flexibility	-	-	-	-	-	-	-	-
Firms that base resource decisions on current needs	-	-	-	Fewer	-	-	-	-
Firms that need to change products quickly	More	-	More	-	-	-	-	-
BU Synergy								
Firms that document how a BU contributes to achievement of firm strategic intent	-	More	-	-	More	-	-	-
Firms that identify cooperation between BUs	-	More	More	-	More	-	More	More
Strategy Formation Processes								
Firms that integrate information and IT needs into the overall process	More	More	More	More	More	More	More	More
Firms that report progress toward the achievement of firm strategic intent	More	More	-	More	More	-	-	More
Firms that name those responsible for tracking achievement toward firm strategic intent	More	More	-	-	More	-	-	More
Firms that describe how to measure achievement toward firm strategic intent	More	More	More	-	More	-	More	-

Figure 5.3 Firm Characteristics and Infrastructure Services Clusters

Firms that focus on identifying business-unit synergies and have well-developed planning processes place more emphasis on the areas of applications, communications, information technology management, and standards. Whereas communications management provides the basic technical integration capability, the other three focus more on the coordination of human expertise. It's the people, not the technology, who are critical in achieving sustained competitive advantage[7] and long-term shareholder value. These four clusters of services are required to enable more integration across the firm. These findings provide useful indicators to assess the extent of infrastructure capability required in a firm.

Indicators for Higher Levels of Infrastructure Capability

Greater information technology infrastructure capability is evident and desirable when firms need to respond more rapidly to changes in the marketplace.[8] This capability comes in the form of more services, particularly in the areas of applications and data management, which facilitate the firm's ability to develop and manage applications based on consistent data. A more extensive Reach and Range are necessary—particularly incorporating the ability to perform complex transactions linking several separate systems. For example, a bank invested tens of millions of dollars creating a customer database to show the bank's full relationship with each customer. The same bank is moving toward an infrastructure shared across different business areas. This dual development allows the bank to have a consolidated and consistent information source to identify opportunities and a common platform from which integrated applications can quickly be developed. The bank has achieved this by extending its Range and offering more firmwide information technology infrastructure services.

Increasing customer desire for a single point of contact is driving a higher interdependence between business units in firms, thus leading to a stronger impetus for shared firmwide services. The trend toward relationship-based services and cross-selling raises the stakes for information sharing across the business, in order to capitalize on opportunities for cross-selling and synergy. This business flexibility requires the information technology capability[9] to share information across products, services, locations, companies, and countries. This leads to a common infrastructure rather than separate information technology platforms and services for separate business activities.

The identification and achievement of business-unit synergies is a key driver for the development of infrastructure capability. Firms in our study that identify the cooperation required between business units have more extensive information technology infrastructure capability in both a higher number of infrastructure services and a larger Reach and Range. The most important service clusters for business-unit synergies are applications, communications, data management, and security.[10]

The complex environment of multibusiness-unit firms requires a high level of strategizing and planning sophistication to achieve strategic objectives.[11] This is particularly true in identifying, specifying, and achieving synergy between business units and in linking business and information technology requirements.[12]

Where infrastructure capability is important to a firm, well-developed strategy formation processes must incorporate deep and timely consideration of technology needs. We found that firms that adopt the sound management practices of having more integration of information and technology considerations in their overall planning processes, and that pay more attention to tracking the success of strategy implementation, generally have more infrastructure capability.

Indicators for Lower Levels of Infrastructure Capability

The demand for information technology infrastructure capability varies among industries due to different levels of information intensity and the different nature and pace of change.[13] Industries generally differ in their extent of cross-selling of products and cross-ownership of customers and processes. For example, in finance firms, customers are likely to utilize several products from different parts of the firm. In retail firms, processes are generally similar across different chains or brands. Manufacturing firms often have fewer synergies and provide fewer information technology infrastructure services than retail or finance firms. Corporate strategies imposing a minimum of mandates on business units also result in minimal firmwide information technology infrastructure capability. Where corporate strategies include the frequent buying and selling of business units, or have a group of businesses with little potential for synergies, minimal infrastructure is desirable.

Firm Characteristic	Critical Infrastructure Services Clusters
1. Integrate IT needs into planning.	IT Services Management Applications Management
2. Identify cooperation between business units.	Standards Management IT Services Management
3. Report progress toward strategic intent.	Communications Management IT Services Management
4. Name responsibilities for strategic intent.	IT Services Management Communications Management
5. Measure achievement toward strategic intent.	Applications Management IT Services Management

Figure 5.4   Firm Characteristics and Infrastructure Capabilities

Important Firm Characteristics and Their Infrastructure Services Clusters

Five firm characteristics are strong predictors of a need for extensive infrastructure capabilities. These characteristics are summarized in Figure 5.4. The strength of the link between the characteristics and the firm's infrastructure capability is indicated by the ranking of the characteristics. If any one of these characteristics is important to a firm, more infrastructure capability is indicated, with the higher list characteristics indicating the need for more extensive infrastructure capability.

The strongest predictor for a high level of infrastructure capability is information technology needs' being an integral part of the firm's planning processes. Alongside each characteristic are the two most important infrastructure services clusters—again, in order of importance. For example, the key infrastructure service clusters for firms with well-integrated information technology planning are information technology services management and applications management.

Reviewing these characteristics will provide a broad pointer to the profile of infrastructure capability that a firm needs. Where firms identify synergies between business units or operate in more information-intensive industries, they need more extensive infrastructure capability in the form of both more shared services and greater Reach and Range. Firms that have strategic formation processes in place to track the achievement of strategic intent need higher levels of infrastructure capability.

Executive managers must take responsibility for clearly specifying what type of infrastructure capability they need. But it is often difficult to know how to identify the specific capabilities that match a firm's strategic context and help deliver on business objectives. In Chapter 6 we describe how business and technology can work together to link strategic decisions and infrastructure capabilities much more precisely.

CHAPTER 6

Management by Maxim: Linking Strategy and Infrastructure

Johnson & Johnson (J & J), the highly successful health care company, began to face new business pressures in the early 1990s when large customers, such as Wal-Mart and Kmart, created new demands. At the same time, the economics of the health care industry itself changed. In response, J & J created new ways of supporting and selling to customers, particularly large customers. It focused on developing long-term relationships with large customers, rethinking the firm's traditional independent operating company model. The new customer services and business and organizational models that J & J developed had significant implications for the firm's information technology investments. Johnson & Johnson's business and technology managers acted in partnership to develop a new set of business and technology principles for the management of information technology and investments—particularly infrastructure capabilities—to balance costs, synergies, and the need for agility.

We've drawn on the experiences of firms like Johnson & Johnson to distill the framework that we call "Management by Maxim." This framework describes how market leaders make investment decisions about the new infrastructure that suit their firm's unique strategic context. These decisions range from having no firmwide infrastructure capabilities at all to extensive infrastructure capabilities encompassing the extended enterprise and including all business units, suppliers, and customers.

We first present an overview of Management by Maxim and then work through each of its components, which provide a practical link between the firm's strategic context and its use of the new infrastructure. Management by Maxim can be used by business and technology managers to shape informed and tailored long-term investments that deliver identifiable business value.

Using Maxims to Make Informed Technology Decisions

Many managers find it difficult to identify the information technology implications of their firm's business strategy. Broad statements of strategic intent, mission statements, and value propositions are valuable starting points, but an informed and appropriate agenda for action requires the joint attention of business and information technology managers.

Management by Maxim involves a series of decision points based on a sound understanding of where the firm is going rather than where it has been. The framework provides a process for surfacing and articulating the information technology implications of long- and medium-term business strategies. This maxims process can also be used for smaller organizational groupings, such as business units, departments, and work groups.

The Management by Maxim framework is presented in Figure 6.1. The framework begins on the left-hand side, with consideration of the firmwide strategic context, synergies among business units, and the extent to which the firm wishes to exploit those synergies. Managers begin defining their strategic context by answering questions such as these:

- What is the firm's strategic intent and its long-term goals?

- What are the synergies among its businesses?

- Do the businesses have overlapping customer and supplier bases?

- Are there similarities in products or in the expertise required in different businesses?

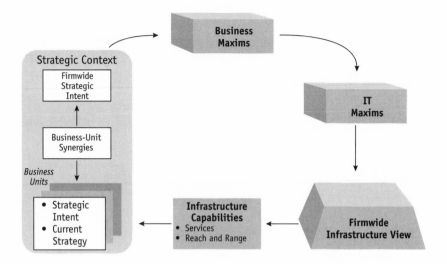

Figure 6.1 Management by Maxim: Linking Strategy and Infrastructure

- To what extent does the firm want or need to capture these synergies?

- What are the strategies, competitive choices, and value propositions of each of the business units, and how are they similar?

Defining the firm's strategic context helps management derive a series of short, sharp strategic statements we call *business maxims*. In using the term *maxim*, we draw on Aristotle's depiction of maxims as statements that indicate a practical course of conduct to be chosen.[1] Business maxims express the shared focus of the business in actionable terms and identify which activities must be centrally coordinated. Maxims, derived from the firm's strategic context, capture the future concerns of the firm as a whole.

Figure 6.2 illustrates the process using the example of Johnson & Johnson. The business maxim "Develop partnerships with customers on a worldwide basis" emerged from changes in Johnson & Johnson's competitive environment and had profound implications for management and investments in information technology. From the business maxims, business and information technology managers together identify a series of *IT maxims*, which express the expectations for technology investments in the firm. IT maxims identify the way information and data need to be accessed and used,

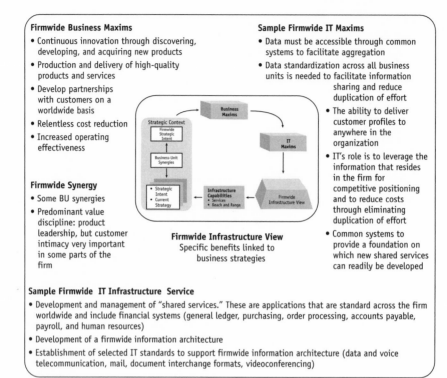

Firmwide Infrastructure View
Specific benefits linked to
business strategies

Firmwide Business Maxims

- Continuous innovation through discovering, developing, and acquiring new products
- Production and delivery of high-quality products and services
- Develop partnerships with customers on a worldwide basis
- Relentless cost reduction
- Increased operating effectiveness

Firmwide Synergy

- Some BU synergies
- Predominant value discipline: product leadership, but customer intimacy very important in some parts of the firm

Sample Firmwide IT Maxims

- Data must be accessible through common systems to facilitate aggregation
- Data standardization across all business units is needed to facilitate information sharing and reduce duplication of effort
- The ability to deliver customer profiles to anywhere in the organization
- IT's role is to leverage the information that resides in the firm for competitive positioning and to reduce costs through eliminating duplication of effort
- Common systems to provide a foundation on which new shared services can readily be developed

Sample Firmwide IT Infrastructure Service

- Development and management of "shared services." These are applications that are standard across the firm worldwide and include financial systems (general ledger, purchasing, order processing, accounts payable, payroll, and human resources)
- Development of a firmwide information architecture
- Establishment of selected IT standards to support firmwide information architecture (data and voice telecommunication, mail, document interchange formats, videoconferencing)

Figure 6.2   Johnson & Johnson's Strategic Context and Infrastructure Services

and what technology resources need to be deployed to ensure adequate technical capabilities, integration, and standards.

Johnson & Johnson's IT maxims expressed the business need to access aggregated data in common systems, deliver customer profiles, reduce duplication of effort, and develop shared services as a foundation for common systems. For Johnson & Johnson, the customer partnerships business maxim required the ability to deliver accurate and up-to-date customer profiles to virtually any location in the firm. Therefore, an important role of information technology was to facilitate leveraging the information about customers that resided in different parts of the firm and to reduce costs through eliminating duplication of effort.

The business and IT maxims lead to identification of the predominant *view of infrastructure* appropriate to achieve these maxims. Do these maxims imply

- No firmwide infrastructure needs, and thus a "None" view of infrastructure?

- Infrastructure investments based primarily on cost savings leading to a utility view?

- Some investments to meet specific business strategies and a dependent view?

- Extensive investments indicating a long-term need for future flexibility and for information technology as a key component of an iterative strategizing process, and thus an enabling view of infrastructure?

Johnson & Johnson had a clearly articulated strategy and infrastructure drivers that led to a dependent view of infrastructure, balancing flexibility and cost savings. The infrastructure view provides a context for decision making about specific infrastructure capabilities across the firm, such as the development of a firmwide communications network or agreed-upon standards to ensure consistency in financial data and applications across the firm.

These infrastructure services provide the human and technical capabilities that then underpin the business capabilities required for competitive positioning. In the late 1980s, the focus of Johnson & Johnson's Corporate Office of Information Technology was the development of systems for the corporate office. Now the major activities relate to what the firm calls "shared services," including applications that are standard across the company.

The changing health care industry resulted in changes to Johnson & Johnson's strategic context and business maxims, which drove new information technology infrastructure capabilities. We now explore how to describe and analyze a firm's directions and characteristics as the starting point for surfacing, articulating, and developing necessary infrastructure capability.

Considering the Firm's Strategic Context

The first step in the Management by Maxim process is to consider the firm's strategic context. We use contrasting examples to high-

Figure 6.3   Components of Strategic Context

light different strategic contexts. Firms like Ralston Purina, Citibank Asia, Johnson & Johnson, and Telstra have different business and organizational objectives and thus need different information technology portfolios. To illustrate these different requirements, the key components of strategic context are depicted in Figure 6.3 and described below.

Firm and Business-Unit Strategic Intent and Current Strategies

A firm's strategic intent and current strategies provide a starting point for describing its strategic context. Strategic intent refers to where the firm desires to be, in order to achieve, as Hamel and Prahalad explain, a "destination which is not only different [but] worthwhile."[2] In providing the strategic focus for the longer-term, stable goals of the firm, strategic intent should create "a substantial misfit between resources and aspirations."[3] In many firms, a key area of misfit is that of information technology resources.

In multibusiness-unit firms, strategic intents can exist at both corporate and business-unit levels. Complementing these longer-term goals are the current strategies aimed at the short to medium term and usually covering a one- to three-year time frame. Current strategies address how the firm does business today and contain details on products, market segments, and pricing. The strategic intents of two banks, Citibank and the Development Bank of Singapore, illustrate how firms make different strategic choices.

Citicorp, the sole shareholder in Citibank, is a global financial services firm operating in more than 90 countries and territories throughout the world.[4] Citibank services individuals, businesses, governments and financial institutions in more than 3,400 locations. In 1991 Citicorp recorded a net loss of $457 million, suspended the dividend on its common stock, and saw the price of that stock fall to a longtime low before rebounding after the year's end. In his letter to stockholders, Citicorp's chairman, John Reed, acknowledged the firm's problems and articulated the strategic intent, which would build on the firm's global presence. Reed's vision was to pursue growth in the consumer banking area through global expansion and leveraging information technology more imaginatively and cost-effectively than competitors. This vision was captured in the strategic intent to create "any time, anywhere banking" now branded as "Citibanking." Five years later, Citicorp announced record pretax earnings of $5.6 billion, a 21 percent increase over the previous year.

The essence of Citibanking is a relationship-based rather than a product-driven customer experience, providing a uniformly high quality customer experience that is readily recognized and valued. "The overriding imperative is globality," explained Citicorp's senior technology officer, Colin Crook, "so that wherever you touch us, the experience is consistent." Citicorp now sees the world as one market, and the same services and products are available "around the world and around the clock."[5] For the customer, the value proposition is ease of banking, as "the Citi never sleeps," together with familiarity of product and service delivery. Citibanking can be conducted 24 hours a day, 7 days a week, at Citicard Banking Centers, through CitiPhone Banking, Citibank Screen Phones, or personal computers, providing customers with greater control over their own funds.

Implementing Citibanking requires constant attention to the development of a global information technology infrastructure and consistent applications throughout the world. Although many of Citibank's systems in different parts of the world appeared to be the same, Crook observed that they were "all broadly the same, but not the same—a bit like making a McDonald's hamburger with noodles. So we have identified exactly how much the same they will be, including software versions, for complete consistency." These technology decisions are essential to make the vision of a global consumer experience real. The Citibanking experience is now delivered to 20 million accounts in 41 countries and contributes more than 60 percent of the total consumer business.

At the regional level, the corporate strategic vision of Citibanking has shaped the evolution of Citibank Asia Pacific. Citibank's retail customers in Singapore represent the more affluent segment of the population. The bank's fees and rates are not the lowest, but the bank is able to offer a high level of service and innovative banking products. The CitiPhone Banking service, available 24 hours a day, 7 days a week, overcomes limitations on the number of branches.

The Development Bank of Singapore (DBS) presents a contrast in strategic vision, intent, and approach to globalization.[6] Whereas global presence is the essence of Citibank's competitiveness, DBS's strength lies in offering a network of cross-border banking and financial services in the Asia Pacific.

Established in 1968 as a development financing institution to give impetus to Singapore's industrialization program, DBS has since evolved into a bank with universal banking capabilities. The development financing heritage gave DBS a competitive edge in providing project finance and venture capital, and in meeting the other related financial needs of emerging economies in the region. This makes the DBS group of companies a natural partner for doing business in Asia.

On the domestic front, DBS is the largest bank in Singapore, with most of its international offices spanning the Asian Pacific. DBS's leadership position in the domestic market has laid a strong foundation for regional expansion, with business activities originating from overseas branches and subsidiaries, as well as from international businesses originating out of Singapore.

The strategic intent, customer profiles, and nature of DBS's international expansion contrast with those of Citibank. Although both banks require considerable information technology infrastructure and consistency in applications, the underlying rationales for their approaches differ, affecting both the process and the outcomes of their decision making.

Competitive Focus: The Three Value Disciplines

The competitive focuses of Citicorp and DBS also differ, affecting their information technology choices. Whereas the success of Citicorp has been based on Citibanking, a relationship-based customer experience, DBS's strategy has been continuing product innovation. Citicorp and DBS have chosen different paths to position themselves in their markets.

Michael Treacy and Fred Wiersema's notion of the three value disciplines[7] is useful in highlighting implications of different current strategies for technology choices. Successful organizations, the "market leaders" according to Treacy and Wiersema, usually excel at delivering one type of business value to their chosen customers. The three value disciplines are

- *Operational excellence*, under which businesses emphasize efficiency and reliability, lead the industry in price and convenience, minimize overhead costs, and streamline the supply chain.

- *Customer intimacy*, with the focus on the cultivation of relationships, lifetime value to the company, satisfaction of unique needs, customer service and responsiveness, and customization based on deep customer knowledge.

- *Product (or service) leadership*, with continuing product innovation, embracing ideas, new solutions to problems, and rapid commercialization.

Market leaders excel in at least one value discipline but also meet a minimum threshold of competence in the other two. The firm's strengths and competitive position in the three value disciplines underpin its value proposition to customers. Market leaders, such as Citibank and DBS, build their organizations around their chosen value discipline emphases. They have a consistency in all areas that is directed toward and reflects their value proposition. In the case of Citibank, we observe that the predominant value discipline is customer intimacy, whereas for DBS it is product leadership. DBS maintains its product leadership position by providing innovative customized solutions to meet the needs of its wide range of customer segments.

As each of the value disciplines has different implications for many aspects of their operations, firms need to understand their value discipline orientation. Figure 6.4 summarizes the major implications of the different value disciplines.[8] The business processes, management systems, and information needs inherent in each of the value disciplines lead to different business and IT maxims.

Different value disciplines also lead to different types of information technology portfolios, often with tailored infrastructure capabilities. Operational excellence requires transactional systems that are fast, robust, and cost-effective, with strong emphasis on systems that automate transactions and reduce costs.

	Operational Excellence	Customer Intimacy	Product Leadership
Business Processes	– End-to-end supply chain optimization – Emphasis on efficiency and reliability	– Customer service, marketplace management – Emphasis on flexibility and responsiveness	– Product development, time-to-market, and market communications – Emphasis on breakthroughs
Management Systems	– Command and control, standard operating procedures – Quality management	– Customer-equity measures like lifetime value – Satisfaction, share management	– Rewarding individuals' innovative capacity – Risk and exposure management
Information and Information Systems	– Integrated low-cost transaction systems – The system is the process	– Granular customer databases, linking internal and external information – Strong analytical tools	– Person-to-person communication systems – Technologies enabling cooperation
Infrastructure Capability Emphasis	– Management of large-scale transaction-processing facilities	– Shared customer databases – Management information re service quality	– Firmwide messaging services – Firmwide groupware applications

Figure 6.4   Three Value Disciplines and Infrastructure Implications

Source: Adapted from "Building the New Information Infrastructure." CSC Index Foundation Working Paper 1, 1993 (Copyright © CSC Index), and M. Treacy and F. Wiersema, *The Discipline of Market Leaders* (Reading, Mass. Addison-Wesley, 1995). Reprinted with permission.

The strategy of customer intimacy requires greater attention to the storage, analysis, and availability of more extensive information on customers than is necessary simply to complete business transactions. More comprehensive customer databases are required, in both structured form and in the form of electronic images of letters and documents, notes, and perhaps phone conversations. Powerful analytic tools are used to extract information to manage customer relationships more proactively. It takes significant focus on integrating all the different points of customer contact to present a consistent face to the customer.

Businesses that compete predominantly on product leadership put more energy into managing flows of ideas, including the interrelationships between many different parts of the organization, such as R&D, engineering, information technology, and marketing. Here, systems to support the management of ideas are concerned with context and communication, rather than with the content of the data, as in transactional systems. Product leadership often involves more emphasis on support for high-performance teams that might be physically dispersed.

Business managers need to identify their predominant value discipline as a step toward understanding the implications for their information technology requirements. In multibusiness-unit firms, different value disciplines can coexist across the different businesses. This pattern has implications for the nature of synergies in the firm and, in turn, for the extent and depth of firmwide infrastructure investments.

Identifying Potential Business-Unit Synergies

Firms vary in the extent to which they have synergies among their different businesses, customers, products, competitive bases, and suppliers. The extent and nature of potential business-unit synergies affect what type of information technology can sensibly be shared across the firm.

A high level of customer overlap across business units provides opportunities to cross-sell products and implies the need for common customer profiles and databases. Where there is a high degree of overlap in suppliers, synergies and cost savings could be derived from a coordinated approach to systems reaching beyond the enterprise, such as links to suppliers by electronic data interchange (EDI) or by extranets utilizing Internet technologies. More effective management of supplier relationships, including lower firmwide costs, was a major driver in the development of firmwide applications at Monsanto.[9]

In some firms, different business units have different competitive bases. This difference reduces the efficacy of shared services, leading to lower investments in information technology at the firmwide level and higher investments in the business units. The extent of shared value disciplines indicates the level of firmwide infrastructure capabilities. If business units share the same predominant value discipline (such as product leadership), a larger number of infrastructure services can be shared across the firm, with larger Reach and Range. If business units compete on different value disciplines, a smaller investment in firmwide infrastructure is appropriate, with more extensive tailored capability in the business units.

An example of different value disciplines' coexisting in one firm is a process manufacturing firm we call ChemCo, which is structured in five relatively autonomous business groups. Two of these business groups—Chemicals and Advanced Materials—illustrate the implications of different value disciplines for firmwide infrastructure investments. The Chemicals group competes in largely mature markets with commodity products, predominantly on the basis of operational excellence. The products in this group face fierce international competition and are very focused on reducing costs and improving quality, usually orienting the portfolio to low-cost transaction systems (see Figure 6.4). Advanced Materials, on the other hand, is a grouping of smaller, newer businesses experiencing considerable growth with a strong export focus. The value discipline of these businesses is product leadership, requiring quite a different information technology portfolio.

Within ChemCo, the range of businesses exhibits different value disciplines, different levels of maturity, and different types of products and markets. Consequently, each of the businesses takes a different approach to its information technology investments. However, because the firm places considerable emphasis on driving economies of scale through shared best practice, there is some shared infrastructure capability, such as a firmwide communications network supporting electronic mail. In recent years, ChemCo has moved steadily to a more extensive firmwide infrastructure capability to achieve economies and synergies in areas such as common applications for accounting and plant management.

Leveraging Potential Synergies

Many firms have a strong corporate desire to exploit synergies to achieve economies of scale, scope, or expertise. Firms with little overlap in customers, suppliers, or products now seek to utilize synergies and sharing in such areas as financial management, human resources management, and information systems. However, some firms prefer to forgo potential synergies in favor of providing maximum autonomy, so that their businesses can move quickly, particularly at the regional and local levels. Forcing similar processes and procedures is seen as contrary to a culture that encourages entrepreneurship among its line managers, particularly in periods of rapid growth. This approach is typical of the entrepreneurial Hong Kong–based trading firms.

In reviewing the strategic context of firms, we begin to appreciate how firms develop different, but appropriate, approaches to infrastructure services based on their synergies. We'll illustrate with examples of Amcor and Honda.

The international paper and packaging company Amcor Ltd. has operations in more than 20 countries and annual revenue of more than $5 billion. From its Australian headquarters base, Amcor is one of the world's top ten paper and packaging firms. Amcor has moved in stages from paper making to packaging, to corrugated boxes, and then to plastic containers and cans.[10] As the CEO describes it, "We now have a very decentralized and very individual set of businesses—each with their own subculture. The overall control mechanism for the Group is based around return on assets."[11] Although there is some vertical integration in Australia and the United States, where the paper group's mills supply some of Amcor Fibre Packaging's (AFP) box factories, generally the businesses do not share customers or products. The emphasis on operational autonomy is echoed in the words of AFP's managing director: "We have a strong focus on local accountability and prefer to run the business with the minimum of mandates."[12] Within AFP, business groups in different locations reflect different value disciplines in their operations.

Honda, on the other hand, seeks to balance high levels of both international integration and local responsiveness. Honda sees its businesses as "a global network with 83 production facilities in 39 countries that supply Honda products to approximately 160 countries."[13] "Product realization"—taking an innovative idea and turning it into a product—is a capability central to Honda's competitiveness in each of its businesses.[14] There is synergy in the competencies required to make motorcycles and automobiles. An efficient parts system for all products is part of the backbone of the business. Honda's communications network aims to both cut costs and enable electronic communication to speed the business. Honda's Systems Division's general manager recalled the justification for the enhanced network: "Each business and IS group saw the benefits as we did and the divisions agreed to share the cost. It then became part of the business plan for each business and region."[15] In Honda, there is a clear desire and capacity to exploit the potential of the synergies that exist among the different businesses.

Surfacing the Synergies

The importance of business-unit synergies is often insufficiently recognized, articulated, or discussed within firms. We've developed three sets of questions that elicit possible synergies and surface the firm's attitude toward gaining these potential benefits. We suggest that managers review their responses to these questions and then consider the extent to which colleagues share their views.

Extent of Potential Business-Unit Synergies

To what extent

- Do the businesses have an overlapping customer base?

- Is there information about customers that you want to share across the firm?

- Do the businesses have an overlapping supplier base?

- Is there information about suppliers that you want to share across the firm?

- Do the businesses offer similar or overlapping products?

- Does each part of the firm share similar business processes, such as servicing a customer, creating a new product or service, and providing a treasury service?

- Are there areas of expertise, competencies, or capabilities (for example, product development, financial management, systems development) that are or could be utilized across the firm?

Similarity of Competitive Base: Common Value Disciplines

- Which of the value disciplines are represented among the businesses in this firm: operational excellence, customer intimacy, and/or product leadership?

- To what extent do the business units in this firm share the same value discipline?

Exploiting Synergies and Encouraging Autonomy

The third group of questions clarifies the balance between encouraging local autonomy and the extent to which the firm wants to exploit potential synergies. How important is it to

- Maximize independence in local operations in this firm?

- Provide local autonomy with a minimum of mandates?

- Utilize the potential synergies that reside in each of the businesses?

The answers to these questions clarify the existence of synergies and the extent to which the firm wants to garner those synergies. To gain an accurate picture of a firm, it is useful to involve corporate executives from different areas of responsibility together with managers from the major businesses. When working in firms, we ask business and information technology managers to prepare by completing these questions from their own individual perspective, and then share the results at a usually lively roundtable meeting.

The attributes of firmwide and business-unit strategies, together with identification of the implications of business-unit synergies, need to be synthesized and captured in a form that is accessible outside the executive team. Such information provides critical input to formulating what should be shared across the firm and what can be devolved to business units or process owners. In most firms, these high-level strategic notions are too abstract to be used for investment decisions. We synthesize these notions into maxims.

Articulating Business Maxims

Consideration of a firm's strategic context provides insights about what should be coordinated across the firm, what can be leveraged from within business units, and what can be left to local options. A useful way to express this synthesis is in the series of short statements that we call business maxims. Business maxims draw on the firm's statements of strategic intent; on output from the strategy formation process, such as mission and value statements; and on other statements of strategic direction. The purpose of maxims is to articulate an agreed-upon position in a form that can be readily understood and communicated. Maxims mix strategic directions with the practical grounding referred to by Aristotle,[16] to create a form that is readily communicated.

An example of a business maxim in an insurance firm with three business units is "All sales employees are decision makers about selling new policies and cross-selling." This maxim implies that the firm's infrastructure needs to provide access for all employees (regardless of business-unit affiliation or location) to the data and systems required to make insurance policy decisions. This business maxim was one of five, which, taken together, provided a strong and concise statement of firmwide business requirements.

Using business maxims overcomes two common problems. First, some firms don't have strategic statements with the required qualities of sharpness and comprehensiveness,[17] and thus much more refinement and insight are needed to surface the information technology implications. Alternatively, some firms have an excess of strategies that aren't sufficiently focused and for which the implications are obscured or not readily actionable.

Business maxims focus the attention of all employees, whether or not they are part of the strategy-making process, on simple and achievable messages. These short and specific statements translate aspects of strategic context into terms that can be easily communicated across the firm. Business maxims can express the competitive stance of the firm; the extent to which the firm coordinates the business units (such as autonomy of business units, or cross-selling; synergies; and sharing of resources); and the implications for the management of information and information technology.

Changes in a firm's competitive environment require reshaping business maxims. The competitive environment of the RACV, a membership-based provider of vehicle insurance, roadside, and other services in Australia, changed substantially when an equivalent organization in a neighboring state extended its base into the RACV's geographic customer catchment area. In response, the RACV developed a strong focus on membership acquisition and customer needs, together with innovative products and services.[18] New business maxims have increased the urgency of cross-selling and of sharing customer databases and transaction-processing systems across the businesses.

Examples of business maxims from a range of firms illustrate our Management by Maxim framework.

Business Maxims and Different Strategic Contexts

Business maxims derived from the firmwide strategic contexts of Amcor, Honda, and the RACV are listed in Figure 6.5. These sets of maxims show differences in emphasis, which have implications for different information technology infrastructures. Amcor has strong pressures for local responsiveness in its businesses and

Amcor
• Provide products and services of the highest quality and the most competitive price. • Expand internationally through creation and acquisition of new businesses. • Extend activities into selected paper and packaging businesses. • Optimize returns on shareholders' funds by focusing on core activities. • Establish local responsibility and accountability with minimal mandates.
Honda
• Innovate continuously by creating and developing new products, and adapting products for major regional markets. • Expedite global operations through maximizing the synergies of production and operations in many countries. • Continue to focus on reducing cycle time from R&D through production and marketing. • Increase flexibility to respond to new opportunities and create new markets. • Hire the highest-caliber staff who excel at working together. • Commit to minimizing costs where possible.
RACV
• Differentiate through product innovation. • Maintain highest possible one-stop service standards from a low-cost base. • Encourage customer-needs–driven product and service development. • Show growth in membership and services cross-selling. • Sustain and develop member and staff loyalty.

Figure 6.5 Business Maxims from Three Firms

emphasizes local accountability with a minimum of mandates. Honda seeks to expedite global operations through maximizing the synergies of production and operations in many countries, while focusing on greater localization. Honda refers to this approach as "glocalization," where there is a need for greater localization, particularly in styling, but within the context of sharing expertise in a firm committed to globalization.

Innovation is now viewed as critical to the future success of the RACV, both in its mission to expand the membership base and in the future survival and growth of its critical revenue earner, insurance. The RACV seeks to remain a low-cost provider, but views its function and role in new ways, resulting in acquiring complementary businesses to assist in the development of new products and services. Cross-selling to the membership base is now also a strategic focus.

Examples of Business Maxims

We've identified business maxims that refer to many different aspects of the business. Figure 6.6 provides examples of generically phrased maxims in six categories:

Cost Focused	Growth
• Price products/services at lowest cost. • Drive economies of scale through shared best practice.	• Expand aggressively into underdeveloped and emerging markets. • Establish international reach and presence as one business. • Carefully grow internationally to meet the needs of customers who are expanding. • Target growth through specific product and customer niches. • Leverage international growth from a domestic base.
Value Differentiation as Perceived by Customer	
• Meet client expectations for quality at reasonable cost. • Make the customer's product selection as easy as possible. • Provide all information needed to service any client from one service point. • Capture the electronic delivery channel to the customer. • Provide strong relationship management with superior customer service. • Provide client service that helps customers reach their potential. • Develop customer partnerships based on long-term relationships. • Develop customer partnerships on a worldwide basis. • Know what is selling and where it is selling. • Develop win/win relationship with key suppliers.	**Human Resources**
	• Create an environment that maximizes intellectual productivity. • Maintain a high level of professional and technical expertise. • Identify and facilitate the movement of talented people. • Attract and retain high-caliber staff committed to our vision of the one corporation.
Flexibility and Agility	**Management Orientation**
• Be flexible to respond to new markets. • Grow in cross-selling capabilities. • Develop new products and services rapidly. • Achieve fastest time to market with new products and services. • Foster ability to detect and respond to subtle shifts in the marketplace. • Innovate continuously through new product development. • Create capacity to manufacture in any location for a particular order. • Foster ability to deploy resources for new products quickly and judiciously.	• Maximize independence in local operations with a minimum of mandates. • Make management decisions close to the line. • Leverage synergies throughout the firm. • Create management culture of information sharing (to maintain or generate new business). • Provide flexibility in operating style to make decisions (for customers) quickly.

Figure 6.6 Sample Business Maxims

1. Cost focused

2. Value differentiation as perceived by customers

3. Flexibility and agility

4. Growth

5. Human resources

6. Management orientation

We've found that five or six maxims are the most that can be communicated by executive management and well understood by operational managers. Thus management needs to prioritize the relative importance of maxims to ensure a set that captures the most important messages. Limiting the number of maxims is a valuable strategic exercise to test the group's focus. A large number of maxims indicates fuzzy or overambitious thinking, reducing the chances of successful implementation.

Let's refer back to the earlier discussion of the strategic intent and vision of Citibank. The firm's value discipline of customer intimacy and its intense focus on Citibanking characterize a high level of commitment to synergies. The strategic context of Citibank translates into these business maxims:

- Develop deep and long-term relationships with customers, with a uniform customer experience that is readily recognized and valued.

- Provide all the information needed to service any customer from any service point.

- Provide a seamless and consistent level of service from market to market, region to region.

- Achieve the highest level of global integration of products and services driving economies of scale through shared best practice.

- Maintain professional staff of the highest caliber, whose outlook and orientation are global.

- Ensure substantial and sustainable growth in emerging markets.

Citibank's corporate policies and shared values are well articulated, known, and understood throughout the firm.

Identifying Information Technology Maxims

Information technology maxims are statements that decree how the firm needs to connect, share, and structure information[19] and deploy information technology across the firm.[20] IT maxims are the outcome of considering the information and technology implications of the firm's strategic context and business maxims.

IT maxims express the strategic intent for information technology and identify the ways the firm needs to

1. Lead or follow in the deployment of information technology in its industry (e.g., the role of information technology and the required level of investment relative to competitors).

2. Electronically process transactions.

3. Connect and share data sources and systems across different parts of the firm.

4. Connect and share data sources and systems across the extended enterprise (customers, suppliers, regulators, strategic alliances).

5. Maintain common information technology architectures across the firm, including policies and standards.

6. Access, use, and standardize different types of data (financial, product, customer).

7. Identify appropriate measures for assessing the business value of information technology.

Citibank's focus on customer intimacy and the uniform customer experience leads to a series of IT maxims, including the following:

- Customer information must be kept in a consistent form and be accessible to both the customer and staff any time and anywhere the customer interacts with Citibank.

- A consistent architecture for hardware, software, communications, data, and work flow is critical to the bank as the basis for the shared infrastructure and shared services to provide the capability for the uniform customer experience.

- Customer entry points to the bank (ATMs, branches, phone services, personal computer access) must provide a consistent interface throughout the world.

- Our network must enable our customers and our businesses easy access to a wide range of applications essential to the delivery of customer-friendly banking.

Samples of generically phrased IT maxims synthesized from our work are listed in Figure 6.7. We identified maxims in five major areas[21] of importance for long-term investments:

Expectations for IT Investments in the Firm
• We use IT to reduce costs through eliminating duplication of effort.
• IT is viewed as a service provider focused on satisfying end-user requirements.
• IT expenditures must improve customer service levels.
• We compete with IT, and our services and products are dependent upon continuing investment in leading-edge business technology.
• We develop innovative business and marketing applications of leading-edge (but stable) technologies.
Data Access and Use
• The usefulness of data must be recognized beyond the area immediately responsible for its capture so that it is not lost.
• Business processes and systems must ensure that financial and sales data are captured and maintained together.
• We need to have a common view of the customer across our businesses.
• Mobile users must have ready access to the same data they have at the desktop.
• Customer service representatives must be empowered with access to a complete file of the customer's relationship with the firm.
Hardware and Software Resources
• We will migrate toward hardware and software resources that can process complex transactions across global reach.
• We will electronically process repetitive transactions.
• Desktop IT must provide all managers and staff with user-transparent applications to empower them to perform complex tasks quickly.
• We will have common order entry systems across business units that can cross-sell.
• New systems will provide a foundation on which new services can be added without major modifications.
Communications Capabilities and Services
• Our corporate network must provide access to a wide range of applications essential to the delivery of consistent customer service.
• Our corporate network must be capable of carrying high-bandwidth applications such as imaging and videoconferencing.
• We require maximum penetration in the use of EDI and related technologies to streamline business processes.
• We need to integrate access to the Internet with our communications network.
• Our external communications are seen as providing future channels to our customers—particularly for electronic commerce and service delivery.
Architecture and Standards Approach
• We have a recommended IT architecture, covering hardware, software, and connectivity requirements only.
• We require data standardization for financial and sales data only.
• We enforce standards for hardware and software selection to streamline resource requirements and reduce incompatibilities and costs.
• We will maintain short lists of supported products and favored vendors in each technology category. Users may purchase other products, but IT will not support them.
• We will centrally coordinate purchasing of IT from major vendors to minimize costs, ensure consistency, and coordinate expertise.

Figure 6.7   Sample Information Technology Maxims

1. Expectations for information technology investments in the firm

2. Data access and use

3. Hardware and software resources

4. Communications capabilities and services

5. Architecture and standards approach

Sample Business Maxims	Sample IT Maxims
Provide all the information to service the client from any service point.	Customer service representatives must have access to a complete file of each customer's relationship with the firm.
Drive economies of scale through shared best practice.	We enforce standards of hardware and software selection to reduce costs and streamline resource requirements. We centrally coordinate purchasing of IT from major vendors, to minimize costs and ensure consistency.
Capture the electronic delivery channel to customers.	Our external communications provide channels to customers that are easy to access, particularly for electronic delivery of services and products.
Be able to detect and respond to subtle shifts in the marketplace.	Centrally coordinated information flow should allow all parts of the firm to more easily and quickly spot trends and use these to the firm's advantage.
We have a management culture of information sharing to generate new business.	The usefulness of data must be recognized beyond the area immediately responsible for its capture so that it is not lost.
Able to develop resources for new products quickly and judiciously.	New systems must provide a foundation on which new products and services can be added without major modifications.

Figure 6.8   Linked Sample Business and IT Maxims

The number of IT maxims varies among firms, depending on the breadth and depth of the business maxims. IT maxims tend to be longer statements than business maxims, as they address implementation issues. One business maxim usually leads to several IT maxims. There is often overlap among the IT maxims generated from several business maxims, requiring some rewording to achieve a concise and comprehensive set. In Figure 6.8 we match some business maxims with key IT maxims.

As a guide, here are some specific examples of IT maxims from firms in different industries:

- Summary information for production, sales, marketing, distribution, and financial management should be readily available to managers in a form that is timely (two hourly), consistent, integrated, and easy to use in making business decisions.

    —A growing firm in the beverage business

- Common interfaces and transaction processing will be used for ATMs across the five countries in which the bank operates.

    —An Asia-headquartered bank that is expanding its operations

- Our corporate network must be capable of carrying high-bandwidth applications, such as imaging and videoconferencing.

    —A manufacturing firm with both headquarters and distributed R&D groups, and a strong focus on product innovation

- Selected enterprisewide, relevant data must be in a consistent form to facilitate aggregation on a worldwide basis. These data will enable global management of customers (accounts receivable, credit), suppliers (accounts payable), materials, and general finance, as well as provide knowledge of suppliers who are customers and customers who are suppliers.

    —A multibusiness international manufacturing firm

The last example above is from a firm we will call WorldCo, where a recently appointed CEO set the context for a different balance between corporate and business-unit operations with these words:

> Each business has its own strategic needs that must be served while sharing information at an enterprise-wide level. Differences among business units that contribute meaningfully to business results are appropriate; differences that don't are not. Information technology, in the context of business redesign, is the single most valuable tool to allow us to become more effective in the marketplace.

WorldCo identified which data and systems should be managed across the firm and which should not.

WorldCo's strategy of sharing and meaningful difference is captured in its IT maxims:

- Our network must enable business units to access selected applications essential to the firm's shared business objectives.

- The network must provide, as a minimum, electronic mail facilities for communication among business groups internationally, and support the ongoing implementation and use of groupware products.

- Communication systems must facilitate high-quality person-to-person interaction among R&D staff and between R&D, production, and marketing personnel.

- We have an agreed-upon architecture for those parts of the information technology infrastructure that support shared services. This architecture includes that required to manage knowledge for enterprise decision support.

- We enforce some standards for hardware and software selection to streamline resource requirements and reduce incompatibilities and costs.

- Provided they meet certain data requirements and selected standards, business units can determine the most appropriate applications for their businesses.

By way of contrast, Amcor's multinational approach to its operations, and business maxims emphasizing a minimum of mandates, leads to an IT maxim:

Information technology expertise and technological solutions are shared on an informal basis.

This maxim implies no investment in firmwide technology infrastructure and is consistent with the firm's strategic context. Amcor is willing to forgo any information technology–related synergies and to emphasize autonomy.

The different strategic context of these multibusiness firms leads to different views of information technology infrastructure and different infrastructure capabilities. Amcor has had a "None" view of infrastructure with no firmwide infrastructure services and low Reach and Range. WorldCo is moving from "None" to a utility view, with a basic set of services driven largely by efforts to lower costs, particularly the costs of supply. Honda has a dependent view of infrastructure, with an above-average number of services and Reach and Range. The RACV is implementing an enabling view of infrastructure, with increased infrastructure services and a higher Reach and Range.

Deriving Maxims and Matching Infrastructure Capabilities

Johnson & Johnson's infrastructure decision-making process reflected the Management by Maxim approach. The firmwide strategic context and the associated business maxims shifted to respond to changes in the health care industry.[22] Managers need to be able to identify large customers who were dealing separately with different autonomous business units. This requirement altered the amount and kinds of information that needed to be communicated and shared across Johnson & Johnson operating companies worldwide (see Johnson & Johnson insert).

When firms apply the Management by Maxim framework, they have a transparent trail of evidence between strategy and infrastructure capabilities. The use of business and IT maxims provides a vehicle for true dialogue between business executives and information technology management.

In articulating IT maxims, business and technology managers are developing an agenda for future information technology investments and reviewing current infrastructure capabilities. The Management by Maxims framework is dynamic; changes in one part of the framework mean rethinking each of the components. Senior management must revisit business and IT maxims regularly, as part of an ongoing process to ensure value from information technology investments, asking

- Are the IT maxims in line with business maxims?

- Do the business maxims on which IT maxims are based continue to reflect the firm's strategic positioning and value proposition?

- What are the market shifts that lead to changes in business strategy with new or different implications for IT maxims?

Johnson & Johnson

For most of its history, Johnson & Johnson has been managed as a group of autonomous businesses. The firm has more than 80,000 employees and 168 operating companies located in more than 50 countries around the world, selling products in more than 150 countries. Johnson & Johnson's decentralized operating structure provided its operating companies with a great deal of autonomy. In the early 1990s, the impact of changes in the health care industry was being realized. Customers were becoming larger, with global reach themselves, and, in some countries, were forming buying groups to increase their power in the supply chain. Johnson & Johnson needed to streamline its business worldwide to make the organization more cost-effective and to respond to changes in its business environment.

In Chapter 7 we examine how firms operationalize the Management by Maxim process and consider an alternate process, Management by Deal.

Johnson & Johnson's Strategic Context

The strategic intent of Johnson & Johnson was clear:

- To be the world's most innovative and competitive health care company
- To grow units and profits at a rate faster than the competition
- To provide superior long-term returns to shareholders

This vision is attained through product innovation and the growth of new products. In the mid-1990s, approximately one-third of the firm's sales were from products introduced into world markets in the past five years and from existing products launched into new markets during the same period.

Johnson & Johnson has placed much greater emphasis on synergies between its businesses. Among many initiatives was the creation of programs to share administrative, financial, and information services among companies and locations; mergers of operating companies; and consolidation of manufacturing locations.

The business maxims derived from Johnson & Johnson's strategic context can be expressed as

- Continuous innovation through discovering, developing, and acquiring new products.
- Production and delivery of high-quality products and services.
- Developing partnerships with customers worldwide.
- Constant cost reduction.
- Increased operating effectiveness.

Information Technology Maxims

Johnson & Johnson seeks specific benefits from its investments in information technology and has identified an extensive set of information technology principles. The thrust of these principles can be summarized as a series of IT maxims:

- Data must be accessible through common systems to facilitate aggregation.

- Centralized information flow should allow all parts of the firm to more easily and quickly spot trends and to use these to the firm's advantage.

- Data standardization across all business units is needed to facilitate information sharing and reduce duplication of effort.

- IT's role is to leverage the information that resides in the firm for competitive positioning and to reduce costs through eliminating duplication of effort.

- We need the ability to deliver customer profiles anywhere in the organization.

- Common systems should provide a foundation on which new shared services can be readily developed.

- Communication systems must facilitate person-to-person interaction among R&D staff and between R&D, marketing, and sales managers.

- Information systems must facilitate the monitoring of product and service quality.

Infrastructure View

These IT maxims guide Johnson & Johnson's firmwide view of information technology infrastructure to balance synergies and flexibility. The firm's Information and Information Technology Vision Statement indicates that the firm "will position [its] IT capabilities and resources in a manner that will ensure competitive readiness." Information technology is being used to maintain Johnson & Johnson's position as the leading health care company worldwide.

Infrastructure Services

The Corporate Office of IT establishes infrastructure directions and standards, and coordinates about 40 percent of all Johnson

& Johnson's systems. The Corporate Office of IT has responsibility for

- Establishing the enterprisewide information policies.

- Establishing selected information technology standards in support of the implementation of the enterprisewide information technology (for example, videoconferencing, data and voice telecommunications, e-mail, document interchange formats).

- Coordinating the investigation and implementation of emerging information technologies across the enterprise.

- Assisting in the identification of business opportunities, and implementing business applications to meet corporate and enterprisewide business requirements.

- Providing selected enterprisewide information technology support services (computing resources, telecommunications networks).

- Providing enterprisewide executive education to improve awareness of the impact of information technology on the business.

This approach to infrastructure services has resulted in Johnson & Johnson's having increased emphasis on shared services either run from the corporate office or standardized across the firm but operated locally. For example, one corporate group manages and operates systems, such as purchasing, accounts payable, and human resources. Other systems, such as the general ledger, are standard across operating companies though supported locally. The remainder of systems reside at the sector or operating company level.

CHAPTER 7

Using Maxims to Drive Change

Each of InvestCo's four business units made large investments in information technology to meet the specific needs of its business. There was no coordination of InvestCo's investments, and the CIO had been unable to convince the business-unit heads to agree on a common approach to information technology infrastructure. Each of the four businesses had different and incompatible systems, and there was no firmwide perspective on infrastructure or shared services. InvestCo did not take a firmwide perspective on its technology investments—or on any other investments, for that matter. As a result, InvestCo was unable to quickly introduce the "Executive Choice" product to match its competitors.

Applying the Management by Maxim framework to InvestCo would help surface firmwide synergies, similar strategies, and synthesized and articulated firmwide business maxims. The result would be a well-informed basis for future investment and resourcing decisions. Management by Maxim is a top-down, strategy-led process that can result in the firm's taking any one of the four infrastructure views: none, utility, dependent, or enabling. The end result is a set of carefully specified and developed infrastructure capabilities tailored to the strategic needs of the firm.

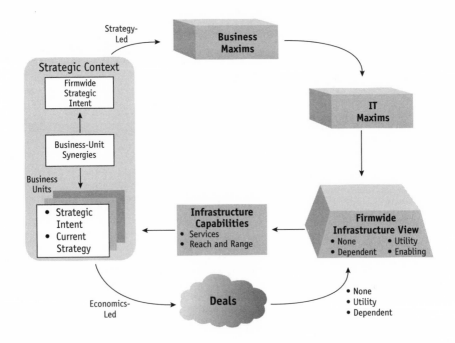

Figure 7.1 Maxims and Deals

However, not all firms are in a position to apply Management by Maxim. In our experience, firms making sound decisions about the new infrastructure have used one of two management processes: either Management by Maxim or Management by Deal. These are illustrated in Figure 7.1.

Management by Deal is primarily an economics-led process driven by the demands of business units. The deal-making process usually results in one of three infrastructure views: "None," utility, and, rarely, dependent. It is difficult using the deal process to achieve the firmwide focus on the longer term required to achieve an enabling or dependent view. The CIO of InvestCo referred to that firm's ad hoc infrastructure decision-making process prior to the formation of the Information Technology Council as "degenerate deal making."

In this chapter we explore how the Management by Maxim and by Deal processes operate in firms, where each is appropriate, and the barriers to their successful implementation. We conclude with a description of how business and information technology managers of a $2 billion global manufacturing firm used a Management by Maxim workshop session to assess and compare current and future infrastructure capabilities.

The Management
by Maxim Route

Management by Maxim is a process of developing business and IT maxims from the strategic context to determine required infrastructure capabilities. Through a series of business maxims, senior managers articulate and communicate the firm's strategic context, including strategic intent, business-unit strategic intents, and current strategies and synergies. These strategic statements capture the essence of the future direction of the firm. Business maxims lead to the identification of IT maxims, which express how technology resources should be deployed and the ways information and data need to be processed, accessed, and used. IT maxims provide a basis for decision making about how the firm should view information technology infrastructure and its required capabilities, in the form of infrastructure services and Reach and Range.

If a firm takes the maxims route, any one of the four views of infrastructure can result and be optimal. The examples of Citicorp and Amcor illustrate how maxims can lead to different views of infrastructure.

Management by Maxim Leading
to Firmwide Infrastructure Capabilities

Citibank expresses its "any time, anywhere" maxim in the phrases "The Citi never sleeps" and "around the world . . . around the clock."[1] The strategic implications are captured in a series of business and information technology maxims described in Chapter 6, which refer to creating and sustaining a global brand, global relationship banking, and commercial customers' ability to gain a worldwide picture of their company's financial situation.

Citibank is a global business providing consistent consumer banking throughout the world, as well as global products and services. The goal of the "Citibanking experience" drives continuing investments in information technology to fully integrate all aspects of the bank's infrastructure services.[3]

In order to meet the demands for consistency in its strategic context, Citibank is increasingly coordinating the management of information technology centrally. Information technology infrastructure decision making is seen as a corporate-level executive management

Citibank: Leading in Applying New Technology[2]

Technology is fundamental to our "Citibanking" strategy. It allows customers to obtain account information, make investments, pay bills, and transfer funds whether they are at a model branch, a Citicard Banking Center, or communicating via CitiPhone or by home computer. When customers travel, they can access their banking relationship in 34 countries because operations are linked from market to market.

Back-office processing activities for both European and US Cards have been converted to a single system. When a German consumer uses a Citibank card at a local restaurant, the transaction transparently travels our global network across the Atlantic to South Dakota and back.

For our corporate customers, we offer globally integrated transaction and information systems that work seamlessly with the existing systems they already have in place, and they can access these systems in Thailand or Kazakhstan as well as New York or Tokyo. Innovations in linking technology globally make Citibank's unmatched network even more valuable to our customers.

responsibility with firmwide strategic, business, and market implications. Citicorp's most senior information systems executive, the senior technology officer, reports directly to the CEO.

The Senior Technology Officer explained,

> Three factors are driving our outlook on technology management and investments. First is the strong emphasis on globality and the priority we are giving to the global consumer experience. Second is the bank's approach to planning and complexity theory where we are aiming to create a constantly adapting and adaptive organization. Third are our efforts to fuse business and information technology cultures so that we do not reflect C. P. Snow's two views of the world.

Citicorp takes an enabling view of information technology infrastructure, recognizing that extensive and coordinated infrastructure capabilities are the basis for Citibank's strategy, for the development of future products and services, and for the shaping of new business strategies.

The strong emphasis on globality has led to the ongoing development of a truly global infrastructure based on a set of architectures and to consistency in applications development and delivery throughout the world. Five years ago, Citibank began the development of its next-generation communications network to replace or link more than 100 disparate networks throughout the world. That global network, the firm's "strategic nexus," now provides the base capability for the Citibanking experience based on standard communications technologies. Citibank's architecture is based on sets of standards for applications, processing, and networking. Businesses now have to demonstrate the business value if they seek to vary from any of the standards in place.

Citibank is standardizing the range of devices that customers use for access throughout the world. These standard service-point devices access one global network to transfer data to a Global Customer Information Facility (GCIF), which in turn accesses the customer information file wherever that is located. Increasingly, those customer files are located at a smaller number of sites. Citibank is drastically reducing the number of its data centers around the world into a small number of centralized facilities, while maintaining customer service operations close to the customer in local markets.

Citibank's architectural planning is based on implementing consistent and integrated approaches to data, hardware, software, and communications across three levels: networking, processes, and applications. Due to the complexity of the bank's products, services, and mix of business environments, it has taken several years to develop a corporate data model. Lack of a firmwide approach to data management was a weakness in the past but is now critical to the implementation of the common customer experience.

Citibank's approach to the development and management of information technology infrastructure demonstrates a Management by Maxim approach resulting in an extensive set of business-driven infrastructure capabilities. The process of infrastructure decision making is driven by an articulated strategic intent, acknowledgment of business synergies, and the identification of business and IT maxims. The maxims shape the nature of infrastructure investments and a consistent set of technology management procedures and architectures directed toward achieving Citibank's strategic vision.

Management by Maxim Leading to No Firmwide Infrastructure Capabilities

Taking a top-down perspective, delineating information technology infrastructure requirements from the firm's strategic context, doesn't necessarily lead to extensive, or even *any*, information technology infrastructure investments. Amcor's paper-making, fiber-packaging, and container businesses had limited business synergies and different value disciplines, both among the three major businesses as well as in different parts of the world within some of those businesses. Amcor placed considerable emphasis on local responsibility and autonomy, with a minimum of mandates, and had a lean corporate structure.[4] Amcor's business maxims led to an IT maxim of sharing information technology expertise and technological solutions, although this would not necessarily be mandated.

Amcor had a "None" view of firmwide information technology infrastructure, although information technology managers in some businesses met on a regular and informal basis.[5] There were no firmwide information technology infrastructure services and very limited Reach and Range. This was consistent with Amcor's considered position on the locus of business responsibility.

Like Citicorp, Amcor had taken a firmwide view of the implications of its strategic context for information technology infrastructure investments. However, the paper and packaging company came to an informed view that no firmwide infrastructure was appropriate. As Amcor's business and competitive environment shifts, this situation is under review.[6]

The Management by Deal-making Route

The maxims route assumes that both business management and information technology management are willing and able to take a firmwide view. This situation existed in about half the firms we studied. The other half adopted a deal-making process in which requirements are defined by the immediate and more parochial needs of each of the businesses. The drivers of the deal-making process are summarized in Figure 7.2.

In the deal-making process, information technology managers talk with business-unit managers, often as part of an annual planning cycle. The aim is to understand the business units' information technology needs based on current business strategies. After making the rounds of all the business units, information technol-

Collective Agreements
– Satisfy short-term needs of the participants
– Initiated by one or more parties through self-interest
– Driven by economies of scale or similar financial benefits
– Benefit more powerful groups
– Driven by economic case, not strategy
– Usually contain reference to:
  • Sharing IT components, processes, or resources
  • Only services perceived as "politically neutral"
  • Voluntary participation

Figure 7.2   The Deal-making Process

ogy managers make firmwide infrastructure recommendations based on the aggregation of the business units' needs. Costs are estimated, and the information technology manager goes back to each business unit with a proposal. Negotiations follow, trading costs off against infrastructure services, and a deal is struck, with the business units usually paying for the services through a charge-back arrangement.

In firms taking a deal-making route, we observed that one of three views of infrastructure emerges: "None," utility, or dependent. No firm took an enabling view of infrastructure through the deal process, and few had a dependent view. An enabling view is hampered by the pressure on costs and dominance of current strategies versus long-term strategic intents in the deal process. This pressure and the parochial perspective of the business unit usually prevent valuing the flexibility inherent in an enabling firmwide view of infrastructure. It takes business maxims set by corporate executive management to have the political weight to justify enabling firmwide infrastructure with extensive infrastructure capabilities.

The deal-making process is the free market of information technology infrastructure formation. The free market often means that powerful, successful, and rich business units are far better served by the information technology infrastructures. In several firms, we found that small, but growing business units often complained about the lack of suitable infrastructure provided centrally by information technology management. Typical examples were the treasury units in banks and the exploration units in mining or resource firms. Each has clusters of expert users with specialized needs who have highly developed, though specific, technology expertise. These smaller business units tended to build their own infrastructures tailored to those specific needs.

Firms with a deal-making approach often provide a utility firmwide infrastructure with more tailored business-unit infrastructures with dependent or enabling views. For example, ResourceCo, a petrochemical firm, has a deal-making process and at least one business unit with an enabling view. The emphasis in infrastructure decision making was on current business-unit needs, accompanied by a strong concern for continuing operational efficiencies. The corporate information technology group managed a sophisticated communications network, e-mail and EDI services, some centralized processing, data consultancy, and recommended standards for office systems. Information systems are a business-unit responsibility, and most information technology staff have been part of business units since the early 1990s. In most instances, the businesses had the option to use external providers. The corporate group aimed to be "the quality information technology service of choice for the firm."

The locus of business responsibility in ResourceCo is the business unit, reflected in a deal-making approach to information technology infrastructure decisions. The nature and extent of infrastructure capability is negotiated with business units, and their aggregated needs determine the requirements and priorities for cost-effective shared services. This is how ResoureCo's sophisticated communications network supporting e-mail and EDI services came about. Managers seeking support for information technology investments needed to show direct improvements in customer service and relationships. Most firmwide information technology services were offered on a chargeback and, in some cases, an outsourced basis. Both the Consumer and Wholesale units made extensive use of leading-edge technology applications, and the information systems groups managed local infrastructure services at the business-unit level.

ResourceCo's experience was common to several manufacturing firms where business units, working in new and less commoditized industries, often desired an enabling information technology infrastructure as a tool to gain market share. The business unit's enabling infrastructure was built in a plug-compatible way on top of the limited infrastructure services provided centrally.

Shifting from Deals to Maxims

Over time, a firm's political, market, and investment climate can drive a shift from one information technology management approach to another: from Management by Maxim to deal making or vice versa.

An international financial services company that we refer to as InterFinCo provides an example of a firm that has shifted from Management by Deals to Management by Maxim in the past five years. InterFinCo has operations in more than 30 countries, and its international presence is a key factor in its competitive positioning.

In the mid- to late 1980s, InterFinCo went through a period of divisionalization, including the devolution and dispersal of most information technology management functions to multiple business divisions. This policy shifted in the early 1990s and is now consolidated in the notion of "one InterFinCo," with business objectives that include all staff working as a team to service the best interests of customers. This has translated into the business maxim "Staff of the highest caliber who excel in working together." A second maxim emerged from a much greater emphasis on synergies across the business units: "International reach and presence as one financial services firm."

InterFinCo's CIO now reports directly to the CEO. The corporate-level information technology group was formed in the early 1990s as a direct result of a review of the decentralized and distributed approach then in place. The result has been greater centralization of key technology-related decision areas and a high degree of coordination across the firm. All technology staff and services were organized as a pool, with each staff member regarded as a resource for allocation to a particular work assignment.

Although the information technology group now has overview responsibility for all technology-related activities within the firm, this is in the context of a shift in senior management's consideration of the way business and technology strategies are integrated. There is an increased sense of priority and greater degree of involvement from senior executives in crucial information technology projects. Benefits have included better control of business investment in information technology, an improved service orientation together with more cost-effective services, and cost savings in the rationalization of the InterFinCo communications infrastructure.

The firm's business and technology planning processes reflect a Management by Maxim approach. The vision of "one InterFinCo" is applied to information technology investments. The firm now provides an extensive range of infrastructure services, including integration of its customer systems, and has a high level of Reach and Range. Common business processes are being implemented, and an integrated cluster of systems, based on a well-developed architecture and set of standards, is being rolled out.

While InterFinCo now takes a Management by Maxim approach, such a route would have been difficult five years ago because of organizational barriers. There was no business maxim relating to the notion of "one InterFinCo," and there was strong devolution of decision making to the business units. The evolution of the firm's strategic intent and a renewed perspective on synergies across the firm has resulted in a Management by Maxim approach with strong executive management involvement.

Overcoming Barriers to Creating Business-driven Infrastructures

Creating and utilizing business-driven information technology infrastructure capabilities is a difficult and challenging process. The impact of the three types of barriers—expression, specification, and implementation—described in Chapter 2 are depicted in Figure 7.3. Expression barriers retard the development of business maxims. Specification barriers hinder the development of IT maxims. Implementation barriers stall the recognition of an appropriate firmwide view and the provision for the appropriate infrastructure capabilities.

Expression Barriers

Clear and concise strategic statements suitable for business maxims emerge from some firms' visioning and strategy formation processes. In other firms, business maxims might not be explicit, but rather implicit and easy to identify. An expression barrier exists where busi-

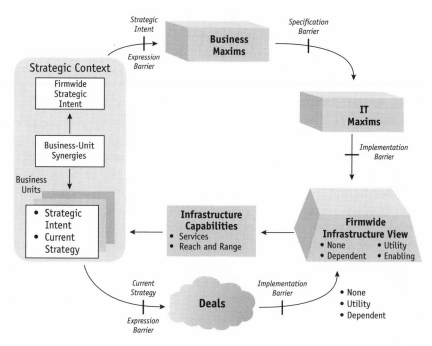

Figure 7.3 Barriers to Creating Information Technology Infrastructures

ness maxims are difficult to locate or articulate. Expression barriers also exist where operational management has insufficient understanding or commitment to the strategic intent of the firm. Insufficient understanding is often created by one of three causes:

- Executive management not achieving clarity in either the strategic intent or the current strategies of the firm

- Executive management having clarity but not articulating and communicating the message successfully to operational management

- Individual reward systems and the culture of the firm working against the successful articulation and use of maxims

Although we've observed organizations with expression barriers caused by lack of strategic clarity, this is less common than the inability to communicate or the existence of nonsupportive cultural and reward systems. Such expression barriers mean that those who manage the information technology resource lack the information on the strategic context of the firm that they need in order to build an appropriate infrastructure. Executive management is unaware of the importance of clear and actionable strategy statements to developing infrastructure capabilities matched to business objectives.

The strategic intent expression barrier prevents the use of business maxims and necessitates the use of Management by Deals. At the business-unit level, the existence of a current strategy expression barrier prevents deals being struck, as the basis on which satisfactory deals can be made is unclear or confused by mixed messages.

In situations where both expression barriers exist, one option is for information technology managers to forge ahead and build infrastructures. This scenario has resulted in the biggest failures in the development of excessive or inappropriate infrastructures.

To overcome expression barriers, we recommend that information technology managers use their knowledge of the firm to develop a set of business maxims, involving whichever business managers they can. This set of maxims forms the basis for dialogue with executive management. Often the maxims they develop aren't quite right, but executive management is impressed with the technology manager's efforts, and time is spent working together to fix the business maxims. The channels for constructive dialogue are open. The final section of this chapter describes a maxims workshop where business and information technology managers work together to identify maxims and the necessary infrastructure capability.

Specification Barriers

Specification barriers can occur where IT maxims are set in isolation and thus are not related to business maxims. For example, the push by information technology groups to set and enforce firmwide data and computing standards, in the absence of an appropriate business maxim providing impetus and credibility, results in comments like "Here comes the IT police again." The lack of business maxims to provide a trail of evidence from strategic intent to IT maxims makes the IT maxims appear as technically motivated rules. These IT maxims, unsupported by business maxims, appear to limit business managers' flexibility to do their job and serve the customer.

In one firm, information technology management set IT maxims based on good technical motivations of reducing complexity, but without consulting the business. The business was given a year to migrate to the new standards. In the year that followed, almost all of the business managers in the business units ignored the new standards and actually increased the diversity and complexity of the information technology portfolio. At the end of the year, frustrated information technology managers started to implement sanctions for not following the new standards, such as refusing to provide assistance to particular business managers. At that point, the CEO stepped in to sort out the problems. By then, both sides were firmly entrenched in their positions and it took some months to resolve the impasse. The situation was caused by information technology management's independently setting IT maxims. The problem was resolved by the CEO's expressing business maxims from which the information technology management then derived well-informed and different IT maxims. The new IT maxims were much more appealing to the business managers, with the credibility of associated business maxims.

To overcome specification barriers, both business and information technology managers must be involved in developing IT maxims. The implication of each business maxim must be clear and mapped onto the IT maxims. In turn, the business relevance of each IT maxim must be traced back to the relevant business maxim. To achieve buy-in, the trail of evidence must be compelling to both business and technology managers.

Implementation Barriers

Implementation barriers occur where there is the will and vision to form the appropriate infrastructure, but the task cannot be completed. There are many possible causes, ranging from organizational, political, cultural, and reward system issues to lack of information technology leadership and technical impediments.

Sometimes technology executive management is unable to gain organizational agreement to invest in infrastructures. This barrier often occurs where the business benefits are not based on immediate cost reduction and executive managers are ill equipped to make infrastructure investment decisions on any other basis. A rapidly expanding Asian bank had recently appointed an executive-level information technology manager. The bank's executive team was inexperienced in considering infrastructure investments. The technology executive explained her approach to overcoming implementation barriers:

> The challenge here is for the business to understand and own the information technology investments. Until a year ago, there was no history of infra-

structure investments and little coordination of information technology across the bank. We are now in Stage 1 of an investment and education process. At present I can't sell the concept of infrastructure without it being linked to specific business applications. The result is that we hide the infrastructure costs in business application cases and thus the infrastructure building process has been piecemeal. But it is following a plan. I expect that next year, the executives will have a much greater understanding of the role of infrastructure. We will have some new applications in place and they will see it for themselves. The justification case for infrastructure can be made differently once they see what it delivers to the business.

This information technology executive was overcoming the implementation barrier with a careful and planned program to educate executive management about the nature of infrastructure investments. She could not achieve the immediate goal of investments in necessary infrastructure based on a separate business case for that infrastructure. The aim was to overcome the immediate implementation barrier and later to decouple the investment cases into infrastructure and applications. A range of infrastructure investment justification approaches are discussed further in Chapter 9.

Implementation barriers can also result from technical constraints of the current infrastructure. Often barriers to increasing the Reach and Range and infrastructure services stem from proprietary operating systems or lack of standard data definitions across the firm. This type of implementation barrier is common in firms where business units are acquired or where the business need for shared infrastructure, as for cross-selling between business units, has only recently occurred. In both these situations, the technical decision to form the separate business unit infrastructures was made without the need to consider integration.

One option is for firms to set agreed-upon architectures across the business units, while continuing to provide only a limited number of firmwide infrastructure services. This option reduces implementation barriers for the business units that do share customers or suppliers. They can more readily integrate specific parts of their portfolios to gain the benefits of synergies. This does not impinge on other business units, where the integration of systems lacks a strong business imperative. We've seen this approach work successfully where firms have grown by acquisition. The setting of architectures delivers both economies of expertise and the option to benefit from synergies where they exist.

In firms we studied that have created business-driven infrastructures, either maxims or deals are evident. Maxims provide focus and credibility for information technology managers as they build the infrastructures necessary for the strategic context of the firm. Sometimes the trail of evidence provided by business maxims makes it clear that contradictions exist. For example, we've observed firms seeking to minimize costs while concurrently attempting to achieve a high degree of future flexibility. This approach requires considerable up-front investment, but executive management balks at the magnitude of this investment and the discipline of setting firmwide architectures. Clarifying business maxims in a workshop can be very useful in prioritizing trade-off situations. Where the firm cannot or will not fund the investment needed, the impact on both business and infrastructure capabilities needs to be articulated and communicated. All stakeholders need to be aware of the ongoing gap between resources and aspirations, and what this means for the firm's strategic intent.

Assessing Future and Current Capabilities Using Management by Maxim

We conclude this chapter by working through an example of how one firm used a Management by Maxim workshop process to articulate future requirements and assess these against its current infrastructure capabilities.

Distilling Future Information Technology Infrastructure Capabilities

The development of business-driven infrastructures requires the joint efforts of executive and information technology management. We've worked with business and technology managers using a workshop process to identify necessary infrastructure capabilities. We outline this process using the example of an international manufacturing firm that we call WestCo. WestCo has revenues of more than $2 billion and 4 business units producing consumer goods and products used by other manufacturers. Much of the growth has been via acquisition, and all the businesses have global operations. This growth had placed strains on the executive team and on the firm's information technology resources, particularly infrastructure. The way ahead was unclear in a firm where there were limited synergies but a strong desire to achieve economies in terms of cost savings and expertise. It was time to consider how to surface and clarify the links between the firm's changing strategic context and its infrastructure capabilities.

Executive and Information Technology Management Workshop

Members of WestCo's corporate management team, together with business-unit and information technology managers, came together to review the future direction of WestCo's infrastructure investments. Before the workshop day, each participant spent 15 minutes responding to a short questionnaire about the nature of business synergies across WestCo and the preferred balance between exploiting these synergies and encouraging autonomy. Copies of the firm's mission, plans, and value statements were also available at the workshop.

The major steps of the workshop were as follows:

1. Identifying the Extent of Business Synergies

Led by a facilitator, the participants spent the first hour of the workshop discussing and confirming the firm's preferred approach to its potential business synergies. Although WestCo appeared to share little by way of products and services, participants agreed that greater synergies could and should be achieved through sharing expertise in generic cross-business processes, such as managing financial resources, managing human resources, environment and safety policy, and information systems infrastructure provision.

2. Articulating Business Maxims

Participants used the generic business maxims in Figure 6.6 as a starting point. Each participant individually scored the importance of each business maxim to WestCo's future performance and then reviewed this to select his or her top six business maxims. Four business maxims were clearly agreed on by all participants and were reworded to be more in line with the terminology used in WestCo. Decisions on the last two generated considerable discussion, highlighting current debate about priorities and directions. Managers agreed on the final six business maxims through iteration of previously agreed-upon mission and vision statements, statements of strategic objectives, and outcomes of ongoing strategizing. These business maxims were short, pithy decrees, easily remembered and communicated, focusing on what must be shared across the firm.

The participants checked to see if the balance among the business maxims reflected the firm's priorities. The difficulty of achieving all six maxims was discussed, together with the need to revisit them if implementation required more extensive investments than the firm was prepared to fund.

3. Identifying Information Technology Maxims

Participants were divided into groups to work on IT maxims. The sample IT maxims in Figure 6.7 were used as a basis, with each group working on two or three categories. Each group then presented its IT maxims. These were discussed and refined, checked for internal consistency and firm specificity, and then compared to the business maxims identified. As part of the process, some barriers to achieving the IT maxims were noted and recorded for later reference.

4. Clarifying Information Technology Infrastructure View

The firm's future expectations for information technology infrastructure investments were articulated by the CFO, who chairs the firm's Information Technology Council. At this point, the nature of current investments, driven by a utility view of infrastructure, was acknowledged and benchmarked using the table in Figure 4.8. The workshop outcome indicated that, to achieve the firm's business maxims, particularly realizing the benefits of acquisitions and firmwide initiatives, the firm would need to change its view of infrastructure from utility to dependent, with the necessary change in investment and approach to justification.

5. Specifying Required Infrastructure Capabilities

Using the list of infrastructure services in Figure 4.2 as a basis, the CIO led the discussion of which services were essential in light of the business and IT maxims identified. To provide the information technology capability necessary for the firm's strategic context and business maxims, 15 of these services were required. The extent of Reach and Range was agreed upon using Figure 4.4 to chart the necessary capabilities.

6. Reviewing the Linkages

As a final step, the participants reviewed the outcome as presented in Figure 7.4. The information technology infrastructure manager stated that two of the required services were not currently offered

Firmwide Business Maxims

- Lowest cost of sales
- Strong long-term relationship management with superior customer service
- Flexibility to respond quickly to market changes
- Realize the benefits of acquisitions and initiatives
- Identify, attract, and facilitate movement of staff committed to one corporation
- Exceed client expectations for quality at reasonable price
- Culture of information sharing for achieving synergies

The Firm

A diversified manufacturing company serving global markets

Potential Synergies

- Presence of all three value disciplines—operational excellence, customer intimacy, and product innovation—across the businesses, with operational excellence the most predominant
- Potential synergies very limited for products, customers, and supplier base across all businesses
- Considerable potential for sharing expertise in generic cross-business processes: managing financial resources and services, managing human resources, environment and safety policy, information systems infrastructure provision

Use of Synergies

- Very important to utilize potential synergies
- Local autonomy of limited value

Sample IT Maxims

- Each IT investment must support the firm's mission and values, and the current business plan
- Capture data once and provide appropriate flexible access. Data to include financial, human resources, key performance indicators, externally sourced
- Enforce firmwide IT open architecture
- Partnering with strong suppliers
- Firmwide communications capability appropriately available, reliable, and of sufficient capacity
- User ownership for IT investments and operations, which are measured on performance

Infrastructure View Utility → Dependent

Sample Firmwide Infrastructure Services

- Wide area network (WAN) linking domestic and international operations
- Firmwide e-mail system
- Recommendations on standards for all components of IT architecture
- Enforcement of selected IT architecture and standards through capital expenditure arrangements
- Technology advice and support services available to the business groups
- Data management advice and consultancy services to the business groups on an ad hoc, but proactive, basis
- Managing and negotiating with suppliers and outsourcers
- Performing IS project management (for firmwide projects)
- Assisting the business groups in their IS planning
- Development and management of on-line and/or EDI linkages to suppliers or customers for all business units

Figure 7.4 WestCo's Strategic Context and Infrastructure Capabilities

and that the extent of some current services would need to be extended, requiring additional investments.

The nature of the current infrastructure investment decision-making process was discussed, and it was agreed that the firm's current approach was largely a deal-making process. This was strongly motivated by efforts to reduce information technology costs within each of the businesses and across the firm. Although in some cases the CFO commented that infrastructure decisions had been made "because we knew we just had to do it," the maxims workshop had highlighted gaps. WestCo's business and IT maxims provided a well-informed base from which to pursue IT infrastructure capabilities in light of the firm's business and competitive aspirations.

Of particular value was the nature of the dialogue that had taken place during the day. Both business and information technology executives now had a deeper understanding of WestCo's business and information technology strategy needs, particularly as they related to longer-term investments. The firm didn't need to start with a blank sheet or even with its own strategy documents. The business and IT maxims generated from other firms provided a time- and energy-saving approach that WestCo's managers adapted to suit their firm-specific needs.

The importance of joint business and technology responsibility for infrastructure became evident as information technology managers explained what investments and time would be needed to operationalize the capabilities to serve some of the emerging business directions. Some changes in the way WestCo usually justified investments in the new infrastructure were identified as necessary to achieve its business objectives.

This workshop process can readily be adapted to any single- or multiple-business-unit firm considering the capabilities of its firmwide infrastructure to meet strategic needs.

Assessing Current Information Technology Infrastructure Capabilities

How can firms assess their current capabilities to see if what is in place is appropriate to the firm's strategic context and goals? The suitability of a firm's current capabilities can be assessed by working through the Management by Maxim framework in reverse, starting with current infrastructure capabilities and drawing on the benchmark data presented in Figure 4.8.

Information Technology Infrastructure Capabilities

- How many of the information technology infrastructure services are offered?

- In what areas is there a comprehensive or selective level of infrastructure services?

- Sketch the current Reach and Range of the infrastructure. Who can be reached by the firm's infrastructure and with what range of services? Is this capability sufficient to achieve the firm's goals?

- What indicators do the first three questions provide about the level and nature of the firm's infrastructure capabilities?

- What view of infrastructure does the level of capability indicate?

View of Information Technology Infrastructure

- What type of infrastructure investment cases have been argued and accepted in the firm—what combination of cost savings, responses to specific current strategies, or need for future flexibility?

- Is information technology infrastructure expenditure viewed by executive management as an administrative expense, a business expense, or a business investment?

Business and IT Maxims

- What IT maxims are implicit in the current infrastructure capabilities?

- What do the IT maxims imply in terms of the business maxims they would support?

- What do the business maxims indicate in terms of the firm's strategic thrusts?

- What do the business and IT maxims indicate about how the firm values synergy among its businesses?

This exercise provides an indication of the current level of information technology infrastructure capability and the extent to which that capability is appropriate to the firm's strategic context.

Management by Maxim describes a business-led approach to identifying information technology infrastructure capabilities used by market leaders. Not all firms are in a position to utilize this process. Many firms develop appropriate infrastructures using Management by Deals. However, where a firm has neither process in place in some form, there is little likelihood that they will develop infrastructure capabilities necessary to support business directions. Good infrastructures rarely just emerge. They are the result of sound and proactive management processes aimed at maximizing business value.

PART 3

Managing and Maximizing Value

Managers wanting to drive change through business transformations must understand the dynamics of the new infrastructure and the capabilities essential for specific transformations. Making information technology decisions driven by business issues involves reconciling pressures to minimize cost, increase business flexibility, and enhance customer responsiveness. These pressures often conflict in terms of the scope and nature of the new infrastructure, as they once did in physical infrastructure decisions involving location, buildings, and plant. Firms that gain value from their technology investments reconcile these pressures through management mechanisms that articulate and communicate business expectations; include appropriate investment justification approaches; and have measures to assess the impact of the information technology portfolio on business performance.

In Part 3 we outline how senior managers accept responsibility for informed business expectations that are well communicated and where the implications for information technology investments are clear. The new infrastructure requires rethinking information technology investment approaches and managing the total investment as a portfolio. Information technology must be part of ongoing firmwide strategizing, management, and planning processes. These processes include measuring the impact (both positive and negative) of the current information technology portfolio on business performance.

Managers may often be certain about implementing transformation, but unclear as to whether their information technology portfolio will be a help or a hindrance. In Chapter 8 we discuss four transformation processes: redesigning business processes, integrating electronic commerce into business, extending international business operations, and proactively managing knowledge. Each transformation process drives change and has different requirements for infrastructure capability. If the capabilities are not in place, the transformation is likely, at best, to stall or, in the worst case, to fail completely.

Chapter 9 explores how firms assemble appropriate business cases to justify information technology investment decisions. Different appraisal approaches are presented for each of the four different investment classes in the information technology portfolio. In particular we look at the strengths and weaknesses of the available approaches to justifying information technology infrastructure and make recommendations for infrastructure investment appraisal. As an input to the appraisal process, we review how managers can assess the health of their information technology portfolio.

In Chapter 10 we consider the importance of leadership and shaping informed expectations between business and information technology management. The choice of governance processes is critical to effective management of information technology investments. Governance practices must be integrated with a firm's strategic context, with business and IT maxims, and with the governance of the firm as a whole. Four examples of best practice are given, together with a summary of leading governance processes. We conclude with our Top Ten Leadership Principles, which synthesize our findings and successful management practices from market leaders who drive business value from the new infrastructure.

CHAPTER 8

Business Transformations and Infrastructure Capabilities

In the early 1990s, the telecommunications firm GTE Corporation faced regulatory changes and increased competition. As Charles Lee, GTE's chairman and chief executive, commented, "GTE needed to become a leaner, quicker and more aggressive player."[1] GTE began a five-year transformation program in 1992, aimed at ensuring the future of the company by rethinking work processes, improving efficiencies, and providing value to the customer. The transformation is on target to achieve annual savings of $1 billion through redesigned processes that enhance current business and support new business growth.

GTE's innovative processes were strongly dependent on information technology capabilities. For example, to support GTE's "one-touch" commitment, in which repair requests are not handed off to another employee, customer representatives have on-line access to the customer database, network switching, and automatic line testing. The "customer zone" concept is about technicians' building stronger relationships with specific customers, managing their own daily schedules, and updating their own records in real time. To support these new processes, technicians use durable high-end laptop computers networked to the home office to schedule service calls and transmit new customer account information to the central database. The technology supporting these new processes requires extensive and sophisticated infrastructure capabilities, including seamless communication networks, and agreed-upon and enforced architectures and standards for customer information.

Shifts in customer expectations, competitive environments, and emerging technologies have made such change a constant for most organizations. Charles Lee called his report on the transformation of GTE "Milestones on a Journey Not Yet Completed."[2]

Many firms are rethinking what business they are in, identifying their core capabilities, searching for that elusive competitive advantage, and preparing for a less certain future. Firms are undergoing transformations in their business processes, in relationships with customers and suppliers, in the international penetration of markets and operations, and in the way they value the expertise of their staff. Successful shifts in how a business operates require understanding the interrelationships between managing people and organizations, changing strategic contexts, and organizational infrastructure. A significant part of that organizational infrastructure is the readiness of the firm's information technology infrastructure capabilities to support or enable such initiatives.

In this chapter we consider four change initiatives currently being pursued in many firms:

- Implementing business process redesign

- Competing with electronic commerce

- Extending international business operations

- Managing knowledge and organizational learning

We identify the business drivers and objectives of these initiatives and the information technology infrastructure capabilities required for implementation. The typical infrastructure capabilities required for each business transformation are contrasted and summarized at the end of the chapter.

Implementing Business Process Redesign

Business process redesign (BPR) is a pervasive tool for transforming organizations.[3] Much has been written about the breakthrough performance improvements it has achieved.[4] Nearly two-thirds of North American and European companies have undertaken process redesign projects,[5] but successfully implementing BPR remains a major challenge.[6] Problems often occur when firms fail to realize that BPR changes the tight and interdependent linkages among many facets of the organization—its leadership, management of change, process management approach, human resources, competitive positioning, and the existing and required information technology portfolio, particularly infrastructure capabilities.

Before embarking on BPR, senior managers need to know the answers to some key questions:

- Will our information technology infrastructure help or hinder the implementation of BPR?

- To what extent do we have a strong core as well as strategic infrastructure services?

- Do these services span the boundaries of business units and functions?

- What is the Reach of the infrastructure in terms of those who are currently connected?

- What Range of services is available: the ability to access information or the capacity to perform multiple and integrated business transactions across all relevant parts of the firm?

The resulting assessment will make management aware of the relative ease of implementing BPR from a technical standpoint, the potential barriers to implementation, and the costs and difficulties of removing those barriers.

In successful process redesigns at GTE, Wal-Mart,[7] and Xerox,[8] the support of enabling technologies and platforms was integral to implementation. Information technology is also a potential constraint or inhibitor[9] through the lack of appropriate infrastructure capability.[10] Firms often have existing investments in incompatible systems in different functional areas or business groups. These systems may have been developed using business rules that were put in place many years ago, with systems built to serve specific local needs. Multiple incompatible systems, with their different standards and technical features, hamper the implementation of cross-functional and cross-business processes.

Details about customers and suppliers often have been recorded quite differently in different functional areas so that it is difficult to get a clear picture of a customer's overall relationship with the firm. Such complete information is critical where there are business maxims to "Provide all the information needed to service any client from one service point" or "Grow cross-selling opportunities." These business maxims require new levels of cross-business integration.

The experiences of four firms illustrate how information technology infrastructure can both enable and constrain the implementation of BPR. A higher level of infrastructure capability and the availability of some specific infrastructure services provided the basis for faster and more extensive change in business processes. Lower levels of infrastructure capability meant that further investment was necessary to implement major changes in cross-functional and cross-business processes. This investment often resulted in delays, frustrations, and missed market opportunities.

CostCo and LeapCo are process manufacturing competitors with different strategic intents leading to different business maxims. StockCo and MergeCo are both nationally operating retail firms, but they differ in size, scope, and product range. Figure 8.1 summarizes the business maxims, BPR motivation, and the extent and role of information technology infrastructure in each firm.

The four firms differed significantly in the initial breadth of their process changes, with CostCo and StockCo beginning with one process, whereas LeapCo and MergeCo decided to design and implement new processes across all business areas. In terms of depth of change sought, CostCo differed from the other three firms in having relatively modest ambitions. CostCo sought to simplify business processes, whereas StockCo, LeapCo, and MergeCo sought radical change in one or more processes.

Extent of Information Technology Infrastructure Capabilities

The infrastructure capabilities of each firm in the first two years of BPR implementation varied. As indicated in Figure 8.1, CostCo and StockCo had a medium level of infrastructure capability, and LeapCo and MergeCo had an above-average or high level of capability.

Different interactions between information technology infrastructure and BPR implementation were evident in the four firms. In CostCo, the infrastructure in place assisted simplification and stream-

	CostCo	StockCo	LeapCo	MergeCo
Business Maxims	Customer responsiveness; Build relationships with suppliers; Cost-consciousness	Flexibility to accommodate change; Capacity to process information; Fast supplier links; Synergy for economies of scale; Continuous margin increases	Provide services for mobile customers; Respond at all phases of the value chain; Differentiate through quality and service	Customer anticipation and response; Know what is selling and where; Manage at the SKU level; Expand product range at marginal cost
Motivation for BPR	Reduce costs in tight market; Maintain profitability; Move to customer responsiveness	Improve competitive position; More efficient replenishment cycles; Reduce inventory costs	Continuing need to reduce costs; More radical gains sought after "best practice"; Rethinking of core business; Leverage infrastructure investments	Merger situation; new practices needed; Necessary to meet strategic vision
IT Infrastructure Capability • **Number of Services**	MEDIUM 15 services	MEDIUM 15 services	EXTENSIVE 20 services	EXTENSIVE 22 services
• **Reach and Range**	Reach: Medium; Range: Low	Reach: High; Range: Low	Reach: High; Range: High	Reach: High; Range: High
Role of Infrastructure	IT infrastructure and systems capabilities adequate for changes to existing processes	Firmwide infrastructure enabled process change to commence; Impact of adequate BU infrastructure capability presented implementation barrier	New IT infrastructure installed; Process changes leveraged from the infrastructure capability	New IT infrastructure provided the basis for radical change to core processes
Impact of IT Infrastructure Capability	NEUTRAL; Existing capability extended	DELAYED AND HINDERED; Major new capability needed	ENABLING; Changes utilized capabilities	ENABLING; Changes and infrastructure implementation iterative

Figure 8.1   BPR and the Role of Information Technology Infrastructure

lining of processes and did not hinder redesign. Incremental investments in enhancing the communications network and in linking suppliers and customers were made to meet the limited and staged
approach to BPR.

In StockCo, the existing infrastructure provided both a sophisticated telecommunications network and the capacity to commence
process redesign. However, other parts of the infrastructure con-
tained incompatible technology and systems, hindering implementation by extending the time and initially reducing the scope of the
changes that were possible. For example, lack of data consistency
across functions meant that much needed data about what was selling could not be integrated with ordering and logistics systems. Time
and money were spent developing a data architecture as a foundation
for cross-functional systems that could then process and exchange
data across the business.

In LeapCo and MergeCo, the information technology infrastructure provided building blocks of capability and stimulated and
enabled implementation of radical new processes. Compatible technologies were implemented, and consistently defined data elements
for the key information were used throughout. Extensive infrastructure services and above-average Reach and Range enabled speedier
implementation of cross-functional and cross-business processes.

The scope and depth of process changes were greater in the two
firms with more extensive infrastructure capability.

LeapCo and MergeCo, but not CostCo or StockCo, had six
boundary-spanning (in bold italic in Figure 8.2) infrastructure services providing a strong basis for implementing cross-business and
cross-functional systems. These services were

- Firmwide or business-unit data management, including
  standards.

- Development of a common systems development
  environment.

- Development of business-unit–specific applications (usually
  on a chargeback or contractual basis).

- Management of business-unit–specific applications.

- Enforcement of information technology architecture and
  standards.

- Electronic provision of management information (EIS).

Required for BPR	5 Core Information Technology Infrastructure Services
√	1. Manage firmwide communications network services
√	2. Manage groupwide or firmwide messaging services
√	3. Recommend standards for at least one component of IT architecture (e.g., hardware, operating systems, data, communications)
√	4. Provide security, disaster planning, and business recovery services for firmwide installations and applications
√	5. Provide technology advice and support services
	20 Additional Information Technology Infrastructure Services
√	6. Manage, maintain, support large-scale data-processing facilities (e.g., mainframe operations)
√	7. Manage firmwide or business-unit applications and databases
√	8. Perform IS project management
√	9. Provide data management advice and consultancy services
√	10. Perform IS planning for business units
√	**11. Enforce IT architecture and standards**
	12. Manage firmwide or business-unit workstation networks (e.g., LANs, POS)
	13. Manage and negotiate with suppliers and outsourcers
	14. Identify and test new technologies for business purposes
√	**15. Develop business-unit–specific applications (usually on a chargeback or contractual basis)**
	16. Implement security, disaster planning, and recovery for business units
√	**17. Provide management information electronically (e.g., EIS)**
√	**18. Manage business-unit–specific applications**
√	**19. Manage firmwide or business-unit data, including standards**
	20. Develop and manage electronic linkages to suppliers or customers
√	**21. Develop a common systems development environment**
	22. Provide technology education services (e.g., training)
	23. Provide multimedia operations and development (e.g., videoconferencing)
	24. Provide firmwide intranet capability (e.g., information access, multiple system access)
	25. Provide firmwide electronic support for groups (e.g., Lotus Notes)

*Bold italic indicates boundary-spanning infrastructure services.

Figure 8.2   Firmwide Infrastructure Services Needed for BPR

In Figure 8.2 we identify 16 such infrastructure services (see those with √ in left column) that are important for implementing BPR across businesses in firms or across functional groups in business units.

Linking BPR and Information Technology Infrastructure

The experiences of these four firms highlight aspects of the relationship between information technology infrastructure and BPR:

- **All four firms had at least an average level of infrastructure that allowed some type of BPR.** All firms had the first ten infrastructure services in Figure 8.2, including communications networks, standards for at least one component of information technology architecture, and management of some firmwide applications and databases. All firms also had some form of on-line or EDI linkage to suppliers or customers.

- **Radical firmwide BPR requires more infrastructure capabilities.** Radical or extensive BPR addresses multiple business processes and integrates more parts of the firm. The required infrastructure capability involves more extensive agreements about architecture and standards, a greater range of data to be processed, more applications, and depth of consistency in work practices across functions or businesses. Six boundary-spanning infrastructure services and an above-average Reach and Range were discriminating capabilities between the firms.

- **Infrastructure capability positively influences BPR implementation.** LeapCo and MergeCo did not have information technology infrastructure implementation barriers in the BPR implementation. They were able to make dramatic business redesign processes and implement those changes. CostCo's aspirations for BPR were limited and achievable with incremental changes to the firm's infrastructure. However, StockCo's BPR aspirations were thwarted by the limitations of the infrastructure in place, and its implementation stalled.

Implications for Business and Technology Management

Extensive IT infrastructure capabilities (as in an enabling view), with a high number of boundary-spanning infrastructure services and above-average Reach and Range, facilitate the implementation of radically redesigned processes. In some firms, excellent returns on significant investment in an enabling infrastructure were realized when BPR was implemented. A dependent view might impose some constraints for BPR, depending on whether the information technology infrastructure in place supports the nature of the process changes required. A firmwide utility view of infrastructure results in less firmwide infrastructure capability and thus less capacity to implement cross-business process changes.

If infrastructure capabilities are not currently in place, costs and time are added to the BPR implementation. Conscious investment in infrastructure capabilities beyond current needs can smooth the BPR path. However, if these capabilities are not utilized, they constitute an overinvestment and an unexercised option. Before embarking on any form of BPR, managers need to complete an audit of their infrastructure capabilities. The current level of the firm's infrastructure capability can be assessed by checking the evidence for the infrastructure services identified in Figure 8.2 (particularly the boundary spanners), and the nature and extent of the firm's Reach and Range.

Firms that have made substantial recent investments in information technology infrastructure capability and have developed a rich set of infrastructure services before undertaking business process redesign are generally able to implement dramatic changes to their business processes over a relatively short time. Less infrastructure capability can suffice where the purpose of the process changes is simplification rather than radical redesign. Inadequate infrastructure capability resulting in the stalling of process change implementation can provide a strong, business-driven case for infrastructure investments.

An integral part of the BPR in many firms is the development of electronic channels to conduct business transactions with customers and suppliers, which is one of the growing opportunities of electronic commerce.

Competing with Electronic Commerce

Electronic commerce has arrived, and with it comes a new set of competitive realities. These realities in turn have specific infrastructure requirements. What links do you need to customers and suppliers to compete in an electronic era? What type of infrastructure capabilities provide a necessary starting point for electronic trading? Internet-based technologies are changing the ground rules for electronic commerce and extending its reach into the home.

Electronic commerce simply means doing business electronically by bringing together sellers and buyers. Some established examples of electronic commerce are

- Electronic funds transfer at the point of sale (EFTPOS) in supermarkets all over the world.

- Electronic filing of more than 91 percent of all individual returns submitted by tax agents to the Australian Taxation Office. More than 70 percent of all individual returns were submitted electronically.[11]

- Stock exchanges that have replaced live floor trading with trading screens.

- Electronic shopping on the Internet for all types of products, including hard-to-find books, wines, clothes, sporting equipment, food, and flowers. All of these products can be searched for, viewed, ordered, and paid for electronically. Reviews and independent ratings of the products are often available to make the choice more informed.

- Microsoft's Internet car search business, CarPoint, sold more than $37 million worth of cars in its first six weeks.[12]

- The Integrated Financial Network (IFN), a consortium of 15 North American banks and IBM, formed to enable customers to bank and use other financial services electronically. IFN will enable transactions through either IBM's proprietary Global Network or the Internet, with additional services added by other providers, such as credit card firms.

- The electronic market, AUCNET,[13] an electronic auction for used cars, facilitates auto dealers' trading in Japan. The system begins with a call or electronic message to AUCNET from a dealer wishing to sell a car. An AUCNET inspector visits, inspects, and photographs the car, noting any faults, and completes a rating sheet. On the weekend, more than 3,000 dealers from all over Japan sit at specially designed terminals to participate in a countrywide auction. Sales are made to the highest bidder and AUCNET completes the transaction and resolves any disputes. AUCNET has more than 10 percent of the unit volume of used cars in Japan and while growing at 15 percent per year has achieved more than 20 percent net income before taxes. The great insight of AUCNET is that information about cars is easier to move than cars themselves and that the competitive auction process with multiple buyers is a very effective sales process.

Electronic commerce is changing the basis of competition. Small companies are able to access large numbers of customers who were previously the domain only of large firms. The economics of conducting business are changing, such that the marginal cost of servicing one more customer, regardless of where he or she is, is trivial. Electronic commerce will continue to significantly reduce the transaction costs of sellers and increase the penetration of the seller's message into the market. Conversely, it will be more difficult for the seller to differentiate its products, and consumers will be more easily able to compare prices and features from a number of sellers.

Participating in electronic commerce is described by John Sviokla and Jeffrey Rayport as competing in both the marketplace and the marketspace.[14] Transactions in the marketplace are the traditional buyer-seller interactions in the physical world, such as a retail store. Transactions in the marketspace occur in the electronic world, using devices such as telephones, personal computers, televisions, and computers connected to the Internet or to information services such as America Online. The marketplace is product and transaction based, whereas the marketspace is service and relationship based.

The description of electronic commerce from the U.S. Information Infrastructure Technology and Applications (IITA) Task Group[15] highlights the connectivity, security, and standardization required for electronic commerce:

> Electronic Commerce *integrates* communications, data management and security services, to allow business applications within different organizations to automatically interchange information. Communications services *transfer* the information from the originator to the recipient. Data management services define the interchange *format* of the information. Security services *authenticate* the source of information, verify the *integrity* of the information received by the recipient, *prevent disclosure* of the information to unauthorized users, and *verify* that the information was *received* by the intended recipient.

The trend toward electronic commerce will accelerate as the penetration of devices capable of ordering goods and services increases. Most businesses already have personal computers with modems that are capable of conducting business electronically, with a large bandwidth allowing for digitized pictures and video clips. As of mid-1996, two of the largest on-line information services in the United States, CompuServe and America Online, had approximately 10 million subscribers.[16] It is estimated that the number of households linked to on-line information services will increase exponentially.

The foundation of all electronic commerce is information technology infrastructure. We now look at the fast-growing phenomenon of electronic commerce and the implications for information technology infrastructures in firms. To conduct electronic commerce, the firm's infrastructure must be capable of performing all of the activities italicized in the definition above.

Types of Electronic Commerce

Electronic commerce[17] can occur between a single buyer and seller, such as the electronic data interchange (EDI) transaction of orders from retail stores like Kmart to suppliers like Levi Strauss. This transaction could be achieved by direct links between the computers of the two firms or through a value-added network (VAN) or service provider. The VAN provides the telecommunications, security, and translation services required between the systems of the two firms, which probably have different data standards and applications. The transaction is initiated by the buyer sending an order message to the seller, who then completes the order. The transaction involves only one buyer and seller at a time, and uses the infrastructure services of the two firms and those of the VAN.

Electronic commerce can also occur between a buyer and multiple sellers shopping on the Internet. The buyer searches the many electronic stores and can make a purchase using a credit card number. The infrastructure used in this case is a combination of the internal infrastructure services of the buyer and the sellers, the Internet, and the credit card company's infrastructure.

Multiple buyers and sellers can all conduct transactions simultaneously. Examples are industry-based infrastructures, such as the IVANS network of U.S. insurance companies and agents. Agents and insurers can complete transactions, such as obtaining a quotation or automatically sending renewal notices from the insurance company to the agent to the customer. IVANS was formed initially as an alliance of property and casualty insurance firms to enable electronic commerce between agents and insurance companies. IVANS has now grown to nearly 500 participating firms, including a broad range of insurance companies, agencies, managed care organizations, reinsurers, brokers, financial service firms, government agencies, and parties selling and delivering services to these groups.[18] IVANS sets an architecture for data and telecommunications, and organizes a VAN provider to supply the infrastructure services shared by the different companies.

The Information Technology
Infrastructure Capabilities Required

The information technology infrastructure capabilities required for electronic commerce include a large Reach and Range extending beyond the firm and several critical infrastructure services. Electronic commerce ideally involves a single electronic point of contact to the firm by a customer. The information technology infrastructure must then integrate the separate business units so that, from the point of contact, the customer can get to the desired business service. Firms taking full advantage of the customer's transaction with one business unit will also attempt to cross-sell other products and services from other business units. Firms with little in the way of synergies may choose to have multiple electronic points of contact with the customer and provide the necessary infrastructure capability at the business-unit level.

The infrastructure services required for electronic commerce are presented in Figure 8.3; 11 of the 25 services are generally necessary, including all 5 of the core infrastructure services. Electronic commerce requires extensive telecommunications networks (services 1 and 2) to customers and suppliers. Across these linkages will run a series of applications and transactions such as EDI, which require additional infrastructure services (service 19). The level of standardization required of information technology architecture is particularly high in the areas of customer, product, and financial data (services 3 and 11), telecommunications, and order-processing applications. Electronic commerce also requires the management of firmwide applications (service 7), such as order processing and accounts receivable.

The need for security and disaster planning (service 16) is paramount for electronic commerce. Also necessary are second-site mirroring systems, which come into operation automatically if problems arise. Particularly rigorous security is necessary, including encryption, firewalls, and other measures to protect the firm's data from accidental or deliberate damage. Authorization and verification of the identity of customers, suppliers, and firm staff are fundamental requirements of electronic commerce. As electronic commerce develops, so will the sophistication of the information transferred and the media used. Advanced multimedia (service 23), combining text, images, video, sound, and graphics, are also likely to be important parts of electronic commerce.

Required for Electronic Commerce	5 Core Information Technology Infrastructure Services
√	1. Manage firmwide communications network services
√	2. Manage groupwide or firmwide messaging services
√	3. Recommend standards for at least one component of IT architecture (e.g., hardware, operating systems, data, communications)
√	4. Provide security, disaster planning, and business recovery services for firmwide installations and applications
√	5. Provide technology advice and support services

	20 Additional Information Technology Infrastructure Services
	6. Manage, maintain, support large-scale data-processing facilities (e.g., mainframe operations)
√	7. Manage firmwide or business-unit applications and databases
	8. Perform IS project management
	9. Provide data management advice and consultancy services
	10. Perform IS planning for business units
√	11. Enforce IT architecture and standards
√	12. Manage firmwide or business-unit workstation networks (e.g., LANs, POS)
	13. Manage and negotiate with suppliers and outsourcers
	14. Identify and test new technologies for business purposes
	15. Develop business-unit–specific applications (usually on a chargeback or contractual basis)
√	16. Implement security, disaster planning, and recovery for business units
	17. Provide management information electronically (e.g., EIS)
	18. Manage business-unit–specific applications
√	19. Manage firmwide or business-unit data, including standards
√	20. Develop and manage electronic linkages to suppliers or customers
	21. Develop a common systems development environment
	22. Provide technology education services (e.g., training)
√	23. Provide multimedia operations and development (e.g., videoconferencing)
	24. Provide firmwide intranet capability (e.g., information access, multiple system access)
	25. Provide firmwide electronic support for groups (e.g., Lotus Notes)

Figure 8.3   Firmwide Infrastructure Services Needed for Electronic Commerce

The dimensions of the infrastructure will need to extend well beyond the firm. The necessary Reach and Range required for electronic commerce is represented in Figure 8.4. The required Reach is to "Customers, suppliers regardless of IT base." Firms engaging in electronic commerce will need to reach any potential customer seamlessly and reliably. This Reach may be achieved through the firm's information technology infrastructure or by linking to the services of a VAN or service provider or perhaps the Internet. The Range needed for electronic commerce will depend on the level of commerce desired. The absolute minimum will be the ability to send messages across the Reach to any customer. This Reach and Range will enable only a primitive form of electronic commerce similar to sending and receiving letters electronically. Adding the ability to

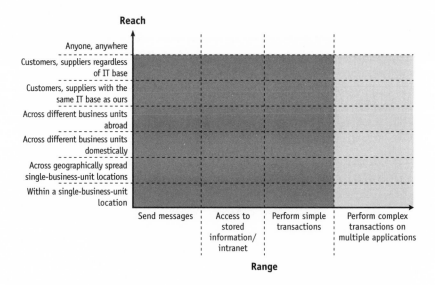

Figure 8.4 Reach and Range Needed for Electronic Commerce

access stored data allows more extensive electronic commerce. For example, Federal Express enables its customers to access a large database to determine the whereabouts of particular packages. This level of Reach and Range is very useful for electronic commerce involving the transfer of information, such as the ability to check airline or rail schedules.

To conduct electronic commerce where buying or selling of products is consummated requires a Range extending to simple transactions, such as processing a payment or taking an order. When a customer in a retail store wishes to purchase an expensive item with a credit card, the swipe of the card triggers the processing of a relatively simple transaction, which seeks approval and completes the sale. The Reach and Range required for this type of electronic commerce is represented by the darker shading in Figure 8.4. The top two layers of Reach and Range can readily be provided by a service provider. For the IVANS network, this Reach and Range was provided by a combination of service providers including IBM Information Network and Sears Communications Services (Advantis). Many applications of electronic commerce require a more extensive Range, extending to complex transactions (the lighter shading in the figure), particularly if the electronic commerce is integrated into the transaction-processing systems of the firm.

A critical component of capturing the electronic channel to the customer is having the infrastructure capability. Firms aggressively pursuing electronic commerce as part of their business strategy are more likely to have an enabling view of infrastructure, with particularly extensive Reach and Range and the 12 infrastructure services identified in Figure 8.3. Often, some of the infrastructure services and part of the extensive Reach will be provided by an outsourcer or VAN provider. The critical strategic issue is that the infrastructure is coordinated centrally to provide an integrated and common platform and an external gateway for electronic commerce. At a minimum, coordination will involve setting an appropriate architecture but will extend to the provision of the firmwide infrastructure capability in many firms.

The technology developments that have underpinned the development of electronic commerce have concurrently facilitated international business operations.

Extending International Business Operations

Many firms are aggressively extending their international operations in search of increased growth and profitability. We studied the implications of international business operations for managing information technology in 26 firms headquartered in Singapore, Japan, Hong Kong, North America, and Australia.[19] Each of these firms generated more than 20 percent of its annual revenues from operations outside the domestic headquarters base. Our aim was to examine how firms' international objectives are supported by their information technology infrastructure capabilities.

Choice and Complexity

Firms with substantial operations outside their domestic base face real challenges in getting the right global-local balance. One component of that balance is the management and governance of information technology. Aligning the management of local operations with firmwide strategic directions is a complex undertaking on multiple sites, in multiple cultures, and in diverse technological environments. Part of this challenge relates to leveraging information technology to achieve business goals through

- Maximizing information flows across the firm, regardless of locations.

- The most appropriate balance for corporate, business-unit, and local information systems management.

- Implementing common systems among different locations.

- Deployment of expertise to support the management and operation of systems.

- Balancing the availability and use of country- and firmwide information technology infrastructures.

International Business Orientations

The strategic orientation of a firm's international business operations provides some guidance for the broad parameters of critical long-term information technology investments. These orientations have been classified into four categories which have different strategic focuses and different configurations for the management of assets and capabilities.[20] Figure 8.5 provides an overview of the four categories.

Firms with a global international business orientation focus on cost advantages and centralize their assets and capabilities on a global basis. Examples in our study included two large banks headquartered in Singapore, where the domestic headquarters continued to be the basis for providing services for large customers expanding and operating internationally.

Transnational firms have a dual emphasis on global efficiency and flexibility, along with the transfer of learning across the firm. Honda and Sony are examples of transnational firms that have strong pressures for both international integration of their operations and local responsiveness in their products.[21] Achievement of these dual aims requires a complex balance of both interdependent and dispersed resources to meet pressures for international integration in areas such as manufacturing and tracking of parts. In addition, these market leaders must be locally responsive, ready to modify products or services at the country or regional level.

Orientation	Strategic Focus	Configuration	Examples
Global	Cost advantages, product and customer experience consistency	Centralized assets, capabilities	Singapore banks
Transnational	Global efficiency and flexibility, learning	Complex balance, interdependent and dispersed	Honda, Sony
International	Worldwide diffusion and parent company adaptation	Mix of centralized and decentralized, based on core competencies	Sun Life of Canada
Multinational	Strong national bases, local autonomy	Decentralized assets, nationally self-sufficient	Amcor

Figure 8.5   International Business Orientations

Firms with an international orientation usually adapt parent company policies and practices for other markets, in a mixed centralized/decentralized structure. Sun Life of Canada is an example of a firm with a strong desire to gain synergies from its strong brand and practices, but in the context of recognition of significant differences between the competitive and regulatory situations across the countries in which it operates. Thus Sun Life has a mixed centralized/decentralized structure, in which local businesses adapt the parent company's policies and practices.

The firms headquartered in Japan and North America tended to have international or transnational orientations that were continuing to evolve. These orientations provided particularly complex decision environments for both business operations and for information technology management. Successful management of transnational and international firms requires integrating strong pressures for both international integration and local responsiveness. The challenge is to ensure the right choices in both areas. Firms with a multinational orientation operate with largely decentralized assets, with strong national bases managed with a high degree of local autonomy.

Matching International Information Technology Management Configurations

These four types of international business orientations, with their differing strategy emphases and mixes of centralization and decentralization lead logically to four different types of information technology configurations[22]—global, transnational, international, and multinational information technologies—which have different patterns of infrastructure capability:[23]

- Firms with *global* information technology patterns, like the Singapore banks, had headquarters-driven information technology configurations, with extensive firmwide infrastructure capabilities. They had an average of 20 services, with the additional services in the areas of shared applications, data management, standards, and information technology management.

- Firms with *transnational* information technology patterns, such as Honda and Sony, had configurations integrating local and worldwide information technology operations. With an average of 16 services, their firmwide infrastructure capabilities were generally less extensive than those of global firms, but were critical to their competitiveness. Transnational firms put more emphasis on information technology research and development than other firms.

- Firms with *international* information technology patterns had information technology configurations emphasizing intellectual synergy among information technology groups in different parts of the firm, and tended to have a limited number of firmwide infrastructure services (six services on average).

- Firms with *multinational* information technology patterns had separate and independent information technology operations in different local and regional areas, with few or no firmwide infrastructure services.

About one-quarter of the firms had mismatched business and information technology configurations, underscoring the dynamic nature of business developments. A few firms were in transition from, for example, an international to a transnational business orientation, and information technology configuration changes were lagging behind these business changes. In some locations, the requisite skills or the national telecommunications infrastructure were not available, so pragmatic processes were put in place to manage technology differently in specific locations. However, a third group of firms lacked realization of the importance or relevance of meshing business orientation and information technology

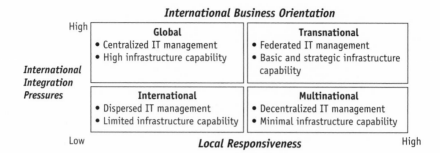

Figure 8.6 Business Pressures and Information Technology Management
Responses

configuration to deliver shared services more effectively. Although
the business changed, information technology did not change at
the same pace or rate, resulting in a mismatched set of services and
considerable frustration.

In Figure 8.6 we summarize the patterns of information technology management and infrastructure services that are appropriate
to the four international business orientations. *Global* firms benefit
from centralized information technology management to deliver the
consistency and extensive range of infrastructure required to match
the firms' centralization of operations and assets. *Transnational*
firms benefit from a federated approach to information technology
management, where some operations and key infrastructure services are managed across the firm while others are managed locally.
International firms can be more dispersed in their management of
information technology, with limited infrastructure services being
offered across all business units. In *multinational* firms, information technology is managed predominantly at the local level, in line
with the business approach of a high degree of local autonomy.
This business orientation requires few, if any, infrastructure services for implementation.

Managers need an intimate knowledge of current and future
business directions to develop appropriate information technology
management structures and infrastructure services. Business-driven
information technology decision making requires an understanding
of the often-conflicting pressures for international integration and
local responsiveness, and the need to balance firmwide control and
local autonomy. Managers can review Figure 8.6 and diagnose the
international business approach of their firm as a basis for identifying the nature and extent of infrastructure services required.

Managing Knowledge and Organizational Learning

Knowledge is a source of competitive advantage that is difficult and time consuming to emulate. In the late 1990s, knowledge is increasingly seen as a primary business asset[24] and knowledge management, as a key differentiation between firms.[25] Knowledge management interacts with a firm's approach to organizational learning, information management, human resources management, and its information technology infrastructure capabilities.

Hoffmann-LaRoche's Right First Time program, launched in 1992, is a knowledge management initiative to help reduce the vital time-to-market factor in new-drug approvals.[26] Delays in the process can cost the Swiss-headquartered pharmaceutical firm as much as $1 million a day in lost revenues.

The original program director, Patricia Seeman, identified three goals of knowledge management against which she developed tools for "knowing what," "understanding why," and "making sense." Hoffmann-LaRoche had to understand its knowledge base, develop process maps and databases, and then use knowledge maps to show linkages between disparate types of knowledge and "Yellow Pages" to catalogue the expertise in the firm. Five years later, the program is still thriving and delivering benefits—for example, in reduced time to prepare clinical reports. The repository of knowledge is locked into the company's organizational infrastructure and is supported by information technology infrastructure capabilities involving a communications network and shared groupware applications.

Integral to the implementation of knowledge management is understanding the firm's information flows and implementing organizational learning practices that make key aspects of the firm's knowledge base explicit, so that they may be shared. We give the example of ReInsureCo, an international reinsurance firm, to explain the interdependencies that underpin the implementation of knowledge management.

One ReInsureCo information resources manager claimed, "We are achieving a major shift in culture where each employee understands that the more information they share with their colleagues and enter into our international knowledge base, the more highly valued is their role at ReInsureCo." This ReInsureCo executive manages a large cadre of information specialists in the firm's European headquarters. The work of these specialists is critical to ReIn-sureCo's core businesses of life and property/casualty reinsurance. Reinsurance generates its profits from sound financial and risk management across multiple countries, firms, and environments. ReIn-sureCo's contact with clients is primarily through multidisciplinary client teams. Client managers, financial analysts, and actuaries must have very accurate and detailed information about each client, the insurance industry, economic and financial indicators, and health and environmental indicators.

ReInsureCo's knowledge base about its clients (insurance firms, governments), as well as factors affecting economic, political, and environmental situations, has been codified and indexed from most parts of the business. Regional offices have local information resource managers, whose work is increasingly integrated with the headquarters knowledge base.

Integral to the development and success of the knowledge base is the firm's ability to manage its information flows and implement the practices of learning organizations—the foundation of knowledge management. Successful application requires a set of information technology infrastructure capabilities that matches the human resource and information management of the firm. These infrastructure capabilities include a well-developed communications network enabling the easy transfer of messages and information between ReInsureCo's staff throughout the world; the use of groupware applications to manage the work of geographically dispersed managers and analysts collaborating on specific clients and projects; and the implementation of worldwide agreements on architecture and standards for specific types of data and selected application systems.

ReInsureCo's Asian Region human resources manager explains how that regional group is integrating its employee appraisal and reward systems to engender a culture shift toward knowledge management and organizational learning practices: "A key criterion of every employee appraisal is the contribution made to the firm's knowledge base. In this way we reinforce what is, for many of our staff, a different approach to sharing information with both local and international colleagues." Supporting this approach are two types of specialists with complementary skills: information resource managers, who are responsible for the access and use of external information, such as financial services, and for supporting internal information flows, and information technologists, whose responsibilities are the development and management of the firm's technology infrastructure and applications. The infrastructure connects people, manages access to the firm's databases, and supports the technical desktop capability so critical to analysts.

ReInsureCo started its knowledge management process by applying four steps of integrating knowledge management into the way the firm works:[27] making knowledge visible, building knowledge intensity, developing a knowledge culture, and building the firm's knowledge infrastructure.

Knowledge management represents a quantum shift for most organizations. It is a form of expertise-centered management, focusing on using human expertise for business advantage. Knowledge management practices draw out and make available to other managers the tacit knowledge people have—what they carry around with them and what they observe and learn from experience.

Structures and Processes for Knowledge Management

In a major study of knowledge management completed by the Economist Intelligence Unit and IBM Consulting Group,[28] a composite set of characteristics of learning organizations was developed. These characteristics focused on the organization's behavior in four areas: leadership, culture, managing people as assets, and structures and processes. The structure and process characteristics of learning organizations include

- Business information on performance, current activities, and best practices is widely accessible and shared.

- The organization encourages—and work routines allow—people to capitalize on opportunities for informed learning.

- Information technology facilitates the rapid dissemination of knowledge and improves communication and collaboration among employees at all levels and all locations.

These statements are similar to the IT maxims that we found in firms where the notion of knowledge as a business asset was understood. Knowledge management involves the accessibility and sharing of business information, rapid dissemination of knowledge, communication and collaboration among employees, and systems designed to codify, capture, and disseminate knowledge.

To manage a firm's knowledge requires a specific set of information technology infrastructure capabilities that match the leadership, culture, human resources policy, structure, and processes of the firm. For the manufacturer Honda, the values of knowledge management are evident in business and IT maxims, and then implemented in the company's infrastructure view and capabilities.

Leveraging Communication for Sharing Expertise at Honda

Honda is a large transnational firm with automotive design and manufacturing teams in multiple locations, balancing pressures of greater localization and globalization of its operations.[29] Although Honda is committed to the globalization of its operations, it has recognized the need for greater localization, particularly in styling. Both objectives are achieved by focusing on the shared expertise and organizational learning that Honda refers to in its international business operations as "glocalization." This refers to global operations that are increasingly self-reliant and able to source locally or from other regions, depending on the most efficient and effective arrangement.

Honda's long-term strategies focus on innovation in automobile development and production technologies, exploiting new markets, expediting global operations, and stabilizing the business against currency fluctuations. Honda's business maxims, which reflect these strategies and the commitment to glocalization, include

- Continuous innovation and originality in creating and developing new products.

- Rapid creation and adaptation of products for major regional markets.

- Expediting of global operations through synergies of production and operations in many countries.

- Continuing focus on reducing the cycle time from R&D through production and marketing.

- Staff of the highest caliber who excel in working together.

- Commitment to minimizing costs in all areas within the context and constraints of the above maxims.

These business maxims, with their emphasis on product leadership, R&D, and cost minimization, result in IT maxims that stress information consistency, accessibility, and the importance of communications networks:

- Information flow throughout Honda should allow all parts of the company to more easily and quickly spot trends and use these to Honda's advantage.

- Honda R&D staff in different parts of the world need ready access to each other to be able to communicate their ideas and output to their colleagues.

- Communications systems must facilitate high-quality person-to-person interactions among R&D staff and between R&D, production, operations, and marketing personnel.

- Communication systems must support the transfer of sophisticated design concepts, data, and documentation in a high-quality and cost-efficient manner.

This selection of Honda's business and IT maxims shows the links between the importance of managing Honda's knowledge base and the expertise to speed development processes. Honda's firmwide infrastructure capability provides both basic and some strategic services. The strategic services include a full-service global communications network and global databases for sales, finance, and parts ordering. There are considerable synergies across these areas, and the systems are required for the effective sharing of information.

Honda's approach to infrastructure investments is highlighted by the efforts made to establish and then upgrade Honda's international network system (INS-III) in the past four years. The network, now named Pentaccord, was developed with three basic functions:

- International telephone and fax communications between Japan and major overseas sites, using an extension number

- International high-speed LAN-to-LAN communications using standard international protocols (TCP/IP)

- International high-speed HOST-to-HOST communications (IBM SNA)

Further functions, driven by strategic needs for enhanced communication among R&D staff, were quickly added. These included an expanded international e-mail facility and the beginnings of multimedia communication. The network allows state-of-the-art design and styling work to be shared among major centers, particularly Los Angeles and Wako-shi. This sharing capability has made a major difference to both the speed and the type of design developments that can now occur. Very-high-resolution photographic and digital images can now be transferred. Wako-shi can now quickly check the styling changes suggested by Los Angeles R&D designers for specifications and feasibility.

The System Division and R&D groups are now experimenting with further multimedia applications. "We know that person-to-person communication and informal communication, is critical in our business—both in the design and development area and amongst senior managers," explained the Systems Division's general manager. "Our people get to know one another quite well, as many come to Japan or go on exchange to Los Angeles or Belgium for training. Some forms of communication need the richness of seeing the person and how they react to various suggestions. We see multimedia as an avenue for supporting high bandwidth technical information and human communication needs in the future." Honda increasingly sees its approach to information and communications systems supporting global shared values, flatter management structures, and the transparency of information throughout the company.

Honda's sharing of expertise, rapid exchange of R&D knowledge, and technical and human communication capabilities reflect the structures and processes of a learning organization. These initiatives are all concerned with managing knowledge and the expertise base for competitive advantage. This focus is not new to Honda,[30] and there is a clear understanding of the implications for infrastructure capabilities of implementing knowledge management.

Knowledge Management and Infrastructure Capabilities

To enable the sharing and transfer of design concepts and data, Honda required a very sophisticated, high-bandwidth communications network, agreement on and enforcement of many parts of the information technology architecture, and the early development of multimedia capability.

The implementation of knowledge management across a firm requires, as a minimum, a comprehensive level of communications network and messaging services (services 1 and 2 in Figure 8.3), together with agreed-upon technical standards that enable the sharing of knowledge and exchange of information (services 3 and 11). The additional infrastructure capabilities required will depend on the type of knowledge to be managed and the individuals and groups who are part of the activity.

Transformation Approaches and Capability Patterns

Dramatic changes in the availability of computer and communications technologies add both opportunity and complexity to the challenges of transforming businesses. These information technology developments have raised the stakes for sustaining competitiveness in many industries while giving firms more options for product and service delivery. In Figure 8.7 we present each transformation with sample business and IT maxims, providing guidance on the types of infrastructure capabilities needed to successfully progress through each transformation.

Driving each type of transformation requires a sound base of core and specific infrastructure capabilities. The extent to which managers recognize the implications of each of the transformation approaches is critical to having those capabilities in place in a timely and appropriate manner.

The efficacy of developing business-driven infrastructure capabilities is intimately bound up with how investment cases for the information technology portfolio are assessed and how the portfolio is managed and governed. These are the topics covered in the remaining two chapters.

Transformation Type	Sample Business Maxims	Sample IT Maxims	Sample IT Infrastructure Features
Business Process Redesign — Multibusiness Retailer	• Know what is selling and where it is selling • Anticipate and respond to the behavior and changing needs of the customer	• Centralized information to quickly and easily spot trends • Integrate once-only data capture with business processes to ensure quick response	• Firmwide data standards and data management and application systems to process point-of-sale data and provide management information • Development and management of EDI linkages to supplier
Electronic Commerce	• Link to suppliers in a fast and efficient way • Provide a single point of contact to the customer • Reach the broadest range of customers at low cost	• Adopt one firmwide standard for EDI • Link different BU IT platforms to single gateway to customer • Develop one firmwide home page	• Development and management of on-line and/or EDI linkages to suppliers or customers • Extend the Reach to a customer and Range to support simple transactions
International Business Operations — Large Bank	• Responsive and consistent customer service at any location • Total service to global customers	• Unified and real-time customer information database that is readily available to all frontline staff • Network that enables access to a wide range of applications essential to competitive customer services	• Customer-centric integrated banking systems implemented consistently throughout the world utilizing a robust international communications network
Knowledge Management — Automotive Manufacturer	• Continuous innovation and originality in creating and developing new products • Staff of the highest caliber who enjoy working together	• R&D staff in different locations need ready access to each other to communicate their ideas and output to colleagues • Communications systems must facilitate high-quality person-to-person interaction among R&D staff and among R&D, production, operations, and marketing personnel	• Sophisticated high-bandwidth network supporting rich forms of human communication (e.g., multimedia) and the ability to transfer design concepts, data, and documentation in a high-quality and cost-effective manner

Figure 8.7 Sample Business and IT Maxims and Infrastructure Capabilities

CHAPTER 9

Making the Investment Decision

In managing any investment portfolio, appraising the investment, and making the investment decision are key steps. The investment appraisal process must reflect the firm's strategic goals and the mix of the current information technology portfolio. The executive vice president for corporate banking and data resources at DBS Bank of Singapore reflects on the bank's approach to information technology investments:

> If our approach had been to determine how much we could save, we would not have invested in technology in the way we did. We view technology as strategic investments—to give us a competitive edge. That's the advantage of having a business manager take charge of IT—we treat IT decisions as business decisions. We do not just follow what other banks are doing. We are not afraid to be the first user of a new technology in the region. We justify IT in terms of business capabilities, and strategic positioning, not merely cost savings. . . . We also watch our costs closely; although annual IT investments have increased from 1985[,] IT costs per transaction ha[ve] been decreasing.[1]

The opportunities and risks of investments in the new infrastructure are significant and require senior management attention to ensure that investments meet the firm's strategic goals. DBS Bank's successful approach illustrates the balance of investments that suits its goals. Three areas critically in need of such senior management attention are appraising new investments, assessing the health of the current portfolio, and governing information technology investments. This chapter addresses appraising investments and assessing the health of the current portfolio. Chapter 10 focuses on senior management's leadership responsibilities for governing and managing the portfolio.

In this chapter, we outline the nature of information technology investments, leading to a comparison of the different approaches to information technology appraisal. We provide recommendations for the information technology appraisal process focusing on using appropriate but different approaches to each of four information technology investment classes. The latter part of this chapter presents an approach we've used to assess the health of the information technology portfolio as an input into the overall appraisal process. Understanding the health of the current portfolio puts proposed investments in context and allows senior management to ensure that new investments complement and support both the existing portfolio and the firm's strategic goals.

The Nature of Information Technology Investments

Information technology is no different from any other investment made by a firm. A return must be made from the investment or eventually the firm will fail. The management of information technology requires no special treatment beyond the attention expected for an investment that now accounts for more capital than any other category of investment in many firms. There are, however, some characteristics of information technology investments that make their management challenging. Seven characteristics affect almost every information technology investment decision:

1. Costs often appear certain.

2. Benefits vary from certain to unauditable.

3. The information technology culture is project based.

4. Information technology decisions are political.

5. Information technology changes the way the work is done.

6. The impact of investments becomes diluted.

7. Information technology investments are strategic choices.

We need to understand these characteristics of information technology investments to make sound decisions with convincing appraisal cases using appropriate tools.

Costs Appear Certain

Estimating the costs of a project with a heavy information technology component is difficult. Costs often appear certain, but the evidence for bringing projects in on budget is poor. An IDC study of software projects reported that only 29 percent of them were delivered on budget.[2] There are many reasons for this poor performance compared with estimates. Software projects, such as airline reservation systems, are some of the most complex artifacts ever produced. It isn't unusual for an airline reservation system to have more than 100,000 fare changes in a single day. Software to cope with this level of complexity has to be an impressive piece of engineering, and programmers are still learning to successfully estimate the costs of such projects.

Projects are completed late partly because specifications change along the way. During the building and implementation phases, new features are added as needs and aspirations change. Integrating a new system with existing systems, which use different infrastructures, is tricky. Often, unexpected complications add time to the project. The disciplines of software project management are developing, but they are not mature, so the industry has a deserved reputation for time overruns. The information technology industry has much to do in this area to become a reliable project manager.

Many firms have chosen to reduce the risk of building their own software by purchasing large-package solutions that can be bought and implemented in modules. SAP, the German software package, is an example of an integrated package with many modules covering the entire business. But estimating the costs of packaged software is as difficult as for internally developed software, and it isn't uncommon to hear of time overruns in such large implementations.

Another useful strategy is outsourcing the systems development or implementation process to firms like Andersen Consulting, EDS, or IBM. Firms like these will offer a fixed price for an agreed-upon system specification. This approach can remove some of the risk of

cost overruns, but outsourcing adds other risks, such as the difficulty of exactly specifying the systems up front or handling changing business needs midproject.

Benefits Vary

The benefits from an investment in information technology come in
three types, requiring different appraisal approaches.

- *Certain benefits*, in which cash-in of the benefits can be
  guaranteed. If the investment in an order-processing system
  will reduce the number of staff, the financial benefit is tangi-
  ble and certain when the next year's budget can be reduced
  accordingly, thus guaranteeing cash-in of the benefits.

- *Estimated benefits*, in which cash-in cannot be guaranteed
  before the investment, but for which the impact can be
  assessed afterward. Improvements in quality, increased sales,
  better information, faster time to market with new products,
  and better customer service are all estimated benefits.
  Through managers' testimonials they can all have value, but
  predicting their impact before investment is difficult.

- *Unauditable benefits*. Even after these occur, it is very difficult to assess their impact. Customer loyalty and quality of
  work life are intuitive examples. We know there is a benefit, but measurement is usually impossible or unconvincing.

Project-based Culture

The field of information technology is very strongly project based.
People work on *projects*; costs are allocated to *projects*; and *projects*
are started, canceled, and completed. However, the benefits of an
information technology investment often rely on the interactions
among many projects—some completed long ago and others still
in progress. The building of a sales analysis system is a project
with certain characteristics, such as size and start date. To be successful, the completed system will use the existing sales database,
wide-area telecommunications network, and local network of per-

sonal computers. The benefits rely on the iterations of these many different projects, making the assessment of benefits difficult.

Australia's largest bank, Westpac, has implemented a very successful Marketing Support System (MSS)[3] for the corporate sales team's relationship managers. MSS consists of six interconnected databases in Lotus Notes and captures all relationship, customer, and sales activity for corporate customers. MSS acts as a reservoir for the group's collective knowledge. Implementation relied on a PC, server, and local area network infrastructure that was already in place. However, success bred its own problems, and soon the response times were unacceptably slow. New technology investments were required to increase the capability of the infrastructure services to support MSS.

MSS illustrates the interrelationships among projects. MSS used the existing infrastructure, which then became a bottleneck. The significantly enhanced infrastructure now has the potential to support other applications. The cycle of exploiting the existing infrastructure, followed by identifying new needs and committing to further investment, will continue.

Politics

Information and technology decisions are often very political. The natural tendency of many managers is not to share information. Simon Narroway, project manager for Westpac's MSS, explains, "It took a while to convince many people to move away from previous work practices of knowledge hoarding . . . but it's now second nature for our sales people to use MSS before a meeting. In the bad old days there could be times when several different areas from Westpac would visit the customer on the same day without each other knowing. Now there is no excuse for this lack of coordination."

Many internal political struggles have been fought over who had access to whose information. Politics is natural and healthy in any organization, but in some organizations politics becomes a significant barrier to progress, soaking up huge amounts of talented managers' time and creative energies. Decisions about technology and information are often the targets of a higher level of political activity than is desirable. Having clear and well-articulated approaches to the appraisal of information technology investments helps to reduce the potential of unproductive politics.

Information Technology Changes the Way Work Is Done

Investments in information technology often result in a radical change in the way a job is done, complicating the process of predicting the benefits. For example, many insurance firms are investing in workflow systems in which tasks such as claims processing are routed via information technology to a claims processor who may be working from home. The technology has completely changed the dynamics of the relationship between supervisor and worker. Predicting and then assessing the exact benefits are difficult. No matter how well planned, the implementation of new systems always has unintended consequences. The potential of information technology to change the way the job is done often confounds the traditional appraisal approach of comparing the costs and benefits before and after the investment.

Many traditional approaches to cost-benefit analysis compare the current costs and benefits with new costs and benefits expected after the investment in information technology has occurred. As Kaplan[4] convincingly points out, competition in most industries is so fierce that one must assume a deteriorating relative position (say, sales falling at 1 percent per year) as the current case. Making the appropriate investment may then lead to maintaining or even improving the firm's relative position. Henry Ford put it best: Those who don't invest in new machinery pay for it without buying it. In an information technology investment decision, it is advisable to compare the "without" case with a deteriorating relative position to the "with" case.

Dilution of Impact

Investments in information technology are usually made to have an influence on how individuals work in the organization. Customers or employees use the systems, but benefits are sought at the level of the business unit or corporate bottom line. Although investments are made at the individual level, to be effective the impacts must work up through the levels of the team, the department, the business unit, and finally the corporation. As the impact moves up through the levels, there is a dilution of the effect of information technology with the influence of other factors, such as pricing decisions or competitor moves. Measuring the impact of an information technology investment at the level of the individual (productivity improvements) will be much easier than at the business-unit level (improved labor productivity and profit), where many other factors dilute the effect. In predicting the impact of information technology during the appraisal process, the sequence (and dilution) of impact moving up from the individual to the business-unit level must be taken into account. It is only by understanding how the investment affects each level that one can build a coherent picture of the payoff of information technology investment.

Strategic Choices

The nature of information technology investments as described makes the process of appraisal challenging. These challenges are much more difficult for information technology infrastructure decisions because of their long-term nature, their size, and the difficulties of predicting business needs and technological change. Positioning an information technology infrastructure is like positioning a strategy.[5] Putting in an infrastructure involves a whole system of choices, activities, and trade-offs that must be made. As with strategic issues, the need for choices provides the potential for competitive advantage. Without the trade-offs and choices, any good idea such as appropriate infrastructure would be quickly imitated. The best infrastructure choices will be unique for a particular firm, based on the fit with other strategic choices, and hard to imitate.

Comparing General Approaches to Information Technology Appraisal

Because the different types of information technology investment have different management objectives and risk-return profiles, they are different asset classes. Thus they should be appraised using different approaches. We outline several approaches to information technology appraisal, drawing on our work with firms and on the evidence for payoff identified in Chapter 3. Based on the strengths of these approaches and the characteristics of each type of information technology in the portfolio, we make recommendations for appraising investments.

Using one approach to appraisal for all information technology investments is doomed to failure. Rather, we advocate using different approaches to suit the different management objectives for each type of investment:

- *Strategic*, to gain competitive advantage via positioning the firm in the marketplace, usually with the aim of gaining sales

- *Informational*, to provide better information to manage, control, account, communicate, analyze, and make decisions

- *Transactional*, to reduce the cost of doing business usually by automating the transactions of the firm and substituting capital for labor

- *Infrastructure*, to provide the base foundation of shared information technology services

Four Approaches

1. Discounted Cash Flow Techniques

Discounted cash flow (DCF) techniques such as net present value (NPV) and internal rate of return (IRR) are generally the most rigorous and defensible approaches to appraising investments. They require knowing with confidence the net cash flow for the investment and a hurdle rate for the investment, such as the weighted average cost of capital. In Bacon's[6] survey of 80 firms, DCF techniques such as NPV and IRR were used in around 50 percent of firms in a little more than 50 percent of their projects. Thus DCF techniques are applied to nearly 30 percent of all information technology projects in these firms. In some information technology investments, such as many transactional investments, the hurdle rate and cash flow are known with some certainty, and DCF approaches work well. However, with the other types of technology investments, such as those made to meet strategic objectives, it is impossible to predict cash flow with great confidence. Yet we have all been tempted to manipulate anticipated cash flow to help achieve the desired outcome. These sound techniques have been abused, and as a result, some senior managers have lost confidence in them, further confounding the investment decision for strategic systems where the aim is to gain sales.

2. Subjective (or Value) Analysis

The difficulty of many information technology investments is that the net cash flows can never be known with certainty beforehand. Most strategic and many infrastructure investments require other approaches. These approaches are generally more subjective and rely on the judgment of experts and senior management. Informed subjective analysis is based on the best estimates of those who should know. Their worth depends on the personal credibility and experience of those doing the estimating. Stating that "we must make this investment in personal computers for our sales force to compete" is a subjective judgment, as is estimating that the new advertising campaign will increase sales by 5 percent on the East Coast. What really matters is the position, experience, information base, and reliability of the intuitive perspective of the decision makers proclaiming these judgments. This type of informed subjective analysis is the province of key business managers, not information technology managers—and it is the business managers in these situations who must be held accountable for delivering the business benefits.

3. Discounted Cash Flow Value Analysis

To address the difficulties of using DCF in more uncertain situations, we advocate using a modified approach called DCF value analysis. Our approach draws on the ideas of Keen[7] and Kaplan[8] and the experiences of firms using this approach. DCF value analysis combines the rigor and discipline of DCF with the reality of subjective value analysis. It works as follows:

- Categorize the benefits of the investment into certain and estimated (including unauditables).

- Determine the cash flows based only on certain benefits.

- Calculate the NPV based on the cash flows, and accept the project if positive. To calculate NPV, use a hurdle rate such as the weighted average cost of capital, which does not include project risk.[9]

- Describe each of the estimated benefits, and provide the expert's best judgment of the expected benefit in dollars. Include the contact details (name and phone number) of the estimator to build accountability into the process. For example, it is much more convincing and accountable when John Citizen, the marketing director, and not an anonymous business analyst, estimates that the new sales analysis system will increase sales by 0.5 percent per year.

- If the NPV is negative by X dollars, then the senior management group must determine whether the firm is willing to pay the X dollars to receive the estimated benefits.

For example, a finance firm was considering an expert system to assess applications for automobile loans. The system would cost $1 million to implement, and the NPV based on certain cash flows was –$250,000. A list of six subjectively estimated benefits totaled $700,000. The senior management team decided to proceed with the project, confident that enough of the higher-risk estimated benefits would be realized to cover the negative NPV. The management team was completely confident that the benefits classified as certain would be achieved, as they would reduce the budgets of the loans area accordingly.

The major benefit of the DCF value analysis approach lies in combining the certain and subjectively estimated benefits into a framework to help make the decision. Both certain and estimated benefits are important, and DCF value analysis uses both appropriately in the decision process.

4. Payback, or Breakeven

Payback and breakeven are very popular approaches for information technology appraisal and are used by more than 60 percent of firms in 50 percent of projects.[10] However, they have problems, as they ignore the time value of money that the DCF approaches consider. They are poor substitutes for DCF when cash flows are known with certainty. However, in more subjective situations they are both popular approaches to determine the scope of the problem. They are quick and simple to explain but should be used with caution.

In providing recommendations for information technology appraisal approaches, we consider strategic, informational, and infrastructure applications separately from infrastructure invest-

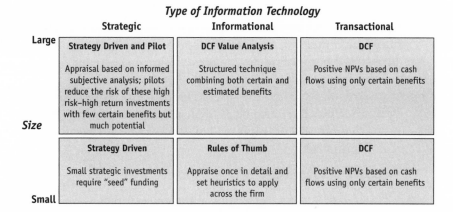

Figure 9.1 Information Technology Investment Appraisal

ments. The shared and long-term nature of infrastructure requires special treatment during the appraisal process.

Recommendations for Strategic, Informational, and Transactional Investments

Our recommendations[11] for appraisal of strategic, informational, and transactional technology investments are summarized in Figure 9.1. They are divided into two size categories (small and large), which are subjective to each firm.

Regardless of size, to be acceptable, a transactional information technology investment must return a positive NPV based on certain benefits. This certainty leads to the strong positive effect that transactional investments have on firm performance. Firms that are good at generating value from their information technology investments have strong disciplines around transactional investment. For example, they ensure cash-in of the benefit of the transactional investment by reducing the budgets of the areas identified in the proposal.

For large informational investments we suggest the DCF value analysis approach. The benefits of most informational investments have some uncertainty, and DCF value analysis works well to combine certain and uncertain benefits. For smaller projects, it is sensible to develop rules of thumb. For example, firms often do the analysis once, for decisions such as who should have a laptop computer, mobile phone, or Internet access, and then set a policy for all staff.

Strategic investments, with their high risk and high return, are quite different. Whether large or small, strategic investments must be driven by the current strategy of the firm. A pilot reduces the risk significantly, particularly when the investment is large. The production of a pilot in a limited geographical area or for a limited number of customers or employees or a limited set of products buys four pieces of critical information:

1. The technical feasibility of the project

2. The organizational feasibility of the project, including insight into how work is done and the resistance to and incentives for using the system

3. The costs and benefits of the project, to allow the use of DCF value analysis

4. The specifications for the production version of the system

Ultimately, strategic information technology investments are a subjective decision. They are risky and have high potential for gain. Like all high-risk investments, strategic information technology initiatives have to fit into the whole portfolio and require confidence and the willingness to lead.

How Firms Appraise Infrastructure Investment

Senior information technology managers are very creative in how they appraise and justify information technology infrastructure investments. They have had to be, as infrastructure has often been a hard sell to senior management teams. First, we discuss the pros and cons of successful approaches we've used and observed. Some have long-term adverse consequences. Then we'll synthesize these approaches into our recommendations for the appropriate approach for each view of infrastructure (see Figure 9.2 on page 223).

Cost Savings Driven by a Utility View

For firms taking a utility view of infrastructure, the appraisal and justification is generally straightforward. Information technology infrastructure investments must save money; thus, the net cash flows of the projects are positive, leading to a positive NPV based on certain benefits. Cash-in of the benefits can be ensured by reducing the budgets of the areas where the cost savings are to occur.

For example, there has been a worldwide trend toward consolidation of data centers. Significant cost savings are achieved by reducing the number of data centers in a firm and taking advantage of the substantial economies of scale offered by the advances in technology performance cost ratios and centralizing some technical people. Also, the continuing reduction in telecommunications costs makes it economically possible to place data centers significant distances from the employees using the systems.

The adoption of a utility view of infrastructure requires tight discipline from senior management to focus on cost savings—the type of discipline found in firms competing successfully with low-cost producer strategies. Managing these firms involves the relentless pursuit of efficiencies. This culture permeates the whole firm, including large and long-life investments, such as information technology infrastructure.

Bundling with Transactional Systems

Senior information technology managers frequently bundle infrastructure into transactional systems investments. Bundling works as a justification or appraisal approach but can have undesirable long-term consequences.

Bundling occurs when a desirable new transactional (or other) application is proposed, such as a claims-processing system that will have significant cost savings in an insurance company. The proposed system has a price tag of $1.5 million, with an internal rate of return (IRR) of 39 percent based on certain benefits. The information technology manager adds to the proposal infrastructure, such as a new set of servers, that isn't required for the claims-processing system. The added infrastructure brings the IRR down to 12.5 percent—just half a percentage point above the hurdle rate of 12 percent set by the firm for information technology investments. By bundling infrastructure with a series of projects, the information technology manager can quietly and successfully put an infrastructure in place for less financially attractive projects to use. The information technology managers who use this approach often have a clear architecture in mind. They are great deal makers, who can build an integrated infrastructure over time on the back of highly desirable applications. A sure indicator of this approach is where there are a large number of information technology projects with returns just above the firm's cut-off. CIOs who are successful in the deal-making route to building infrastructures described in Chapter 7 often use this approach.

Bundling helps get projects approved. Many information technology managers argue that it's the only way to build infrastructure, as their senior management team or board wouldn't support stand-alone infrastructure business cases. However, negative consequences follow as infrastructure investments are hidden from senior management who subsequently do not value them. In many ways, this approach is akin to giving infrastructure away with an application and thus allocating it a value of zero.

When bundling is used on a regular basis, senior management gets a distorted picture of the information technology portfolio and assumes it to be all applications with little or no infrastructure. When the firm needs—and the CIO proposes—a large infrastructure investment, real problems occur. Naturally, the senior management team, unfamiliar with valuing infrastructure, turns down the proposal. Senior managers are unfamiliar with the characteristics and dynamics of infrastructure investments and their benefits.

Instead of bundling, we recommend that managers

- Identify infrastructure separately, based on the family of applications it enables. Infrastructure is about providing a capability to enable business applications that create business value.

- Appraise and justify infrastructure investments separately from applications, due to their shared nature and concurrent use by multiple applications.

- Require business areas responsible for each application to contribute to the cost of the infrastructure.

Differential Hurdle Rates

In recognizing the different risk-return natures of the different types of information technology investments, some firms have adopted distinct hurdle rates for each type. For example, in one large telecommunications firm, the hurdle rate for information technology is set at 11 percent, and the following differential percentage rates are used for investments:

- Strategic information technology   25%
- Informational information technology   20%
- Transactional information technology   11%
- Infrastructure information technology   8%

This approach is successful in allocating different risk profiles to each type of investment. It would encourage infrastructure and discourage strategic information technology. It is rather a clumsy and misleading approach, as the hurdle rates are arbitrarily decided for all investments in a category. Successful use depends on the availability of accurate net cash flows for all projects, even for strategic and infrastructure investments. This approach leads to a culture of "doing it by the numbers" and forces the subjective aspects of the process to be folded into the numbers and thus indistinguishable from the benefits about which there is certainty. The result is often a loss of confidence in the accuracy of the numbers—which in fact occurred in this particular firm.

Value Flexibility

For a firm to implement an enabling infrastructure, it must value flexibility. The primary business benefit of an enabling infrastructure is the ability to produce a broader range of products more quickly and cheaply than competitors, without requiring further infrastructure investment. Obtaining this flexibility has a cost that business managers must view as investment in flexibility. It is similar to the idea of purchasing a financial option.[12] An investment is made in infrastructure as an option. If the option is called and applications are built utilizing the infrastructure, then the option is successful. The more applications exercising the option of the infrastructure, the better the investment. However, if the option isn't exercised, then the investment is wasted. Much research is under way to apply financial (or real) options theory to information technology infrastructure. So far, no practical techniques have appeared, although they will in time.

A practical way to implement the concept of an option to value flexibility is to identify the family of applications that may be required by the business. Then information technology management can determine and cost the infrastructure services required to enable those applications. The broader the family of applications specified by senior management, the more expensive the infrastructure option will be, leading to greater infrastructure capability in the form of more extensive services and a larger Reach and Range.

A member of the board of directors of a medium-sized bank explained his approach to buying information technology options with the example of Internet banking:

> I am not sure when or whether Internet banking will take off in our industry but we can't be left behind. I advocate buying the option by acquiring or building the infrastructure and expertise to give us a capability in the area. If and when Internet banking takes off we can ramp up quickly to deliver a product. If not we haven't bet the business. Acquiring capability and perhaps building a small pilot buys us the option which [we] can exercise in a hurry.[13]

In earlier chapters, we discussed three practical ways to specify a firm's required infrastructure capability: maxims, deals, and business transformations. Although not strictly methods of investment appraisal, they do set the agenda for investment appraisal and deserve comment, as they are all used successfully.

Maxims

The use of business and IT maxims as a lead-in to appraisal and justification ensures a trail of evidence from the strategic context of the firm, through business and information technology maxims, to a view of infrastructure. The process ultimately leads to investments in infrastructure capability. Once senior management has determined the infrastructure capability needed, then it is up to information technology management to build or acquire effective infrastructure at minimum cost and agreed-upon quality. This approach radically changes the appraisal approach, as senior management takes responsibility for specifying the required infrastructure capability. The focus of information technology management then is to implement the requirements at world-class levels of efficiency, to benchmark costs, and to provide the quality of infrastructure services needed to ensure the delivery of business capability. The appraisal process then moves from the need to justify the infrastructure, which is achieved via the maxim, to appraising the alternatives to determine the most efficient way to provide the capability.

Deals

Firms using the deals approach to infrastructure are adopting a more free-market process than firms using maxims. The deals approach is used where the locus of power is predominantly with the business units. Deals approaches to infrastructure are funded as an outcome of the CIO or the senior information technology managers going to all the business-unit managers to determine their needs. A suitable infrastructure is identified, and then funding is sought from some combination of the business-unit heads and corporate management.

Most often, the deals approach will lead to a utility infrastructure. For many firms, the deals approach is an excellent cultural fit and perhaps the only workable approach. The appraisal and justification is a negotiated process between information technology and business-unit management, with deal making occurring to trade off cost versus infrastructure capability.

However, if an enabling view of infrastructure is required, the deals approach is inappropriate, as it indicates a lack of mandate for extensive firmwide infrastructure investments. An enabling view would not be successfully implemented, nor its business value realized, due to the short-term and volatile nature of the deal-making process and the voluntary nature of funding. Either the firm needs to move to a maxim approach or review its business and IT maxims in the light of political reality.

To handle the appraisal and justification for infrastructure in a deals situation, the information technology manager acts as a broker bringing together a community of interested business areas who can benefit from sharing. DCF-type approaches are usually most appropriate, as there is often a clear case of cost savings from sharing, when compared with each business unit's going alone and acquiring separate infrastructures.

Business Transformations

Managers are constantly considering ways to significantly transform their businesses and make them more successful. In Chapter 8 we discussed the infrastructure requirements for four approaches to business transformation: reengineering, electronic commerce, international expansion, and knowledge management. New approaches will continue to emerge in the coming years; all of them need information technology infrastructure, and thus all provide a way to justify information technology infrastructure.

One of the most compelling motivations for justifying new infrastructure is to successfully complete a business transformation initiative. We've seen initiatives such as reengineering stall due to lack of information technology infrastructure, either firmwide or within a business unit. Once the barrier is confronted, the justification becomes straightforward, as the success of the entire initiative rests on the new infrastructure.

Firms with enabling infrastructures meet far fewer infrastructure barriers due to their more extensive and flexible services and their Reach and Range. Firms with less extensive infrastructures must consider the infrastructure capability during the business transformation initiative proposal. Appraising and justifying the infrastructure proposal is part of the transformation initiative justification, even though the infrastructure will often be more broadly applicable.

Recommendations: Infrastructure Investments by Views

Fundamentally different approaches to the management of information technology infrastructure are needed for different views of infrastructure. For each of the views, different approaches are needed—in areas including management expectations, strategic thinking, positioning of the information technology group in the organizational structure, and measures for performance, as well as the appraisal process.

Figure 9.2 contains our recommendations for the appraisal of information technology infrastructure investments. Recommendations are given for both firmwide and business-unit–specific infra-

View of Infrastructure

	Utility	Dependent	Enabling
Firmwide	Driven by cost cutting	Driven by corporate IT strategy	Driven by corporate strategic intent
	DCF	*Business case plus DCF value analysis*	*Maxims or value flexibility*
Business Unit	Driven by cost cutting	Driven by BU current strategy	Driven by BU strategic intent
	DCF	*Business case plus DCF value analysis*	*Maxims or value flexibility*

Figure 9.2   Recommendations for Appraisal of Information Technology Infrastructure

structures, which often have different characteristics. For both firmwide and business-unit utility infrastructures, the driver is cost cutting, and the appraisal should be made by traditional DCF approaches. Desirable utility infrastructures will lead to positive NPVs and acceptable IRRs based on cash flows with certain benefits.

Dependent business-unit infrastructures must be driven by the current strategies of the business unit, such as the desire for phone banking, which requires a different infrastructure than can be provided by the existing branch banking infrastructure. The appraisal and justification must be made as part of a business case, and we suggest using maxims or deals, depending on the firm. A powerful approach is to use maxims to provide the strategic motivation in the business case and then appraise using DCF value analysis. The DCF value analysis facilitates the trade-off required between the certain and subjective benefits intrinsic in a dependent view. For firms where there are insurmountable barriers to using maxims, the deals approach is recommended with DCF value analysis.

Dependent views of firmwide infrastructure are complex to implement, as they require the combination of the current strategies of all or many of the business units. These business-unit current strategies must be analyzed by the information technology group and through a corporate information technology strategy process to determine the infrastructure requirements to be shared. Firmwide infrastructures are based on the synthesis of the business cases of all the business units. Again, maxims are recommended, with DCF value analysis, although deals are quite common.

Enabling views of infrastructure are quite different. To take an enabling view, the firm must value flexibility, see information technology as a core competence, and take a long-term view. Therefore, the driver for taking an enabling view is the synthesis of the strategic intents of the firm and business units. It is the long-term nature of the strategic intents and associated goals that give credibility to a large investment in infrastructure. Whether appraising firmwide or business-unit enabling infrastructures, the firm must find a way to value the flexibility that is required. We have found maxims to be a most successful approach. Business maxims must be clear, succinct, and few in number and, most important, promulgated by the CEO. It is the top management expression of the business maxims, which lead to the information technology maxims, which lead to the view and capabilities of the infrastructure, that provides the trail of evidence and credibility required for enabling infrastructure justification. If maxims are not used, then another method to value flexibility is required.

The condition of the current information technology portfolio is an important investment consideration when investing in the new infrastructure. We now outline a practical way to assess the health of the total portfolio that is in place.

Assessing the Health of the Information Technology Portfolio

Assessing the health of the information technology portfolio requires two steps. First, assess the infrastructure capability (Reach and Range and infrastructure services) to determine the fit with the firm and business unit's strategic context. (This assessment of fit was the subject of Chapters 5, 6, and 7.) Second, the health of the applications that use the infrastructure must be assessed and is the subject of this section. The concept of the information technology applications Health Grid is introduced as a tool to assess the health of the portfolio.

To assess the health of the portfolio requires senior managers' value judgments based on measuring the management value, technical quality, investment, and importance of each of the major systems in the manager's domain. Each senior manager will judge the health of the portfolio differently, based on his or her specific needs and biases.

Assessing the health of the portfolio is important in a number of ways. An essential part of the information technology investment process is understanding and evaluating the current portfolio. Evaluating the health of the current portfolio provides a starting point for identifying problem areas and opportunities for better coverage of business needs. These problem areas and opportunities can then be translated into plans for investments in systems building or renewal.

We have applied the Health Grid as a vehicle to convey the required information to judge the health of the information technology portfolio. The Health Grid is based on the idea[14] that systems can be represented on a grid with technical quality on one axis and management value on the other.

Assessing the health of the portfolio also provides a vehicle for turning the two independent monologues often found between information technology managers and line managers into a meaningful dialogue. Used together, the Health Grid and the Management by Maxim process provide a base on which to develop a higher level of shared understanding. The Health Grid provides evidence that appeals to both business and technical personnel. It forms the basis for discussions on where the portfolio is (or is not) delivering value.

Constructing Health Grids is useful for systems supporting a functional area, a business process, or any other area of a business. The information technology managers of a large process manufacturing firm asked us to assess the health of their information technology portfolio, as they were puzzled. There was much dissatisfaction in the business with the value achieved from their information technology investment, but information technology management thought that the portfolio was fairly good. Figures 9.3 and 9.4 are Health Grids for the materials and operations functions in one business unit of the firm. The Health Grid contains information on four aspects of each system: investment, importance, technical quality, and management value.

Investment is the total cost of the information system in dollars. The diameters of the circles in Figures 9.3 and 9.4 are proportional to a year's investment in the system; for this firm, 1 centimeter is equivalent to $100,000. Investment in the system has three major components:

1. *Acquisition* is the up-front cost of building or purchasing, tailoring, and installing the system and includes major modifications made during the life of the system.

2. *Operations* is the annual cost of running the system.

3. *Maintenance* is the annual cost of maintaining and performing minor modifications.

The technical quality of a system has a number of characteristics, including data accuracy and reliability, technical support, understandable reports and screens, structured code, speedy response times, and little downtime.

The importance of the system for assisting the business unit in meeting its goals is a key attribute of any system. We assess importance using a questionnaire and an interview with senior management of the area concerned. "System Importance" specifies the system's potential to generate value, whereas "Management Value" specifies the actual value delivered.

The management value of each system is the deliverable of the investment in terms of senior management perception. The management value describes how useful a system is to the senior manager in the performance of his or her job, which includes responsibility for the group, function, or process. Thus the view of the senior manager on the value of a system includes not only the direct value, but also implicitly the indirect value from use of the system by employees within the manager's domain. We've developed questionnaires to assess all the information presented on the Health Grids in Figures 9.3 and 9.4.

One telling question is: Has the system delivered management value in line with its importance? A healthy portfolio will have all the important systems delivering high management value. These important systems will have good technical quality and be used regularly. The investments in each system will represent a sensible resource allocation, with the important and high-management-value systems consuming the most funds.

The power of the Health Grid is to combine this information in ways for managers to then judge the portfolio's health. To aid this judgment, the grid is divided into four quadrants.[15] Systems in each of these quadrants have different characteristics, and different management action is suggested.

- *Nurture:* These systems are the lifeblood of the business unit. They provide high management value and have good

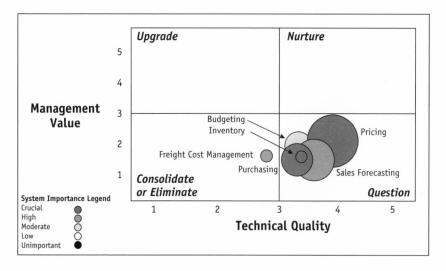

Figure 9.3   Information Systems Health Grid of the Materials Area

technical quality. They must be carefully nurtured, as they form a basis for the business to operate.

- *Upgrade:* These systems are rated highly by users on management value but are poor technically. They are potential business risks and require immediate attention.

- *Consolidate or Eliminate:* These systems have neither high management value nor good technical quality. They may have been of value once but are no longer useful and are also technically deteriorating. These systems need to be carefully examined for consolidation or elimination.

- *Question:* These systems are technically sound but have questionable management value as rated by senior managers. Systems can be in this quadrant for a number of reasons. For example, the system may be a technology looking for a business application that didn't quite fit. Or it could be that line managers and users didn't help specify the system or have failed to use or support it. Or it could be that the system once served a business need, but needs have changed. These systems need to be seriously questioned. Perhaps they can be modified to add more management value, or perhaps training is required to increase the use of a fundamentally good system. The system importance rating (crucial, high

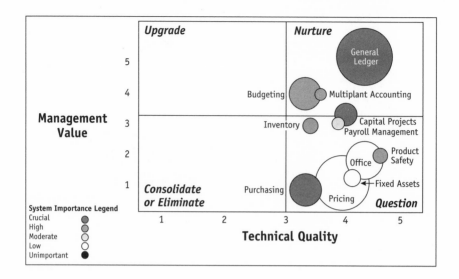

Figure 9.4   Information Systems Health Grid of the Operations Area

importance, moderate importance, and so on) is used as an indicator of the urgency and importance of corrective action.

For example, the Health Grid for the materials area in our manufacturing firm has six systems. Five of the systems, and most of the investment, fall into the "Question" quadrant (see Figure 9.3). The system importance legend identifies each of the systems as being of either crucial, high, or moderate importance to the business-area management. Although pricing is technically good, it is also relatively costly and provides only limited management value. However, senior materials management views pricing and sales as crucial to the business; therefore, action to update or replace is urgently needed.

At our first feedback meeting, the senior managers of the materials area judged the health of the portfolio as quite poor. In contrast, information technology management felt the health was reasonable given the good technical quality. The two groups were looking at different characteristics of the portfolio. The Health Grid was useful in highlighting this difference of judgment about the same set of systems and explained why there had been conflict.

The systems in Operations fall into both the "Question" and the "Nurture" quadrants (see Figure 9.4). General ledger, budgeting, multiplant accounting, and capital projects all provide significant management value. Furthermore, they are perceived as of crucial or

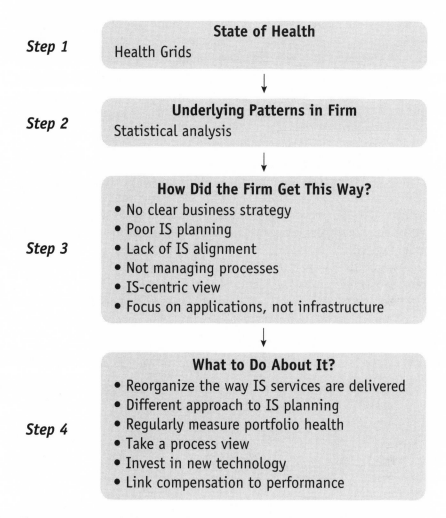

Step 1 **State of Health**
Health Grids

↓

Step 2 **Underlying Patterns in Firm**
Statistical analysis

↓

Step 3 **How Did the Firm Get This Way?**
- No clear business strategy
- Poor IS planning
- Lack of IS alignment
- Not managing processes
- IS-centric view
- Focus on applications, not infrastructure

↓

Step 4 **What to Do About It?**
- Reorganize the way IS services are delivered
- Different approach to IS planning
- Regularly measure portfolio health
- Take a process view
- Invest in new technology
- Link compensation to performance

Figure 9.5 Four Steps to Improving the Health of the Portfolio

high importance to the business and are candidates for careful nurturing. These systems are very important to the business. The purchasing system is perceived as delivering little management value despite its size, cost, and use. However, purchasing is crucial to the operation of the business, so urgent attention is needed to rectify this situation. For the manufacturing firm, the grids provided a basis on which the business and technology managers could work together to improve the firm's health.

Our approach to assessing the health of the information technology portfolio is summarized in Figure 9.5 as a four-step process.

We suggest that the health be assessed once every two years or before a large information technology investment decision is made. The first step uses the grids to assess the health of the portfolio. The second step statistically analyzes the data collected to produce the grid, to look for patterns. For example, analyzing the data used to produce Figures 9.3 and 9.4 revealed that there was no correlation between system importance and investment. Therefore, the process for allocating information technology investment was flawed, as generally the more important systems should have the most investment. Step 3 uses the information available to determine the causes of the current situation, and step 4 focuses on what to do about it. Too often, we've seen senior managers continue to approve large investments in information technology when the track record of producing value is poor. Before new investment is made, the processes or behavior that caused limited business value from previous investments must be changed.

Subsequent to our analysis of the health of the portfolio at the process manufacturing firm, the following changes and investments were made to improve the portfolio:

1. An extensive PC and LAN infrastructure was implemented.

2. Lotus Notes was implemented with a dedicated server. (Lotus Notes is used for messaging, text, discussion databases, and some applications, such as customer complaints.)

3. The integrated package SAP R3 is currently being implemented with a dedicated server using the existing PC and LAN infrastructure. As the CIO summarized, "Basically we are using SAP for transaction processing and Lotus Notes for information and knowledge management."

4. The management of the new systems (client and server hardware, software, training) has changed. The corporate information technology group now performs a facilities management role while information technology staff in the business unit manages the systems.

CHAPTER 10

Leading and Managing the New Infrastructure

When the international financial services firm InterFinCo shifted from deal making to Management by Maxim (Chapter 7), it needed new governance processes. Implementing Management by Maxim meant more focus on balancing firmwide processes and capabilities with those that remained the responsibility of each business unit. In the words of InterFinCo's director of international operations,

> We have made major changes in our governance processes, starting with executive committee responsibility for information technology infrastructure decisions across the firm. We will never get the governance and management responsibilities exactly right. In fact we struggle to know what "right" is—what is right for one firm is not necessarily right for us. We are constantly reviewing how decisions are made to make sure the right people are involved in the right decisions—and that those decisions encourage the behaviors we want. Then we check to see that the management responsibilities across our diverse and strong business units are in place. In our tough markets we know we need the best possible combination of executive and business responsibilities, technology leadership, and practices and incentives that result in innovation in products and services, and in sharing our expertise and best practices.

The governance of this technology-dependent business will never be easy and will need constant management attention. There are multiple layers of businesses, technologies, and management that must be integrated and balanced to encourage innovation while maintaining the necessary consistency in products and services. This means constant attention to management and governance processes, particularly the infrastructure component of the information technology portfolio. InterFinCo has made a sound start, with a creative approach to both capturing economies of scale and encouraging innovation in the business units.

InterFinCo's executive management team has articulated the business role for information technology. Its members have specified business and IT maxims, and set the policy and goals for information technology infrastructure across the firm, including principles to guide an agreed-upon information technology architecture.

The CIO and the corporate information technology group develop the information technology architecture and standards for the shared infrastructure. This is done following the principles set by the executive committee, after consultation with the business-unit managing directors and their senior information technology managers.

InterFinCo's firmwide infrastructure is maintained, supported, and paid for centrally and is available for use by all business units. All business units are also encouraged to use any technology they like, from their own budgets, to create local applications. Often, business units develop or acquire stand-alone applications quickly, without any reference to the firmwide architecture and standards.

Each year the CIO conducts a study to find successful local applications that have been used in various parts of the organization. These applications are assessed for their suitability for wider implementation. The new applications are made robust by the corporate information technology group, often by porting to another hardware or software platform or by stress testing. They are then included in the firmwide infrastructure, where they are supported and funded centrally. Managers are then encouraged to consider them for their own business areas. The originating business units are delighted, as they no longer have to support the new systems and they now have others to share their cost.

This market leader is now more successful at generating value from information technology by using sensible governance processes and careful central coordination of the portfolio, recognizing and capitalizing on its competitive environment, culture, governance, and information politics. The new infrastructure and the associated architecture were used as a way to reduce costs and then share innovation. Over time, the infrastructure grew to capture and share innovative solutions.

The new infrastructure can be a powerful vehicle for innovation with new and current customers, suppliers, and alliance partners. But it requires careful and deliberate leadership and governance to ensure that successful innovations are not isolated incidents, that they are sustained and the learning from them captured to provide well-understood ways of creating new business.

The example of InterFinCo illustrates the powerful combination of governance and leadership—and some of its difficulties. The governance challenge is to have the right people making decisions to integrate the portfolio with strategy, while balancing the decision rights across multiple constituencies. In addition, each firm needs robust management and decision-making mechanisms that facilitate and sustain informed expectations of both business and information technology management. In this chapter, several examples from market leaders illustrate how these governance mechanisms are integrated with the structures and cultures of those businesses.

The leadership challenge is to set the agenda and ensure management practices that maximize return on information technology portfolio investments. Without senior management leadership, the best managers in the world will struggle to achieve superior business value from the information technology portfolio. We have consolidated the leadership responsibility of senior management into what we call the "Top Ten Leadership Principles," which together help generate superior business value from the new infrastructure. We estimate that, on average, these principles can achieve up to a 40 percent premium for the same level of investment. These leadership principles are also useful as a checklist to inform and evaluate the management practices of the firm's information technology portfolio.

Meeting governance and leadership challenges also rests on creating and sustaining informed business and information technology expectations. Let's explore why the expectations of these two groups often differ before outlining how some firms have brought these expectations closer together through their governance and leadership processes.

Shaping Informed Expectations

Most managers want their information technology investments to assist in the delivery of some combination of improved customer service, increased revenues, shorter cycle times, reduced costs, less paperwork, less inventory, faster product development, cross-selling opportunities, easier access to information for decision making, and synergies across their business. Most managers want to do this with the minimum of expense and disruption, within a short time frame, and keeping their future options open. It's no surprise that our research indicates that all these worthy objectives are rather difficult to achieve at the same time!

For many executive managers there is a gap between the rhetoric pervading the technologies now available and their conversion into a portfolio that creates value for the organization. Managers don't necessarily see the challenges of deploying the technologies they've read about into an integrated and tailored portfolio with capabilities appropriate for their firm. In turn, information technology management has often overpromised and underdelivered. These two situations provide fertile ground for a credibility gap.

The challenges for information technology management in fulfilling technology's promise to business are

- Ensuring that executive and business management shape information technology goals and expectations.

- Business and technology management's developing mutually agreed-upon expectations.

- Delivering systems that meet or surpass those expectations.

- Both executive managers and information technology managers' recognizing that the challenges are ongoing.

Decisions about the new infrastructure are the joint responsibility of executive and information technology management. Within this joint responsibility it is the role of senior management to articulate the firm's strategic intent and the required infrastructure capabilities. The role of information technology management is to help senior management determine and cost out the infrastructure capabilities and then provide those capabilities effectively. The Management by Maxim approach facilitates this joint responsibility. An intrinsic part of the process is information technology and executive management's dialogue resulting in the articulation, in business terms, of the expectations for the new infrastructure.

A key factor in the quality of the business and information technology dialogue is the nature of a firm's governance processes for the information technology portfolio.

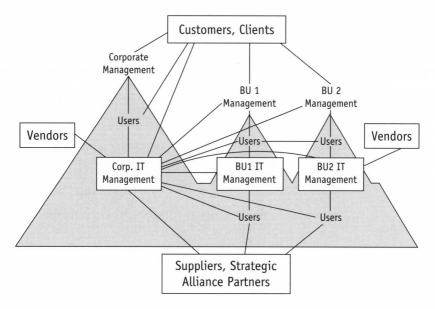

Figure 10.1   Multiple Constituencies in Managing Information Technology

Meeting the Governance Challenge

Firms that make well-considered investments in the new infrastructure usually have a careful and deliberate process of governance. This governance process balances decision rights[1] across multiple constituencies—for example, between corporate and business-unit management, between business and information technology executives, and between management and users—as these interests sometimes diverge. The complexity of these constituencies is illustrated in Figure 10.1. The number and orientation of the constituencies and the communication required leave plenty of room for different perceptions, different agendas, misunderstandings, and lack of coordination.

Many firms struggle with the roles and responsibilities of these different constituencies and put in place formal governance mechanisms, such as information technology councils or steering committees.

We describe how four market leaders have developed governance approaches that facilitated informed expectations and joint responsibility for decision making about the new infrastructure investments. These four exemplars of best practice are

- Fusing business and technology decision making through overlapping participation in global councils.

- Implementing a balance of executive committee and user management responsibilities.

- Integrating budget monitoring and standards setting.

- Linking governance mechanisms and leadership behaviors.

Each approach is focused on governing and developing an information technology portfolio to meet its specific business aspirations with the understanding that the aspirations, and thus the information technology portfolio, will continue to change.

Fusing Business and Technology at Citicorp

Citicorp's strategic context requires that business and information technology managers both have a sound understanding of their mutual challenges and responsibilities.[2] Citicorp is aiming for the fusion of its business and technology foci. To create this fusion in the high-priority consumer banking area, two overlapping committees that meet quarterly provide technology policy and oversight in the bank. The Global Consumer Council, chaired by the senior vice president of marketing, brings together the senior marketing managers and includes the senior technology officer, Citicorp's top information technology executive. The Global Consumer Technology Group, chaired by the senior technology officer, brings together the senior technology managers from the consumer banking area and includes the senior marketing vice president. The two groups have adjacent meeting times, and some of their meetings are held jointly. As the senior technology officer explains,

> Our marketers must listen to a new lexicon. If they cannot come to terms with the process of discovery of the significance of information technology to their business, they will no longer be Citibank employees. An increasingly important characteristic of bank employees in

> our world is immense curiosity about the outside world. For marketers, this includes curiosity about the fusion of technology and the banking businesses.

Key information technology decisions are made jointly by corporate and international operations. The corporate information systems group runs the global technology processes, while local information systems staff reports in to local businesses. However, all major expenditures must go through the office of the senior technology officer, who is also responsible for career-related decision making for information technology staff. These two sets of responsibilities provide powerful leverage for purposeful coordination of information technology policy and decision making. In Citicorp there is a major effort to transparently integrate these aspects of governance, decision making, and people management responsibilities.

Executive Committee Responsibility and User Management at DBS

The Development Bank of Singapore (DBS) provides a different emphasis in its approach to information technology governance, combining executive committee responsibility for long-term technology decision making with strong user leadership on specific projects.[3] One in five senior bank staff members are employed in Data Resources, the information technology group. The first head of Data Resources was, in his words, "a banker, not a technologist," as the bank wanted "somebody senior to head information technology because of its strategic importance to its business mission." Following the establishment of the Data Resources group and its integration with the business, the head was promoted. His successor was chosen for a combination of technical capabilities and a strong business focus.

The establishment of a business-led Data Resources group in the mid-1980s encouraged business-driven information technology infrastructure investments that were argued for at the firm's executive committee. In DBS, significant infrastructure decisions are part of the executive committee's responsibilities through the strategy-setting and budgeting processes. DBS competes predominantly through product leadership, and technology take-up is critical to this competitive strategy, particularly in the sophisticated technological base of banking and finance in Singapore. The DBS approach to technology decisions is to invest for the future, as described by the current Data Resources senior vice president:

> We view technology as strategic investments—to give us a competitive edge. That's the advantage of having a business manager take charge of information technology—we treat technology decisions as business decisions. . . . We are not afraid to be the first user of a new technology in the region. We justify information technology in terms of business capabilities, and strategic positioning, not merely cost savings.

The ongoing development of DBS's Customer Information System (CIS) illustrates two of the firm's goals for all information technology projects: They must be led by user management, and they must be completed in nine months. Systems projects are initiated and led by user departments, and user managers often spend several months full time on the projects they are leading. Concurrently, even large and complex systems are broken into nine-month cycles. The executive vice president for Corporate Banking and Data Resources outlines how these two features are an important part of the governance of information technology in DBS: "Letting users play a central role encourages them to make information technology work for their business, and gives them a greater stake in the successful implementation of the system. Also, since users are responsible for their bottom line, they can see the relationship between technology and the bottom line." As the Data Resources senior vice president wryly observes, "Nine months is a natural waiting time," and users become impatient if systems delivery takes longer than this. When the system affects several departments, a main user is identified. The strong user competence in technology projects is a result of the bank's heavy emphasis on staff training and development.

DBS is an exemplar of the integration of governance, information technology management, infrastructure justification approaches, and human resources management.

Integrating Budget Monitoring and Standards Setting at Southcorp Holdings

Southcorp Holdings has businesses in a number of distinct industries, including packaging, wine production and marketing, appliances, and water heaters.[4] Southcorp operates with a largely decentralized information technology structure. Each of the business groups is responsible for its own systems, with corporate information technology responsible for firmwide systems and the identification of information systems synergies across the firm. The corporate group is small, employing nine information technology professionals, and doesn't manage any large-scale systems.

The main role of Southcorp's corporate information technology group is facilitation, with the aim of identifying opportunities for sharing knowledge and resources across disparate businesses. The corporate group has the following responsibilities across the firm:

- Establishing the firm's overall information systems policy and strategic objectives

- Developing key information systems strategies

- Recommending information technology architecture and standards

- Reviewing acquisitions as part of due diligence

- Facilitating business group information systems strategies and activities

- Managing negotiations with information technology vendors

- Monitoring budgets and benchmarks

- Approving and supporting capital expenditure programs to go before the executive committee

Although Southcorp's general manager for information systems does not directly manage a large group of people, the governance and management of information technology at the corporate level ensure that considerable influence is exerted at both the corporate and the business-unit level through the last two responsibilities listed. The facilitation and coordination role is also a conduit for budget monitoring, benchmarking responsibilities, and guidance of capital expenditure requests to the executive committee.

Southcorp has limited synergies among its businesses but utilizes governance and management mechanisms to provide leadership across these businesses and to achieve economies of scale and expertise.

Linking Governance Mechanisms and Leadership Behavior

Joint planning committees, high-level steering groups, the rotation of business and information technology staff, and the devolution of applications development into business units have contributed to the integration of business and technology expectations in many organizations. However, few have gone as far as the Canadian-based insurance firm Sun Life in ensuring that future expectations are shaped by the reality—and limitations—of experience. In addition to Canada, Sun Life has major operations in Great Britain, Ireland, the United States, the Philippines, and Hong Kong.[5] The corporate information technology function provides infrastructure services (mainly communications and a data center) across the firm, and each national office has an information technology group responsible for local infrastructure and applications development. This division of responsibilities is aimed at forcing close cooperation and greater creativity between business and technology staff.

Like other firms, Sun Life has interlocking business and information technology committees at several levels of the business. However, Sun Life puts more effort than most into recording and disseminating the deliberations of these groups and making the content and outcomes readily accessible to both business and technology managers. The aim is to "make the whole more than the sum of its parts" by leveraging information technology, sharing knowledge, and fostering innovation. Information technology is seen as a cost-effective business investment, and there is a high level of knowledge of the value that technology brings to the business. This knowledge in turn feeds into business expectations which are adventurous but informed, and able to be openly discussed and negotiated.

A major contributor to this process since the early 1990s has been the president's review and the subsequent dissemination of "lessons learned." Each year, the president of Sun Life undertakes a personal review of a specific initiative, with advice from the corporate information systems planning group. These high-profile reviews result in the publication of "lessons learned," which are distributed to all locations. Sun Life sees this as integrating learning experiences into the processes of the firm. It provides an explicit mechanism for mutually informed expectations about the performance and value of the information technology portfolio to Sun Life's management.

Leading Governance Processes

Citicorp, DBS, Southcorp Holdings, and Sun Life have taken different approaches to governance. In our opinion, they represent best practice. Each approach is clearly integrated and consistent with that firm's unique strategic context, its business and IT maxims, and the governance of the firm as a whole. For example, a key component of strategy in Citicorp is to both widen and fuse the perspectives of marketers and technologists. Both the membership and the meeting arrangements of the Consumer and Consumer Technology groups are structured to meet this objective. Southcorp Holdings, though, is a diversified corporation where there is less synergy among the businesses and the corporate information systems group is small. However, the mechanism for the general manager for information systems to approve and present business-unit information technology capital expenditures to the executive committee is integral to the desired role of corporate monitoring, benchmarking, and coordination.

The role and membership of technology decision-making councils and committees often provide an indication of the awareness of the value of information technology infrastructure in a firm. In Chapter 1 we gave the example of InvestCo, which had just instituted an Information Technology Council after a two-year campaign by the CIO. In InvestCo there was initially little realization of the importance of firmwide infrastructure—or lack of such infrastructure—in the business units. There was resentment at the time about time spent in meetings and concerns about possible loss of autonomy in local decision making. After all, each InvestCo business had an information technology group providing the support for that business unit's products and services. However, the governance process needed to change in line with market realities. The CIO could not provide the information technology service needed to respond quickly to new products that were, in InvestCo's structure, essentially cross-business initiatives. InvestCo had to concurrently renew its business processes and business and technology decision making so that it would have the management infrastructure to tackle more agile competitors.

Some well-crafted processes that we've observed and recommend for information technology councils are as follows:

1. Operate an information technology council with membership from the executive committee, the CIO, and managing directors of busi-

ness units. Active participation in the council illustrates top management's commitment to effectively using information technology.

2. Ensure that the information technology council has responsibilities for the information technology strategy of the firm, including

- Articulating the business role of information technology in the firm.

- Linking the firm's strategic context and business and IT maxims.

- Understanding the firm's total information technology investment and portfolio.

- Setting the goals and policies for and owning the information technology infrastructure.

- Setting the principles that guide the firm's information technology architecture.

- Ensuring that there are mechanisms in place to monitor the costs of the information technology portfolio.

- Ensuring that there are mechanisms in place to track the benefits from investment in the information technology portfolio.

3. Operate business-unit technology councils with membership from the business-unit management committees and senior information technology managers from the business units. Responsibilities include the information technology strategy of the business units, including business-unit equivalents of each area mentioned in item 2 above.

Key Questions of Governance

Governance processes must be thought through and regularly revisited. We've synthesized a checklist of questions to help managers do this. Each constituency in the firm depicted in Figure 10.1

has some responsibilities for decision making, implementation, and use of the information technology portfolio. Check the process to ensure that each relevant constituency is included. When reading the questions, think through your firm's current governance arrangements and constituencies, and the current problem areas and hot spots.

- How do managers develop informed and realistic business expectations for information technology investments?

- What mechanisms are in place to sustain informed expectations of the key players in Figure 10.1?

- Does executive management shape the goals for information technology infrastructure investments?

- How do we ensure firmwide involvement, commitment, and acceptance of responsibility for the success of the new infrastructure?

- Are the current governance mechanisms consistent with the future directions of the firm?

- How do we shape behavior and attitudes that will facilitate and enable the achievement of those future directions?

- To what extent are governance mechanisms integrated with our firm's other business decision-making and governance processes?

- How did we structure our governance mechanisms to ensure the contribution to informed decisions of the right people, at the right levels, in a timely manner?

- To what extent do the managers making business decisions understand their implications and consequences for the information technology portfolio?

- To what extent do the managers making information technology–related decisions understand their business implications and consequences?

We now summarize the book's messages on how to generate business value through the new infrastructure by identifying the Top Ten Leadership Principles, which incorporate these governance issues.

The Top Ten
Leadership Principles

The leadership principles that we enumerate in the following pages provide advice for senior managers who want to drive business value from their information technology investments. These principles synthesize the findings of our research and our observations of market leaders into successful management practices. We suggest that senior management use the Top Ten as a checklist to inform and audit the way their firm manages and governs its information technology portfolio.

1. Take a Portfolio Approach to Meet Strategic Goals While Balancing Risk Versus Return

Apply the portfolio approach, which has proven so successful in financial investments, to information technology investments. Different mixes of information technology portfolios are appropriate for different firms, depending on their strategic contexts. At Johnson & Johnson, Citibank, Sun Life, and the other market leaders described in this book, senior business and information technology managers have worked together to identify and implement the unique information technology portfolio for their business. A portfolio approach encourages senior management to understand the relative size of the entire portfolio, as well as the different management objectives, proportions, and risk-return profiles of the different parts of the portfolio.

When they take a portfolio approach, firms need a central coordinating group to oversee all information technology investment in the firm. This group can either proactively determine the desired mix in the portfolio or assess proposed projects for their effect on the balance of the portfolio and strategic goals. For example, in tough times, gently bias the portfolio away from more risky, more expansive strategic information technology investments that are volatile in their production of business value.

With a portfolio approach, managers shift the emphasis from the information technology project to the whole information technology portfolio. Firms will still use and implement information technology in projects but actively manage the total portfolio to deliver a return in the context of the business strategy. Assess projects against the usual criteria of business need and financial and technical risk, as well as costs and benefits, but treat them as part of the firmwide information technology portfolio, which is the ultimate vehicle for business value. It is not necessary for each project to meet the firm's desired level of return, but they must build together to achieve the return.

If there are no synergies between the business units, then it is appropriate to have separate portfolios for, and managed by, each business unit. However, if there is potential for synergies (such as cost savings through sharing or cross-selling), then a person or group with enough standing to get commitment and buy-in must work with all constituencies to take a firmwide portfolio view.

The firm can balance risk versus return for the entire firm when taking a portfolio approach. Like any investment portfolio, this balance will depend on the firm's goals, capabilities, and attitude toward risk. To manage the portfolio, senior management must understand the characteristics of different types of information technology investments (strategic, informational, transactional, and infrastructure, as in Figure 3.2). This process is analogous to assessing the characteristics of different classes of financial investment (bonds, blue chip stock) to balance a financial portfolio.

In taking a portfolio perspective, managers

- Assess the existing and proposed information technology investments, checking the level of alignment of the portfolio as changes occur in the strategic context. Compare the information technology portfolio with benchmarks in Chapter 2 (see Figure 2.4). Check two aspects of alignment and benchmarking: the amount of resources (percentage revenues or expenses) invested in information technology and the mix of types of management objectives within the portfolio (strategic, informational, transactional, and infrastructure).

- Check the health of the applications. How healthy is your application portfolio? (See Chapter 9.)

- Check the infrastructure capability. Do you have the appropriate infrastructure services and Reach and Range? (See Chapter 5.)

2. Integrate the Portfolio with Strategy, Using Management by Maxim

Together, business and information technology management must link the information technology portfolio to the strategic context of the firm. The link is a two-way proposition: strategic context driving information technology decisions and the portfolio providing opportunities for new current strategies. Managing by Maxim helps managers identify the firm's long-term needs for the infrastructure investment component of the portfolio. Chapters 6 and 7 describe the phases of the Management by Maxim process, how to overcome barriers to implementation, and situations where Management by Deal is more appropriate.

Complement Management by Maxim with business planning processes where each business unit's plan identifies the information technology implications of its strategies. Business managers should write the information technology component into their business plans with the help of information technology managers or consultants. Forcing business management to take responsibility will ensure solid linking between the strategic context and the information technology portfolio. In addition, the corporate information technology group must be responsible for providing the firmwide infrastructure to facilitate economies of scale, sharing of information, cross-selling, electronic commerce, and integration. Use mechanisms such as information technology councils to govern the firmwide infrastructure and check for synergies among the business-unit portfolios.

3. Determine Required Service Levels and Outsource Commodities to Save Costs While Retaining Architecture Responsibility

Business and information technology management should carefully specify the information technology services required and determine appropriate measures for each service. These measures become the basis for service-level agreements to assess the performance of the information technology provider, whether internal or outsourced.

If the service is vital and not a commodity, such as a bank's consolidated customer database, use an internal information technology group—particularly where information technology is a core competence. Outsourcing places more barriers in the way of the difficult process of integrating the information technology provider and the business. For example, firms that outsource more information technology have longer times to bring new products to market (see Chapter 3). The longer time is partly due to outsourcing's adding another layer of complexity to the communications between business and provider. When information technology requirements are not known precisely, outsourcing is bound to increase time to market. Also, if the service is vital, then the skills required to manage this asset should be nurtured and developed as a core competence within the organization.

If the service is a commodity, or if the firm's business strategy is to be the low-cost producer, test the marketplace to identify the best source, because outsourcing usually results in lower information technology costs (see Chapter 3). Once you have specified service levels, outsource as many services as possible, using performance-based contracts for relatively short periods (three years).

Use a mix of sourcing. At firms where information technology is a core competence, the number of services outsourced will be fewer and focused on commodities such as PC/desktop maintenance or standard telecommunications networks. For other firms, particularly those with a cost focus, outsource more of the services. Where time to market and synergies between business units are important, the services critical to achieving these goals (such as managing shared customer databases) should be retained in house.

Never outsource the decision rights or the setting of the information technology architecture to any other group, be it service provider or consultant. Drive the architecture from the strategic intent of the firm. Information technology architecture is a key decision for the firm's competitive position, and outsourcing it would be like outsourcing the decision of what capabilities the firm should have. Setting an architecture requires a partnership between business and information technology management. Outsource the provision of the service only after that architecture is set.

4. Agree on Business Value Indicators and Responsibilities

As for any investment portfolio, managing the information technology portfolio requires the providers and consumers to agree on indicators of success. Different strategic contexts lead to firms' having different levels of information technology investment, different portfolio makeups, and different indicators of success. Each year, as part of the justification process, business and information technology management should agree on the appropriate indicators for the business value of the portfolio and who is responsible.

Use a set of indicators that balances lagging measures such as financial performance with leading indicators such as operational performance. Use as a starting point the hierarchy of business value measures in Chapter 3 (Figure 3.1), tailored and supplemented to suit. The value of the information technology is more directly evaluated by the measures in the lower two levels of the hierarchy, whereas many other factors as well as information technology affect the measures in the top two levels. Although it is not possible to determine the exact business value of the portfolio, this approach provides strong evidence. Without agreement on these measures, there is no way to track the success of the management of the information technology portfolio.

Determine who has organizational responsibility for both costs and benefits, and include them in those individuals' performance appraisal systems. Typically, some type of joint responsibility between the business and technology managers works best. Holding the information technology group responsible for both costs and benefits is doomed to failure. The primary role of the information technology group is to help the business determine its information technology needs and then meet those needs with systems delivered at world-class cost and quality levels. The responsibility for information technology costs can lie with the information technology group, the business, or an outsourcer. Where the information technology portfolio is actively managed by the business, it is sensible that the business also take responsibility for information technology cost. Ultimately, business management must take responsibility for delivering the benefits, as it is the actions of the business, using the systems in place, that generate the value.

A powerful approach is a partnership in which the business takes responsibility for specifying the information technology needs and the delivery of the business benefits. The information technology group then takes responsibility for delivering (either insourced or outsourced) the information technology capabilities on time and budget at the agreed-upon quality levels. Whatever approach is taken, the critical point is that a specific group or person has responsibility for the information technology costs, and a specific group or person has responsibility for the benefits. Too many organizations fail to specify who is responsible for either, and in the end, no responsibility is taken.

5. Appraise, Justify, and Manage Infrastructure Separately

Manage the information technology infrastructure and the applications that use the infrastructure separately, as they have different characteristics. Infrastructures have long lives, are shared by multiple business units and many applications, and must be put in place before the precise business needs are known. The applications will change often and are specific to a function or business process. Different approaches to specification, justification, management, and evaluation are necessary for infrastructure and applications. Therefore, separate processes for management are necessary—but the two processes must interlink.

Centrally coordinate the management process for the infrastructure, and involve all constituencies. The process takes a long-term, strategic view, focusing on issues of integration, synergies, shared services, economies of scale, and consensus. The justification and investment decisions are complex and require a combination of informed judgment and instinct, as well as strategic and financial analysis. Clearly specify firmwide infrastructures so that more tailored local infrastructures can be added in a compatible way.

Ensure that the management processes of specification, justification, and implementation occur at the point of organizational focus for the business process and are financial and business decisions. The process for managing applications is usually more clear-cut than for managing infrastructure. The application must have a clear business need, cost, and benefit. The precise processes for the management of infrastructures and applications will depend on the firm's governance characteristics. Managing infrastructures and applications separately is important in encouraging infrastructure sharing and reuse, and in realizing the portfolio's strategic opportunities.

6. Actively Manage Conversion Effectiveness

Firms that achieve better business value from the same level of information technology investment have better conversion effectiveness. Better conversion effectiveness occurs because of a strong information technology management culture that has a mature and deliberate approach to generating maximum value. See Chapter 3 for more details.

Don't increase information technology investment without first assessing the firm's conversion effectiveness. Increasing the investment in information technology in a situation of poor conversion effectiveness is likely to lead to serious problems and wasted resources.

Actively manage and measure conversion effectiveness. Firms that achieve better business value from information technology investments have the following characteristics of stronger conversion effectiveness:

- Top management commitment to information technology

- Less internal political turbulence

- More satisfied system users

- More integrated business and information technology planning

- More experience with information technology

Excelling in these five characteristics relative to competitors can increase the business value from the same level of information technology investment by more than 40 percent. Smart users of the new infrastructure often provide differentiation by under- or overinvesting relative to competitors. They are smart because they extract every last modicum of business value from their investments. Improving conversion effectiveness requires active management of the five characteristics. Although these characteristics aren't all that is required, they are indicative of an effective and business-focused information technology management culture.

7. Manage the Benefits and Learn from the Implementation

Two activities are critical for improving the business value achieved from information technology investments: managing the benefits and reviewing completed projects. Both activities are fundamental but often not well done. First, put a purposeful benefits management process in place to identify what benefits are expected and delivered, and who is responsible. The key is to track benefits over time so that midproject adjustments can be made if necessary. Second, do a postimplementation review to examine what went well and where you can learn for the future. Unfortunately, few firms seem able to conduct postimplementation assessments without turning them into witch hunts. The guilty parties or perhaps scapegoats are pilloried, potential organizational learning is lost, and the disincentives for any form of innovation are clear.

We recommend that managers put in place a benefits management process, identifying the person or group responsible for achieving the benefits identified in the appraisal process, and then carefully track the benefits gained (or not achieved). The named person or group should be a business manager or area that funded the investment and whose business benefits from the new systems. We've seen such a process work successfully at BP Australia. The agenda for capturing and tracking benefits is clear and monitored regularly. The named accountabilities increase the likelihood of capturing the benefits, as the responsibilities and incentives are clear. If a manager becomes concerned about achieving the benefits, this is reported and discussed, and commitments and accountabilities are renegotiated if necessary. But the process is transparent to all parties. This tracking process minimizes slippage in organizational memory, as there is a shared understanding of why the systems were implemented in the first place and an ongoing and overt commitment to cashing in on the benefits.

Managers should review the implementation in terms of agreed-upon expectations, in the spirit of organizational learning. What agreements were made as part of the appraisal and approval processes concerning cost, time, quality, and functionality? Which of these did you achieve and which did you not achieve? Why and how did you achieve these agreements? What insights can you gain into successful management practices? How and why did you fail to achieve some agreements? What can you learn from the delays and problems? How can you use the learning you've gained in future implementations, and how can you add to your knowledge base of good practices? Compile a list of successful practices from the review process, and use these to guide future projects. Sun Life of Canada's structured process of the president's review and "lessons learned" is a powerful approach.

8. Manage Information Politics

Effective management of information technology infrastructure requires careful understanding and management of the firm's information politics.[6] Both business and information technology management often make poor assumptions about how people in the firm generate, process, and use information and about their attitudes toward sharing information. For example, the manufacturing director of consumer product manufacturer championed the creation of a firmwide customer database, including reactions of current customers to new products. Information technology management incorrectly assumed that all parts of the business were positively disposed to sharing their information. But several areas of the firm, including marketing, either overtly refused to be involved or scuttled the project more quietly.

These assumptions are often poorly based, and the reward systems, promotion patterns, and behaviors modeled by management don't always encourage cooperative efforts across businesses, products, or customer groupings. In some firms, information gained by one manager creates a competitive advantage in internal promotions. Firms with cultures where there is more internal competitiveness and political turbulence are poor converters of information technology investment into business value.

Appreciating the dynamics of information politics is essential when planning the development of information technology infrastructure capabilities, as destructive behaviors can make the investment not worth the effort. For example, two particular situations that inhibit business value are

- Where individual business functions define their own information needs and report only limited information to the business unit or firm. In our introductory example (Chapter 1), the managers in InvestCo defined their own information needs and implemented individual systems that supported these. The business units saw themselves as completely separate entities, though the market now demanded different behavior. InvestCo's reward systems were geared to the performance of a manager's own business unit. We've seen other firms where performance bonuses were tied to the financial performance of each business unit, with no consideration of firmwide achievements. This practice encourages a high level of internal competitiveness, increases the disincentives for cooperation, and in turn reduces the likelihood that pertinent information will be shared across business areas.

- Where there is no policy about use of and access to critical information, leaving individuals to obtain and manage their own information. Professional services, such as law and consulting firms, are often interesting studies in contrasts. In some law firms where the professional or partner "owns" the client, there is minimal sharing of information; the incentives militate against this. In consulting firms, such as Ernst & Young, Andersen Consulting, and Booz•Allen & Hamilton,[7] though, there are more open processes identifying the key information elements for each assignment. Information systems support the tracking of client contacts and experiences into knowledge bases, where the information is regularly reused for business advantage. The sharing of information is expected, and can be made part of the appraisal process and rewarded. Avoiding the sharing of information is regarded as inappropriate behavior. In ReInsureCo (Chapter 8), we saw that the extent and nature of an individual's contribution to the firm's knowledge base was a key criterion in every employee's appraisal. Consistent and constructive management of information and politics, where reinforced by appropriate governance, reporting, and reward structures, creates an environment where investment in capabilities across business and functional groups is more likely to deliver business value.

9. Implement Transparent Governance Processes

Governance processes are an important part of achieving business value from information technology investments. They provide transparent pathways for different levels of involvement, decision making, and the allocation and acceptance of responsibilities. Carefully think through governance processes to ensure that they facilitate the achievement of the type of business value sought from the firm's information technology investments and are consistent with the governance of the firm. For example, the governance processes of Citicorp and Southcorp Holdings, discussed earlier in this chapter, differ in their focus and distribution of responsibilities. However, each is consistent with that firm's strategic context and business and IT maxims, and effective in terms of the achievement of business goals.

Governance processes provide the mechanisms that enable business and technology executives, managers, and professionals to integrate business and technology planning, implement and monitor key business and technology initiatives, and track and learn from their effectiveness.

10. Start with Lower-Risk Transactional Systems

Transactional systems are the most reliable generators of business value in the information technology portfolio and will generally provide a reliable and acceptable return on their investment. As with new investors of any kind, start out with the lower-risk, more reliable choices. When building or integrating a total information technology portfolio for the first time, initially bias your investments to the reliable and lower-risk transactional systems supported by modest infrastructure capabilities. Use the same approach when replacing an aging portfolio. Transactional systems are also less sensitive to conversion effectiveness. Firms scoring low on any of the elements of conversion effectiveness also benefit from biasing their portfolio toward transactional information technology.

Differentiation Through Executive Leadership

Senior management responsibility is integral to achieving business value from the new infrastructure. Information technology decision-making is the joint responsibility of executive and information technology management. These decisions and their implementation either help or hinder the achievement of the firm's strategies. Management by Maxim provides a way to proceed in engaging business and information technology management in focused and sustained dialogue to deliver the capabilities the business needs. Management by Maxim is facilitated by governance processes that apportion rights, responsibilities, and incentives in line with strategic objectives. The quality of executive leadership for the new infrastructure will become a source of competitive differentiation.

List of Participating Companies

We owe thanks to the insights and frankness of many managers from more than eighty businesses who spent time with us working through their information technology management and decision-making approaches. They provided us with detailed data and descriptions about their business and technology investments and performance. We are very grateful to all these firms and the many executives who met with us. We would particularly like to acknowledge those who participated in the intensive and time consuming Infrastructure Study funded by IBM Consulting Group:

ANZ Banking Group
BP Asia Pacific
BP Australia
Brashs Holdings
Caltex Australia
Carlton & United Breweries (Fosters)
Citibank Asia Pacific
Coles Myer (including Kmart and Target department stores)
Commonwealth Bank of Australia
Development and Commercial Bank of Malaysia
Development Bank of Singapore
Hoffmann-LaRoche Switzerland

ICI Australia
Johnson & Johnson (Asia and Pacific)
Johnson & Johnson International
Maybank of Malaysia
Metway Bank
Monier/PGH
National Australia Bank
Ralston Purina
Royal Automobile Club of Victoria (RACV)
S. G. Warburg
Southcorp Holdings
Sun Life Assurance Company of Canada
Times Publishing
UNUM Corporation
Woolworth Australia (incorporating Safeway)

We also thank executives at more than thirty firms who participated in the study of international business operations and the Melbourne Business School case study program. We are particularly grateful to Amcor, Citicorp, and Honda, who have been very generous in allowing us to draw on and share their experiences.

Checking Your Level of Alignment

To assess your firm's level of alignment between information technology and strategic context, we suggest the following diagnostic. It is quick, easy to use, and from our experience with hundreds of executives, a reliable indicator of the urgency for action—particularly if several senior managers complete the questions. We suggest that you use this at your next firm management meeting, retreat, or conference, and ask many managers to provide responses. We've found that the results are an excellent stimulant to discussion and action to find out why alignment is poor or excellent.

You might first ask each participant to indicate his or her area of responsibility, in particular differentiating business and technology managers. There are ten questions in Figure A2.1, each requiring a response ranging from "Always True" (1) to "Never True" (5). An answer of 3 indicates a firm where the statement is sometimes true and sometimes not.

1. *Senior management has no vision for the role of information technology.*

   Senior management isn't involved in setting the broad directions for the use of information technology in the firm. Rather, it's the responsibility of information technology management or middle-level line management.

	Always True				Never True
1. Senior management has no vision for the role of IT.	1	2	3	4	5
2. The IT group drives IT projects.	1	2	3	4	5
3. There is no IT component in the divisions' strategy.	1	2	3	4	5
4. Vital information necessary to make decisions is often missing.	1	2	3	4	5
5. Islands of automation exist.	1	2	3	4	5
6. Management perceives little value from computing.	1	2	3	4	5
7. A "them and us" mentality prevails.	1	2	3	4	5
8. IT doesn't help for the hard tasks.	1	2	3	4	5
9. It's hard to get financial approval for IT projects.	1	2	3	4	5
10. Senior management sees outsourcing as a way to control IT.	1	2	3	4	5
	Average				

Figure A2.1   Diagnostic to Assess Alignment

2. *The information technology group drives major information technology projects.*

The information technology group drives all new computing projects in terms of idea generation, specifications, financial justification, and implementation.

3. *There is no information technology component in the divisions' or business units' strategic plans.*

The business units' strategic plans are silent on the information technology needs to support or enable the strategies. In these cases, the information technology issues are delegated to the information systems groups.

4. *The vital information necessary to make management decisions is often missing.*

In the daily process of making important management decisions, the vital information that would significantly help make a better decision isn't available, current, or readily accessible.

5. *Islands of automation and information exist.*

The organization has several different information technology portfolios in different areas, businesses, or departments that aren't compatible. Thus information and processes cannot easily be shared or linked.

6. *Management perceives little value from computing.*

Deep down, do the firm's managers perceive or measure little business value from information technology investments?

7. *A "them and us" mentality prevails.*

A "them and us" mentality exists between the information technology group and the business. There is a general lack of confidence that "they" really understand the issues.

8. *Information technology doesn't help for the hard tasks.*

For the really difficult tasks (employment decisions, pricing decisions, timing decisions) in the firm, the information systems don't really help.

9. *It's hard to get financial approval for information technology.*

It's always difficult to get financial approval for information technology investments, particularly infrastructure investments, due to _____. (Fill in the blank to fit your firm.)

10. *Senior management sees outsourcing as a way to control information technology.*

Contracting out the provision of information technology services is adopted by senior management as a way to control the investment and use of information technology in the firm.

Once Figure A2.1 has been completed, calculate the overall average; the average score across many firms is 2.8. The following are general indicators of urgency:

- **Greater than 4:** This indicates a high level of alignment. Processes are working well and must be codified for future use.

- **Greater than 3 and less than 4:** This is good-level alignment, but there are areas that need attention.

- **Greater than 2 and less than 3:** Alignment needs attention.

- **Greater than 1 and less than 2:** Alignment needs urgent attention.

Calculating the Components of Infrastructure View

Firms can calculate the components of their infrastructure view using the five items listed in Chapter 4 (see the list on page 103). Although three of the items are self-explanatory, two of the items, numbers 3 and 4, require further explanation. This appendix contains details of how to calculate motivation for information technology infrastructure justification (item 3) and how to calculate Reach and Range (item 4).

Calculating Motivation for Information Technology Infrastructure Justification

A series of questions in Figure A3.1 identifies the view of infrastructure adopted by board and investment committees. In your answers, consider the last two years of information technology

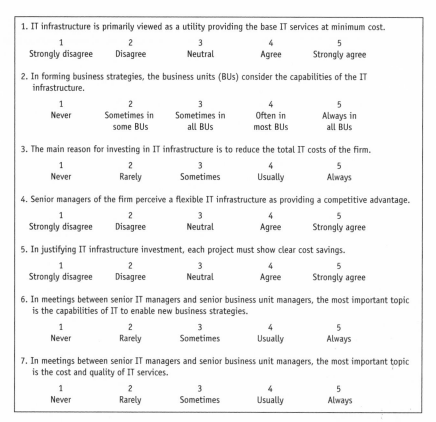

1. IT infrastructure is primarily viewed as a utility providing the base IT services at minimum cost.

1	2	3	4	5
Strongly disagree	Disagree	Neutral	Agree	Strongly agree

2. In forming business strategies, the business units (BUs) consider the capabilities of the IT infrastructure.

1	2	3	4	5
Never	Sometimes in some BUs	Sometimes in all BUs	Often in most BUs	Always in all BUs

3. The main reason for investing in IT infrastructure is to reduce the total IT costs of the firm.

1	2	3	4	5
Never	Rarely	Sometimes	Usually	Always

4. Senior managers of the firm perceive a flexible IT infrastructure as providing a competitive advantage.

1	2	3	4	5
Strongly disagree	Disagree	Neutral	Agree	Strongly agree

5. In justifying IT infrastructure investment, each project must show clear cost savings.

1	2	3	4	5
Strongly disagree	Disagree	Neutral	Agree	Strongly agree

6. In meetings between senior IT managers and senior business unit managers, the most important topic is the capabilities of IT to enable new business strategies.

1	2	3	4	5
Never	Rarely	Sometimes	Usually	Always

7. In meetings between senior IT managers and senior business unit managers, the most important topic is the cost and quality of IT services.

1	2	3	4	5
Never	Rarely	Sometimes	Usually	Always

Figure A3.1   Information Technology Infrastructure Motivation

infrastructure investment cases put to senior management and discussions between business and information technology managers.

We've found that the answers to these questions are good indicators of the approach to information technology justification by firms taking different views. Ask as many business and information technology managers as you can to complete the questions. High scores on the odd-numbered questions indicate a utility view, whereas high scores on the even-numbered questions indicate an enabling view. The justification benchmark equals

$$\frac{(Q2 + Q4 + Q6)}{3} + \left[6 - \frac{(Q1 + Q3 + Q5 + Q7)}{4} \right]$$

where Q1, Q2, and others are the answers to the questions 1, 2, and so on, on a scale of 1 to 5. It is often instructive to compare the

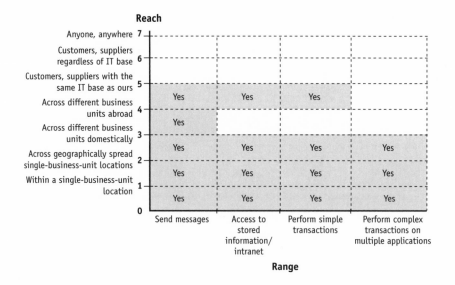

Figure A3.2   Company X's Reach and Range

answers from the information technology professionals in the firm with those of the business managers. Significant differences are a strong indicator of a poor partnership between the two groups, which often leads to poor alignment of strategy and the information technology portfolio.

Calculating Reach and Range

In the following example, the Reach and Range score is calculated for company X. Figure A3.2 shows a plot of company X's Reach and Range.

When calculating the Reach and Range score, each level of Range (each column) should be considered in isolation. For a given Range, there are seven levels of Reach, or seven groups to which the company can extend that Range capability. The first four levels of Reach are groups *internal* to the company. The final three levels of Reach are groups *external* to the company.

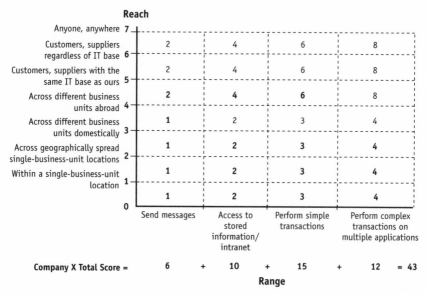

Figure A3.3 Calculating Reach and Range

To facilitate comparison, a formula was developed to convert the plot into a score ranging from 0 to 100, using the grid in Figure A3.3 and a simple point counting procedure. As a company extends its Reach for a particular Range capability, it accumulates "points." In providing the most basic Range capability, "Send messages," a company accumulates 1 point for each internal group to which it can send messages, and 2 points for each external group to which it can send messages (see Figure A3.3).

Hence, each cell in the Reach and Range grid represents a value that may contribute to the Reach and Range score. The cell values are shown in Figure A3.3. Simply add the points for each level of Reach and Range provided. If a company was able to provide complete Reach and Range, it would score the maximum 100 points. Company X's points, totaling 43, are shown in boldface type in Figure A3.3.

As it is more difficult to extend a service to external groups than to internal groups, due to such issues as security, standardization, and connectivity, an external connection is given twice the weight of an internal connection.

As it is more difficult to extend Reach as the Range capability moves from left to right on Figure A3.3, due to such issues as incompatible systems, politics, security, and data incompatibilities, the four levels of Range are weighted 1, 2, 3, and 4.

To calculate a firm's Reach and Range, first circle the cells in Figure A3.3 that represent the current Reach and Range. Then count the points for each cell to get a score between 0 and 100. To put a score in context, compare the mean Reach and Range scores in Figures 4.6 and 4.8 in Chapter 4 for firms in our study. Of the firms covered by the study, the highest Reach and Range score was 80 and the lowest, 9.

Clusters of Infrastructure Services

This appendix lists the 25 infrastructure services we identified while working with the companies listed in Appendix 1. Here they are grouped by functionality into 8 management clusters.

Applications Management

7. Manage firmwide or business-unit applications and databases

15. Develop business-unit–specific applications (usually on a charge-back or contractual basis)

17. Electronic provision of management information (e.g., EIS)

18. Manage business-unit–specific applications

20. Develop and manage electronic linkages to suppliers or customers

21. Develop a common systems development environment

23. Provide multimedia operations and development (e.g., video-conferencing)

25. Provide firmwide electronic support for groups (e.g., Lotus Notes)

Communications Management

1. Manage firmwide communications network services

2. Manage groupwide or firmwide messaging services

12. Manage firmwide or business-unit workstation networks (e.g., LANs, POS)

Data Management

9. Provide data management advice and consultancy services

19. Manage firmwide or business-unit data, including standards

IT Education

5. Provide technology advice and support services

22. Provide technology education services (e.g., training)

Services Management

6. Manage, maintain, support large-scale data processing facilities (e.g., mainframe operations)

8. Perform IS project management

10. Perform IS planning for business units

13. Manage and negotiate with suppliers and outsourcers

24. Provide firmwide intranet capability (e.g., videoconferencing)

IT R&D

14. Identify and test new technologies for business purposes

Security

4. Provide security, disaster planning, and business recovery services for firmwide installations and applications

16. Implement security, disaster planning, and recovery for business units

Standards Management

3. Recommend standards for at least one component of IT architecture (e.g., hardware, operating systems, data, communications)

11. Enforce IT architecture and standards

Notes

Chapter 1

1. See T. Davenport, with L. Prusack, *Information Ecology* (New York: Oxford University Press, 1997).

2. D. G. Copeland, "Information Technology for First Mover Advantage: The U.S. Airline Experience" (DBA diss., Harvard Business School, 1990), referenced in J. L. McKenney, *Waves of Change: Business Evolution through Information Technology* (Boston: Harvard Business School, 1995).

3. M. Banaghan, "Banks Overlook the Technology Trap," *Business Review Weekly*, 4 August 1997, 22–26; S. Plunkett, "Westpac Abandons High-Tech Hopes," *Business Review Weekly*, 8 November (1991): 26.

4. The address for SFNB is http://www.sfnb.com. The address for the Electronic Banking Resources Center is http://www2.cob.ohio-state.edu/~richards/banklist.htm.

5. P. Moore, "Banks Launch a Money Highway," *The Australian*, 17 September 1996.

6. See the excellent work of Konsynski and Warbalow on classifying different types of electronic commerce (http://www.cc.emory.edu/BUSINESS/BRK_home.html) and the pioneering work of T. Malone, J. Yates, and R.

Benjamin, "The Logic of Electronic Markets," *Harvard Business Review* 67, no. 3 (1989).

7. As reported in *Financial Times* and *The Australian*.

8. For a detailed discussion of the payoff of public infrastructure and the similarities to information technology infrastructure, see P. Weill, "The Role and Value of Information Technology Infrastructure: Some Empirical Observations," in *Strategic Information Technology Management: Perspectives on Organizational Growth and Competitive Advantage,* ed. R. D. Banker, R. J. Kauffman, and M. A. Mahmood (Middleton, Pa.: Idea Group Publishing, 1993), 547–572.

9. J. Whitman, A. Farhoomand, and B. Tricker, "How Hong Kong Firms View Information Technology: Information Technology Infrastructure Study"(Melbourne, Australia: Melbourne Business School, The University of Melbourne, 1995).

10. M. Broadbent, "The Role of Information Technology in International Business Operations: The Case of Honda Motor Co., Ltd." (Melbourne, Australia: Melbourne Business School, The University of Melbourne, 1995).

11. C. Butler, M. Broadbent, and S. Niemann, "Management of Information Technology at Amcor Ltd.," CL334 (Melbourne, Australia: Melbourne Case Study Services, Melbourne Business School, The University of Melbourne, 1995).

12. *Monsanto Magazine*, no. 2 (1995).

13. B. S. Neo and C. Soh, "Case Vignette of Citibank Asia Pacific: Information Technology Infrastructure Study" (Melbourne, Australia: Melbourne Business School, The University of Melbourne, 1995).

14. *Monsanto Magazine*, no. 2 (1995).

15. *IT Dialog: Pepsi-Cola International,* vol. 4, 1995.

16. For two excellent discussions of information technology architecture, see P. G. W. Keen, *Every Manager's Guide to Information Technology,* 2nd ed. (Boston: Harvard Business School Press, 1995); M. J. Earl, *Management Strategies for Information Technology* (London: Prentice-Hall, 1989).

17. To reach this description of information technology architecture, we have drawn on the written work of and discussions with a number of people. We would like to acknowledge Peter Keen, Margrethe Olson, Michael Earl, Stewart Neimann, and B. Robertson-Dunn.

18. T. O'Brien and M. Broadbent, "Case Vignette of Southcorp Holdings Ltd.: Information Technology Infrastructure Study" (Melbourne, Australia: Melbourne Business School, The University of Melbourne, 1995).

19. J. Ross, "Johnson & Johnson: Building an Infrastructure to Support Global Operations," CISR working paper no. 283 (Cambridge, Mass.: Center for Information Systems Research, Sloan School of Management, MIT, September 1995); C. Lentz, J. Ross, and J. Henderson, "Case Vignette of Johnson & Johnson Company: Information Technology Infrastructure Study" (Mel-

bourne, Australia: Melbourne Business School, The University of Melbourne, 1994).

20. See Chapter 6 in P. G. W. Keen, *Shaping the Future: Business Redesign through Information Technology* (Boston: Harvard Business School Press, 1991).

Chapter 2

1. B. Harrington, "Commentary on 'Making Local Knowledge Global,'" *Harvard Business Review* 74, no. 3 (1996): 30–31.

2. S. Alter, *Information Systems: A Management Perspective,* 2nd ed. (Menlo Park, Calif.: Benjamin/Cummings, 1996).

3. C. Lentz and J. Henderson, "Case Vignette of Sun Life Assurance Company of Canada: Information Technology Infrastructure Study" (Melbourne, Australia: Melbourne Business School, The University of Melbourne, 1994).

4. Yolanda Chan and her colleagues demonstrated that companies with better alignment between their business strategy and information technology investment were also superior performers. See Y. E. Chan, S. Huff, D. Barclay, and D. Copeland, "Business Strategic Orientation, Information Systems Strategic Orientation, and Strategic Alignment," *Information Systems Research* 8, no. 2 (June 1997): 125–150.

5. M. E. Porter, *Competitive Strategy: Techniques for Analyzing Industries and Competitors* (New York: Free Press, 1980).

6. M. E. Porter, "What Is Strategy?" *Harvard Business Review* 74, no. 6 (1996): 61–78.

7. H. Mintzberg, *Mintzberg on Management: Inside Our Strange World of Organizations* (New York: Free Press, 1989).

8. J. Kay, *Foundations of Corporate Success: How Business Strategies Add Value* (Oxford, Eng.: Oxford University Press, 1993).

9. K. Dery and P. Weill, "Case Vignette of RACV: Information Technology Infrastructure Study" (Melbourne, Australia: Melbourne Business School, The University of Melbourne, 1995).

10. See the work of Hamel and Prahalad, whose influential work popularized the notion of strategic intent. For example, G. Hamel and C. K. Prahalad, "Strategic Intent," *Harvard Business Review* 67, no. 3 (1989): 63–76.

11. R. Kaplan and D. Norton, "Putting the Balanced Scorecard to Work," *Harvard Business Review* 71, no. 5 (1993).

12. Porter, "What Is Strategy?"

13. P. G. W. Keen, *Shaping the Future: Business Redesign through Information Technology* (Boston: Harvard Business School Press, 1991).

Chapter 3

1. Two comprehensive reviews of the literature on the business value of information technology investments are E. Brynjolfsson, "The Productivity Paradox of Information Technology," *Communication of the ACM* 36, no. 12 (December 1993): 66–77; and R. J. Kauffman and P. Weill, "An Evaluative Framework for Research on the Performance Effects of Information Technology Investment" (paper presented at Tenth International Conference on Information Systems, Boston, December 1989), 377–388. The work of Strassmann is also highly recommended, particularly P. Strassmann, *The Business Value of Computers* (New Canaan, Conn.: Information Economics Press, 1990).

2. See E. Brynjolfsson and L. Hitt, "Paradox Lost? Firm Level Evidence on the Returns to Information Systems Spending," *Management Science* 42, no. 4 (April 1996): 541–558; and "Productivity, Profit and Consumer Welfare: Three Different Measures of Information Technology's Value," *MIS Quarterly* 20, no. 2 (June 1996): 121–142.

3. Details of these findings can be found in several studies: P. Weill, *Do Computers Pay Off?* (Washington, D.C.: ICIT Press, 1990); P. Weill, "Strategic Investment in Information Technology: An Empirical Study," *Information Technology* 12, no. 3 (July 1990): 141–147; P. Weill, M. Broadbent, and T. O'Brien, "Does IT Infrastructure Investment Pay Off?" *MIS Magazine* (December 1995): 28–30.

4. The statistical techniques used in this chapter are based on correlations with the likelihood that these effects are based on chance set at 5 percent. Therefore, we cannot usually say that the information technology investments caused the business value impact even if we look over time. Cohen and Cohen suggest that we need three conditions to infer causality: (1) a convincing theoretical model, (2) statistically significant correlations, and (3) the investment occurring earlier in time than the measure of business value. The first condition is the most difficult to achieve. To be convincing, the model of information technology investment must include other factors that are likely to influence business value. In an organizational setting it is very difficult to include all the other important factors, such as culture, management skill, and expertise of the systems user. See J. Cohen and P. Cohen, *Applied Multiple Regression/Correlation Analysis for Behavioral Sciences*, 2nd ed. (Hillsdale, N.J.: Erlbaum, 1983), 80.

5. C. Lentz and J. Henderson, "Case Vignette of UNUM Corporation: Information Technology Infrastructure Study" (Melbourne, Australia: Melbourne Business School, The University of Melbourne, 1995).

6. For more details, see P. Weill, "The Relationship Between Investment in Information Technology and Firm Performance: A Study of the Valve Manufacturing Sector," *Information Systems Research* 3, no. 4 (1992): 307–333.

7. P. G. W. Keen, *Shaping the Future: Business Redesign through Information Technology* (Boston: Harvard Business School Press, 1991), 48.

8. The relationships described in Figure 3.3 are based on five years of data and are all statistically significant after controlling for the effects of industry.

9. H. Zampatakis, "Why Bendigo Went Back in House," *The Australian Financial Review*, 6 February 1997.

10. These five characteristics were identified by statistical analysis using the five characteristics as moderating variables between information technology investment and performance.

11. M. Broadbent and P. Weill, "Improving Business and Information Strategy Alignment: Learning from the Banking Industry," *IBM Systems Journal* 32, no. 1 (February 1993): 162–179.

12. Peter Keen makes this point very convincingly in his chapter titled "Thoughts of an Explorer of Two Worlds: Business and Information Technology," in *The Decade of Relevance*, ed. P. B. Duffey (Boston: Harvard Business School Press, 1994), 47–70.

Chapter 4

1. B. S. Neo and C. Soh, "Case Vignette of Citibank–Asia Pacific: Information Technology Infrastructure Study" (Melbourne, Australia: Melbourne Business School, The University of Melbourne, 1994).

2. Telstra was formerly known as Telecom, then AOTC (the merger of Telecom Australia and the Overseas Telecommunications Corporation).

3. C. Butler and P. Weill, "Standardising the Information Technology Environment at Telecom Australia," CL333 (Melbourne, Australia: Melbourne Case Study Services, Melbourne Business School, The University of Melbourne, 1995).

4. Ibid.

5. Keppel Corporation Limited, *Annual Report 1993*; *Annual Report 1995*.

6. Inspired by and adapted from the work of D. T. McKay and D. W. Brockway, "Building I/T Infrastructure for the 1990s," *Stage by Stage (Nolan Norton & Company)* 9, no. 3 (1989): 1–11.

7. See J. Barney, "Firm Resources and Sustained Competitive Advantage," *Journal of Management* 17, no. 1 (1991): 99–120.

8. Services numbers 24 and 25 emerged as important after the study and no firms had these services in place at the time. Both services are being implemented in many firms today. To facilitate comparison, we have used the 25 services.

9. See P. G. W. Keen, *Shaping the Future: Business Redesign through Information Technology* (Boston: Harvard Business School Press, 1991).

10. The process of statistical confirmation involved collecting data from 27 firms on their information technology infrastructure investments and capabilities across five different dimensions. The firms were categorized into the four views and then were tested to see whether all seven dimensions increased when comparing none to utility to dependent to enabling views. All the dimensions increased together, verifying that the four types of views were internally consistent.

11. For a detailed description of how the views were identified during the research process, see the following articles. They are listed in chronological order to show the development process. P. Weill, "The Role and Value of Information Technology Infrastructure: Some Empirical Observations," in *Strategic Information Technology Management: Perspectives on Organisational Growth and Competitive Advantage,* ed. R. Banker, R. Kauffman, and M. A. Mahmood (Middleton, Pa.: Idea Group Publishing, 1993), 547–572; P. Weill and M. Broadbent, "Infrastructure Goes Industry Specific," *MIS Magazine,* July 1994, 35–39; P. Weill, M. Broadbent, and D. St. Clair, "IT Value and the Role of IT Infrastructure Investments," in *Strategic Alignment,* ed. J. Luftman (New York: Oxford University Press, 1996), 361–384.

12. C. Lentz and J. Ross, "Case Vignette of Ralston Purina: Information Technology Infrastructure Study" (Melbourne, Australia: Melbourne Business School, The University of Melbourne, 1995).

13. K. Dery and P. Weill, "Case Vignette of Carlton & United Breweries: Information Technology Infrastructure Study" (Melbourne, Australia: Melbourne Business School, The University of Melbourne, 1993).

14. D. T. McKay and M. J. Connolly, "It's Not Business as Usual in the Data Center," *Journal of Information Systems* (Spring 1991): 80–83.

15. C. Soh and D. Leow, "Case Vignette of Maybank: Information Technology Infrastructure Study" (Melbourne, Australia: Melbourne Business School, The University of Melbourne, 1995).

16. K. Dery and P. Weill, "Case Vignette of the Commonwealth Bank of Australia: Information Technology Infrastructure Study" (Melbourne, Australia: Melbourne Business School, The University of Melbourne, 1993).

17. The measures for each of these items are converted statistically into a score from 0 to 100, with an average of 50. As different units of measure were involved, each component was converted into a set of standard (or z) scores. With the exception of component 3 (firmwide information technology infrastructure investment as a proportion of revenue), the set of z scores was based on the entire sample of firms in the study. To remove the industry effects for component 3, the z scores were calculated using only the firms within industry groupings. In order to generate a score out of 100 to represent the view, the set of z scores for each component was converted linearly to a set of numbers between 0 and 100, with a mean of 50 and a standard deviation of 50/3. The view of information technology infrastructure was calculated as the mean of 5 components and had a mean of approximately 50. To fit the measure of view into our theoretical classification, ranges were arbitrarily defined, with the objective of having a similar number of firms classified as both utility and enabling, and the majority classified as dependent.

18. These relationships were demonstrated statistically. For more details, see P. Weill, M. Broadbent, C. Butler, and C. Soh, "Firm-wide Information Technology Infrastructure Investment and Services" (Proceedings, 16th International Conference on Information Systems, Amsterdam, December 1995); P. Weill, M. Broadbent, and C. Butler, "Exploring How Firms View Information Technology Infrastructure," working paper 4, Melbourne Business School, University of Melbourne, September 1996.

Chapter 5

1. P. G. W. Keen, *Shaping the Future: Business Design through Information Technology* (Boston: Harvard Business School Press, 1991).

2. C. Lentz and J. Henderson, "Case Vignette of Sun Life: Information Technology Infrastructure Study" (Melbourne, Australia: Melbourne Business School, The University of Melbourne, 1994).

3. K. Dery and P. Weill, "Information Technology Infrastructure Study: Case Vignette of Commonwealth Bank of Australia" (Melbourne, Australia: Melbourne Business School, 1993).

4. J. Gray and D. Crowe, "CBA Rewrites the IT Book with $5bn EDS Deal"; D. Crowe, "The Bank That Ate IT"; J. Gray, "CBA's Push into the Unknown," *The Australian Financial Review* August 1997, 1, 15.

5. M. Broadbent, P. Weill, T. O'Brien, and B. S. Neo, "Firm Context and Patterns and IT Infrastructure Capability" (Proceedings, 17th Annual Interna-

tional Conference on Information Systems, Cleveland, Ohio, December 1996), 174–194.

6. All entries in the figure marked "More," "Higher," or "Fewer" are statistically significant and thus not due to chance.

7. F. J. Mata, W. L. Fuerst, and J. G. Barner, "Information Technology and Sustained Competitive Advantage: A Resource-based Analysis," *MIS Quarterly* 19, no. 4 (1995): 487–505.

8. J. B. Quinn, *Intelligent Enterprise: A Knowledge and Service Based Paradigm for Industry* (New York: Free Press, 1992).

9. N. B. Duncan, "Capturing Flexibility of Information Technology Infrastructure: A Study of Resource Characteristics and Their Measure," *Journal of Management Information Systems* 12, no. 2 (Fall 1995): 37–57.

10. These relationships were all statistically significant. For details, see M. Broadbent, P. Weill, T. O'Brien, and B. S. Neo.

11. J. A. Pearce, D. K. Robbins, and R. B. Robinson, "The Impact of Grand Strategy and Planning Formality on Financial Performance," *Strategic Management Journal* 8, no. 2 (1987): 125–134; C. Christodoulou, "Australian Industry: Sophisticated Planning and Weak R&D?" *Long Range Planning* 21, no. 1 (1988): 82–89.

12. N. Venkatraman, J. Henderson, and S. Oldach, "Continuous Strategy Alignment: Exploiting Information Technology Capabilities for Competitive Success," *European Management Journal* 11, no. 2 (1993): 139–149.

13. M. E. Porter and V. E. Millar, "How Information Gives You a Competitive Advantage," *Harvard Business Review* 73, no. 4 (1995): 149–160; S. P. Bradley, J. A. Hausman, and R. L. Nolan, "Globalization and Technology," in *Globalization, Technology, and Competition: The Fusion of Computers and Telecommunications in the 1990s*, ed. S. Bradley, J. Hausman, and R. Nolan (Boston: Harvard Business School Press, 1993), 3–32.

Chapter 6

1. Aristotle, "Rhetoric Book II Chapters 20–22," in *The Complete Works of Aristotle*, ed. J. Barnes, vol. 2 (Princeton, N.J.: Princeton University Press, 1984), 2219–2224.

2. G. Hamel and C. K. Prahalad, *Competing for the Future* (Boston: Harvard Business School Press, 1994), 133.

3. Ibid., 129.

4. M. Broadbent, "The Role of Information Technology in International Business Operations: The Case of Citicorp" (Melbourne, Australia: Melbourne Business School, The University of Melbourne, 1996); B. S. Neo and C. Soh, "Case Vignette of Citibank Asia Pacific: Information Technology Infrastructure Study" (Melbourne, Australia: Melbourne Business School, The University of Melbourne, 1995).

5. *Citibank Annual Report 1995.*

6. B. S. Neo and C. Soh, "Case Vignette of DBS Bank: Information Technology Infrastructure Study" (Melbourne, Australia: Melbourne Business School, The University of Melbourne, 1994).

7. M. Treacy and F. Wiersema, *The Discipline of Market Leaders* (Reading, Mass.: Addison-Wesley, 1995).

8. We draw here on "Building the New Information Infrastructure: Relating Strategic Positioning to Information Needs," CSC Index Foundation working paper 1, 1993.

9. *Monsanto Magazine*, no. 2, 1995.

10. J. Jost, "Amcor's New Paperchase," *Australian Business Monthly*, February 1994, 42.

11. C. Butler, M. Broadbent, and S. Niemann, "Management of Information Technology at Amcor Ltd.," case CL334 (Melbourne, Australia: Melbourne Business School, The University of Melbourne, 1995).

12. M. Broadbent and C. Butler, "Amcor Fibre Packaging Deployment of Information Technology: The Case of an International Business," case CL331 (Melbourne, Australia: Melbourne Business School, The University of Melbourne, 1995).

13. *Honda 1995 Annual Report.*

14. G. Stalk, P. Evans, and L. E. Shulman, "Competing on Capabilities: The New Rules of Corporate Strategy," *Harvard Business Review* 70, no. 2 (1992): 57–69.

15. M. Broadbent, "The Role of Information Technology."

16. Aristotle, "Rhetoric."

17. A. C. Hax and N. S. Majluf, *The Strategy Concept and Process: A Pragmatic Approach,* 2nd ed. (Upper Saddle River, N.J.: Prentice Hall, 1996); H. Mintzberg, J. B. Quinn, and J. Voyer, *The Strategy Process* (Upper Saddle River, N.J.: Prentice Hall, 1995); P. J. Below, G. L. Morrisey, and B. L. Acomb, *The Executive Guide to Strategic Planning* (San Francisco: Jossey-Bass, 1987).

18. K. Dery and P. Weill, "Case Vignette of RACV: Information Technology Infrastructure Study" (Melbourne, Australia: Melbourne Business School, The University of Melbourne, 1995).

19. S. H. Haeckel and R. L. Nolan, "Managing by Wire," *Harvard Business Review* 71, no. 5 (1993): 123–132.

20. Drawing on T. H. Davenport, M. Hammer, and T. J. Metsisto, "How Executives Can Shape Their Company's Information Systems," *Harvard Business Review* 67, no. 2 (1989): 130–134.

21. Drawing on M. J. Earl, *Management Strategies for Information Technology* (London: Prentice-Hall, 1989); G. L. Richardson, B. M. Jackson, and G. W. Dickson, "A Principles-based Enterprise Architecture: Lessons from Texaco and Star Enterprise," *MIS Quarterly* 14, no. 4 (December 1990): 385–402; S. H. Haeckel and R. L. Nolan, "Managing by Wire," *Harvard Business Review* 71, no. 5 (1993): 123–132.

22. J. Ross, "Johnson & Johnson: Building an Infrastructure to Support Global Operations," CISR working paper no. 283 (Cambridge, Mass.: Sloan School of Management, 1995); C. Lentz, J. Ross, and J. Henderson, "Case Vignette of Johnson and Johnson Company: Information Technology Infrastructure Study" (Melbourne, Australia: Melbourne Business School, The University of Melbourne, 1995).

Chapter 7

1. *Citicorp Annual Report, 1995.*

2. Ibid.

3. M. Broadbent, "The Role of Information Technology in International Business Operations: The Case of Citicorp" (Melbourne, Australia: Melbourne Business School, The University of Melbourne, 1996).

4. M. Broadbent and C. Butler, "Amcor Fibre Packaging Deployment of Information Technology: The Case of an International Business," case CL331 (Melbourne, Australia: Melbourne Business School, The University of Melbourne, 1995); C. Butler, M. Broadbent, and S. Niemann, "Management of Information Technology at Amcor Ltd," case CL334 (Melbourne, Australia: Melbourne Business School, The University of Melbourne, 1995).

5. Personal communication with Rod Pyne, Amcor Fibre Packaging.

6. See, for example, M. Skulley, "Amcor Hopes to Cut $30m More," *Australian Financial Review*, 18 April 1997.

Chapter 8

1. C. Lee, "Milestones on a Journey Not Yet Completed: Process Re-engineering at GTE," *Strategy & Business* 5 (1996): 58–67.

2. Ibid.

3. T. Grover, J. T. C. Teng, and K. D. Fiedler, "Information Technology Enabled Business Process Redesign: An Integrated Planning Framework," *OMEGA, International Journal of Management Science* 21, no. 4 (1993): 433–447.

4. T. Davenport, *Process Innovation: Reengineering Work Through IT* (Boston: Harvard Business School Press, 1993); M. Hammer and J. Champy, *Reengineering the Corporation: A Manifesto for Business Revolution* (London: Nicholas Brealey Publishing, 1993); H. J. Johansson et al., *Business Process Reengineering: Breakpoint Strategies for Market Dominance* (Chichester, West Sussex: Wiley, 1993).

5. Index Group, *Critical Issues of Information Systems Management for 1993: The Sixth Annual Survey of IS Management Issues* (Boston: CSC Index, 1993).

6. J. C. Brancheau, B. D. Janz, and J. C. Wetherbe, "Key Issues in Information Systems Management: 1994–95 SIM Delphi Results," *MIS Quarterly* 20, no. 2 (June 1996): 225–242; M. Snell, "Dissatisfied Companies Blast Reengineering," *The Australian*, 28 June 1994, 22 (reporting the findings of a study of 350 companies by Arthur D. Little, Inc., that over two-thirds of firms encounter unanticipated obstacles).

7. T. R. Furey and S. G. Diorio, "Making Reengineering Strategic," *Planning Review* 22, no. 2 (1994): 7–11, 43.

8. E. Ramcharamdas, "Xerox Creates a Continuous Learning Environment for Business Transformation," *Planning Review* 22, no. 2 (1994): 34–38.

9. Davenport; see also R. I. Benjamin, "Managing Information Technology Enabled Change," *Human Organizational and Social Dimensions of Information Systems Development*, ed. D. Avison, J. Kendall, and J. DeGross (North Holland: Amsterdam, 1993), 381–398; M. Broadbent and C. Butler, "Implementing Business Process Redesign: Early Lessons from the Australian Experience" (paper presented at the 5th Australian Conference on Information Systems, Melbourne, Australia, 27–29 September 1994); M. J. Earl, "The New and the Old of Business Process Redesign," *Journal of Strategic Information Systems* 3, no. 1 (1994): 5–22.

10. D. G. Wastell, P. White, and P. Kawalek, "A Methodology for Business Process Redesign: Experiences and Issues," *Journal of Strategic Information Systems* 3, no. 1 (1994): 23–40; J. R. Caron, S. L. Jarvenpaa, and D. Stoddard, "Business Reengineering at CIGNA Corporation: Experiences and Lessons from the First Five Years," *MIS Quarterly* 18, no. 3 (1994): 233–250.

11. From Australian Taxation Office.

12. Reported by c_net at http://www.cnet.com/ on 8 August 1997.

13. See B. Konsynski, A. Warbelow, and J. Kokuryo, "AUCNET: TV Auction Network System," Case 9–190–001, and "AUCNET: The Story Continues," Case 9–195–122 (Boston: Harvard Business School, 1989). The description of AUCNET draws heavily on a paper by J. J. Sviokla, "Marketspace Markets: Factors for Success and Failure" (Boston: Harvard Business School Publishing, 1996); and J. Sviokla, "Managing the Marketspace: Instructor's Course Overview" (Boston: Harvard Business School, Winter 1996).

14. See J. J. Sviokla and J. F. Rayport, "Managing the Marketspace," *Harvard Business Review* 72, no. 6 (1994): 141–150.

15. Information Infrastructure Technology and Applications (IITA) Task Group, "Electronic Commerce and the NII," National Coordination Office for High Performance Computing and Communications, February 1994, 18 pp. Online. Available: http://www.sda.uni-bocconi.it/fm/mktg/newmedia/cluecom.htm. 23 March 1998.

16. Subscriber numbers compiled by NEXIS reported in J. J. Sviokla, "Managing the Marketspace: Instructors Course Overview."

17. This section is heavily influenced by the thinking of Ben Konsynski and several of his colleagues. For further information, see Ben Konsynski's home page, http://www.cc.emory.edu/BUSINESS/BRK_home.html.

18. J. Owens, "IVANS: Taking the Bite out of Administration Costs," *EDI Forum* 6, no. 2 (1993).

19. This study is partially funded by Hewlett Packard Australia and the Melbourne Business School Foundation. Four of these firms were in the International Infrastructure Study, and the other 22 constituted an additional set of firms. Further details can be found in M. Broadbent and C. Butler, "Managing Information Technology Infrastructure Capability for International Business Operations" (Proceedings of the Pacific Asia Conference of Information Systems, Brisbane, Australia, April 1997, ed. G. Gable and R. Weber, Queensland University of Technology ISMRC, 1997), 598–612; M. Broadbent, "Managing Information Technology for International Business Operations," *The Journal*, no. 4 (1996): 4–21.

20. C. A. Bartlett and S. Ghoshal, *Managing across Borders: The Transnational Solution* (Boston: Harvard Business School Press, 1989).

21. The concepts of international integration and local responsiveness were developed by C. K. Prahalad and Y. L. Doz, *The Multinational Mission* (New York: Free Press, 1987).

22. B. Ives and S. L. Jarvenpaa, "Applications of Global Information Technology," *MIS Quarterly* (March 1991): 33–49.

23. Characteristics of information technology configuration were measured independently of strategic business orientation and infrastructure capability, allowing presentation of typical infrastructure patterns for each information technology configuration.

24. J. Movizzo, Executive summary introduction, in *The Learning Organization: Managing Knowledge for Business Success* (New York: The Economist Intelligence Unit and IBM Consulting Group, 1995).

25. P. Drucker, *Managing in a Time of Great Change* (New York: Truman Alley Books/Dutton, 1995).

26. The Hoffmann-LaRoche experiences are drawn from two sources: P. Seeman, *Real-World Knowledge Management: What's Working for Hoffmann-LaRoche*, CBI310 (Boston: Centre for Business Innovation, Ernst & Young, 1996); D. M. Amidon and D. Skyrme, "Hoffman-LaRoche Profits from Knowledge Management," *Knowledge Inc: The Executive Report on Knowledge, Technology & Performance* 2, no. 7 (July 1997): 1–4.

27. A. Boynton, "How to Get Started with Knowledge Management," extracted from "Exploring Opportunities in Knowledge Management" (Knowledge Management Symposium: Leveraging Knowledge for Business Impact, IBM Consulting Group, Sydney, November 1996).

28. Ibid., 17–18.

29. M. Broadbent, "The Role of Information Technology in International Business Operations: The Case of Honda Motor Company" (Melbourne, Australia: Melbourne Business School, The University of Melbourne, 1995); E. H. Updike, D. Woodruff, and L. Armstrong, "Honda's Civic Lesson," *Business Week*, 18 September 1995, 26–28.

30. L. Ealey and L. G. Soderberg, "How Honda Cures 'Design Amnesia,'" *McKinsey Quarterly* (Spring 1990): 3–14.

Chapter 9

1. B. S. Neo and C. Soh, "Case Vignette of DBS Bank: Information Technology Infrastructure Study" (Melbourne, Australia: Melbourne Business School, The University of Melbourne, 1994).

2. *IDC Australia*, 1993.

3. For more details, see R. Chalmers, "Group Dynamic," *MIS* 7, no. 6 (August 1997): 30–36.

4. R. Kaplan, "Must CIM Be Justified on Faith Alone?" *Harvard Business Review* 64, no. 1 (1986): 87–95.

5. See the discussion on sustainable competitive advantage in M. Porter, "What Is Strategy?" *Harvard Business Review* 74, no. 6 (1996): 61–78.

6. C. J. Bacon, "The Use of Decision Criteria in Selecting Information Technology Investments," *MIS Quarterly* 16, no. 3 (1992): 335–372.

7. For more information on DCF value analysis, see P. G. W. Keen, "Value Analysis: Justifying Decision Support Systems," *MIS Quarterly* 5, no. 1 (March 1981): 1–15; P. G. W. Keen and M. S. Scott Morton, *Decision Support Systems: An Organizational Perspective* (Reading, Mass.: Addison-Wesley, 1978).

8. Kaplan, "Must CIM Be Justified on Faith Alone?"

9. A comprehensive reference on performing NPV and similar analysis is R. Brealy and S. Meyers, *Principles of Corporate Finance,* 5th ed. (New York: McGraw-Hill, 1996).

10. Bacon, "Use of Decision Criteria," 335–372.

11. For a more detailed discussion of these recommendations, see P. Weill, "The Information Technology Payoff: Implications for Investment," *Australian Accounting Review* (1991): 2–11.

12. For a very interesting discussion of using the financial option analogy for infrastructure, see A. Kambil, J. C. Henderson, and H. Mohsenzadeh, "Strategic Management of Information Technology Investments: An Options Perspective," in *Perspectives on the Strategic and Economic Value of Information Technology,* ed. R. D. Banker, R. J. Kauffman, and M. A. Mahmood (Middletown, Pa.: Idea Group Publishing, 1993).

13. Personal communication with author.

14. For example, see M. J. Earl, *Management Strategies for Information Technology* (New York: Prentice-Hall, 1989), 74.

15. These quadrants and definitions were adapted from Earl's (1989) work but have slightly different names.

Chapter 10

1. N. Venkatraman, J. Henderson, and S. Oldach, "Continuous Strategy Alignment: Exploiting Information Technology Capabilities for Competitive Success," *European Management Journal* 11, no. 2 (1993): 139–149.

2. M. Broadbent, "The Role of Information Technology in International Business Operations: The Case of Citicorp" (Melbourne, Australia: Melbourne Business School, The University of Melbourne, 1996).

3. B. S. Neo and C. Soh, "Case Vignette of DBS Bank: Information Technology Infrastructure Study" (Melbourne, Australia: Melbourne Business School, The University of Melbourne, 1994).

4. T. O'Brien and M. Broadbent, "Case Vignette of Southcorp Holdings: Information Technology Infrastructure Study" (Melbourne, Australia: Melbourne Business School, The University of Melbourne, 1995).

5. C. Lentz and J. Henderson, "Case Vignette of Sun Life: Information Technology Infrastructure Study" (Melbourne, Australia: Melbourne Business School, The University of Melbourne, 1994); J. Henderson and C. Lentz, "Learning, Working, and Innovation in the Insurance Industry," *Journal of Management Information Systems* 12, no. 3 (Winter 1995–1996): 43–64.

6. R. H. Davenport, R. G. Eccles, and L. Prusak, "Information Politics," *Sloan Management Review* 34, no. 1 (Fall 1992): 53–65.

7. B. Harrington, "Response to Lexington Labs: Making Local Knowledge Global," *Harvard Business Review* 74, no. 3 (1996): 11–12.

Index

About the Authors

Professor Weill is the Foundation Chair of Management (Information Systems) and a member of the board of directors of the Melbourne Business School at the University of Melbourne, Australia. Dr. Weill has also held visiting professorial positions at the Sloan School of Business, Massachusetts Institute of Technology, and the College of Business Administration at Georgia State University. He has developed and presented in several countries MBA programs that focus on the business value of information technology as well as public and private programs for senior management executive education. His research and advising activities center around the role and value of information technology (IT) in organizations. Dr. Weill has been published widely, including award-winning books, case studies, and articles in the both the business and academic presses. He regularly advises corporations and governments on issues of IT investment and pay off and the alignment of the IT portfolio with business strategy. Recently, Peter testified about IT outsourcing in front of the Australian Government Senate Enquiry on Contracting Out of Government Services. Peter was educated at the University of Melbourne and New York University and lives in Melbourne.

Dr. Marianne Broadbent was appointed Gartner Group's IT executive program director for Australia and New Zealand in January 1998. Dr. Broadbent was previously a professor of the management of information systems at the Melbourne Business School, University of Melbourne, a visiting researcher at Boston University, and head of the department of information services at the Royal Melbourne Institute of Technology. Her industry research, consulting, and advising activities have involved more than eighty businesses in nine countries, and she has managed her own successful consulting and advisory services firm. Marianne has been published extensively in both the industry and academic presses. Recently, Marianne was the lead author of two papers that won international awards, as well as an article in *Sloan Management Review* on linking business strategy and long-term information technology investments. Marianne has a bachelor's and master's degree from Sydney and Macquarie Universities, respectively, and a doctorate from the University of Melbourne.